Study Guide

for

Zillmer and Spiers's

Principles of Neuropsychology

Carrie Hill Kennedy

Eric A. Zillmer
Drexel University

WADSWORTH

THOMSON LEARNING

Australia • Canada • Mexico • Singapore • Spain • United Kingdom • United States

For more information, contact
Wadsworth/Thomson Learning
10 Davis Drive
Belmont, CA 94002-3098
USA

For more information about our products, contact us:
Thomson Learning Academic Resource Center
1-800-423-0563
http://www.wadsworth.com

International Headquarters
Thomson Learning
International Division
290 Harbor Drive, 2nd Floor
Stamford, CT 06902-7477
USA

UK/Europe/Middle East/South Africa
Thomson Learning
Berkshire House
168-173 High Holborn
London WC1V 7AA
United Kingdom

Asia
Thomson Learning
60 Albert Complex, #15-01
Singapore 189969

Canada
Nelson Thomson Learning
1120 Birchmount Road
Toronto, Ontario M1K 5G4
Canada

ISBN 0-534-50700-X

Contents

Preface

As a student, *Principles of Neuropsychology* was my favorite class and one reason why I entered the profession of neuropsychology. Neuropsychology, I believe, is so interesting because it combines neuroscience, biology, and anatomy with cognitive, experimental, and clinical psychology. Since I have become a teacher I have taught the course *Principles of Neuropsychology* many times, at both the undergraduate and graduate level. One obstacle in teaching the course however, has been related to communicating a large amount of complex material that is often associated with neuropsychology and the functions of the brain. Like many teachers, I have had the experience of examining books on the topic of neuropsychology that presented the material in an esoteric manner, removed from real life situations. Undergraduate students have found the material in such texts difficult to absorb. Graduate students have complained that previous texts on neuropsychology were also clinically irrelevant, since there was little coverage on topics such as pathology, assessment, intervention, rehabilitation, and imaging procedures.

The goal of *Principles of Neuropsychology* was to write an undergraduate, beginning graduate level textbook that teaches brain functioning in a clear, interesting, and progressive manner. The task of studying the brain by examining its behavioral product is a complex proposition and necessitates a firm grounding in psychology, neurophysiology, neuroanatomy, and neuropathology. If presented in the proper context, neuropsychology is an exciting and dynamic field that readily stimulates and inspires students and teachers alike. It was with this goal in mind that we have written a text with the central "theme" of how behavior makes neuropsychological sense. An applied and functional approach to neuropsychology, we hope, will make the detailed and often complex material accessible and understandable. Many didactic and pedagogic aids have been introduced to facilitate the learning of the material. These include:

Timeline of Significant Developments in Neuropsychology and *Structure-Function Relationships* that provide useful summaries at the beginning of the text and that can easily be referred to from any point of the text.

Keep in Mind questions at the beginning of each chapter to prepare you for the material that follows and help you focus on key topics as you read.

Neuropsychology in Action boxes (51 in total) contributed by over 20 prominent neuropsychologists that appear throughout the text to provide special insight into the actual clinical application and practice of neuropsychology.

Web Connections, located at the end of every chapter invite you to explore additional learning environments.

Conclusion, *Key Terms*, and *Critical Thinking Questions* sections at the end of each chapter in the main text help students gauge their mastery of the material. The answers to the critical thinking questions are in the appendix of the textbook.

The *Study Guide* was intended to complement the text *Principles of Neuropsychology* to assist you in reviewing the materials in the context of questions and answers. In essence, the *Study Guide* is a study tool for you. Everybody learns differently, but it is not a secret that good preparation, the completion of homework assignments, good class attendance, and detailed note taking is the key to academic success. Thus, the *Study Guide* was not designed to be a substitute for reading the text or attending class. Rather, the *Study Guide* provides different formats of question-answer exercises that will help you master the material in an exam-like context. For each chapter the *Study Guide* features specific sections that review the material in different exam-like formats. Those include an Overview, Learning Objectives, Key Terms and Concepts, Sentence Completion, Matching, True/False Questions, Post-Test Multiple Choice Questions, and examples of possible Essay Questions. At the end of each chapter you can review the answers by examining the Answer Key. If you need additional help you can find, in parentheses, the page number next to the answer which corresponds to the main text page where you can review the topic in more detail. The Post-Test provides an excellent way to find out if you have mastered the material once you have studied the text and completed the questions preceding the Post-Test.

The principal author of the Study Guide is Carrie Hill Kennedy, Ph.D. I am very grateful to Carrie that she took on this project. She not only has very extensive experience as a psychology teacher and is a talented and accomplished neuropsychologist, but Carrie also likes to "get things right." She took this project seriously and focused on finishing a *Study Guide* of the highest quality. Many of the unique features in the *Study Guide* should be credited to her. Special recognition should also go to Stephanie Cosentino and Bill Culbertson who helped with the editing and proofing. Jennifer Wilkinson, Senior Assistant Editor at Wadsworth Publishing, helped with the editing process. The assistance of all these individuals enabled us to provide you with this resource.

Eric A. Zillmer
Drexel University
Zillmer@Drexel.edu

Chapter 1

Introduction
The History of Neuropsychology

Chapter Outline

Overview

The introductory chapter of Principles of Neuropsychology focuses on the history of the field, from antiquity to the future. It has often been said that the history of neuropsychology is long but its past short. This is true. While neuropsychology as a specialization and profession has its roots in the 20th century, early writings and investigations in biology, philosophy, and anatomy have detailed the functions of the brain from a very early period. This history has shaped how we currently conceptualize the brain and its relationship to behavior. It is important for the neuropsychology student to understand this history and the different theories about brain functions that were endorsed along the way. Surprisingly, many of those theories were anything but accurate. The goal of this introductory chapter is to provide a foundation in the historical, theoretical, and philosophical aspects of neuropsychology upon which you can build. By charting the work of noted scholars, the development of neuropsychology is outlined. As you shall see, the history of neuropsychology has been most interesting and taking a look back at the principles that shaped neuropsychological thinking can also be fun.

Learning Objectives

- To obtain an appreciation for the historical aspects of neuropsychology, from antiquity to the decade of the brain, in order to understand the progression of how scholars at various times have conceptualized brain functioning.
- To understand early theories on brain functioning, especially as they relate to theories promoting the specific localization of functioning in the brain, as opposed to those that promote a more generalized approach to brain functioning.
- To learn about integrated approaches to neuropsychology, particularly the functional model suggested by Russian neuropsychologist Alexander Luria.

Key Terms and Concepts

Psychologist	Neuropsychiatrist	Neuropsychologist
Neurosurgeon	Neurologist	Neuroscientist
neurons	vitalism	materialism

Sentence Completion

1. A medical doctor who specializes in surgery of the nervous system is a _____.

2. Brain cells are also termed _____.

3. A _____ is a researcher who studies the molecular nature of the nervous system.

4. The notion of _____ would attribute brain functions to the presence of spirits.

5. A psychologist who studies the relationship between brain functions and behavior is better known as a _____.

6. A medical doctor trained in psychiatry and interested in the organic nature of mental illness is a _____ .

7. A medical doctor trained in neuroanatomical functioning is also called a _____ .

8. _____ is a theory which would compare brain function to a mechanical device.

9. An individual with a Ph.D. or Psy.D. who studies human behavior is a _____ .

The Brain in Antiquity: Early Hypotheses

Key Terms, Concepts, and Theorists

Trephination	Heraclitus	Pythagoras
brain hypothesis	Hippocrates	Plato
Aristotle	cardiac hypothesis	The Cell Doctrine
ventricular localization hypothesis	Leonardo da Vinci	Galen
humors	Albertus Magnus	Andreas Vesalius
Rene Descartes	Thomas Willis	Giovanni Lancisi
Atharva-Veda		

Matching

10. Believed that the ventricles, frontal lobes, midbrain and cerebellum worked together.
    a.   Galen

11. Researched the aneurysm.
    b.   Rene Descartes

12. Believed that emotions originated in the brain.
    c.   Thomas Willis

13. One of the first to suggest that the brain was responsible for reasoning.
    d.   Hippocrates

14. Corrected Galen's mistakes with regards to neuroanatomy.
    e.   Plato

15. Described behavioral changes resulting from brain damage.
    f.   Leonardo da Vinci

16. Best known for his work on blood circulation in the brain.
    g.   Pythagoras

17. Drew an inaccurate rendition of spherical cerebral ventricles.
    h.   Andreas Vesalius

18. Believed the soul was divided into three parts: appetite, reason and temper.
    i.   Giovanni Lancisi

19. Believed the brain cooled the blood coming from the heart.
    j.   Aristotle

20. Related physical functioning to that of mechanistic concepts and machines.
    k.   Albertus Magnus

True/False

21. _____ Trephination is a technique used to remove specific brain structures.

22._____ Individuals who underwent trephination almost always died as a result of the procedure.

23._____ Trephination may have been performed as a treatment for schizophrenia.

24._____ Trephinations were most commonly used to treat skull fractures.

25._____ Procedures similar to trephinations are routinely used today.

26._____ Heraclitis felt the mind was an enormous space whose boundaries could never be reached.

27._____ Hippocrates was the first person to suggest that the brain was responsible for human reasoning.

28._____ The brain hypothesis questions whether or not the brain is necessary for human cognition.

29._____ Hippocrates recognized that epilepsy was a medical problem.

30._____ Dissections enabled Hippocrates to come to many of his conclusions regarding the human brain.

31._____ Sigmund Freud may have modeled his famous personality theory after an original idea by Plato.

32._____ Plato felt that the seat of human reason was located in the brain.

33._____ Aristotle agreed with Plato and noted the importance of the human brain for all mental processes.

34._____ Public dissections were encouraged in Egypt in the 3rd and 4th centuries.

35._____ The ventricular localization hypothesis states that cognition is located in the cerebral ventricles but that spiritual processes originate in the heart.

36._____ The cell doctrine is the same as the ventricular localization hypothesis.

37._____ Leonardo da Vinci originally made a precise sketch of the cerebral ventricles which has uncanny similarity to photographs of the modern age.

38._____ Cerebral spinal fluid (CSF) has been called "the urine of the brain."

39._____ Galen was able to study brain structures and function via his appointment as surgeon to Roman gladiators.

40._____ Galen generally supported the ventricular localization hypothesis.

41._____ According to Galen, the four humors were: blood, black bile, yellow bile and saliva.

42._____ Albertus Magnus believed that behavior was the result of the interaction of numerous brain structures.

43._____ The first precise drawings of human anatomy were done by Andreas Vesalius.

44._____ Andreas Vesalius promoted the theory of dualism.

45._____ According to Rene Descartes, the pineal gland is the seat of all mental processes.

46. _____	The exact function of the pineal gland is well-understood today.
47. _____	Descartes' ideas were so well-received that he received significant recognition by the government and church.
48. _____	Thomas Willis surmised that all mental processes were located in the corpus callosum.
49. _____	Giovanni Lancisi hypothesized that the corpus striatum was the seat of all cognition.
50. _____	The Artharva-Veda was an Indian medical text which endorsed the role of the brain in all mental processes.
51. _____	In the middle ages, Arab countries provided individuals with mental illness, whether rich or poor, equal opportunities for treatment.

Localization Theory

Key Terms, Concepts, and Theorists

Franz Gall	craniology	faculty psychology
localization theory	phrenology	Johann Spurzheim
Paul Broca	aphasia	double-dissociation
Carl Wernicke	fluent aphasia	Sigmund Freud
agnosia	Pierre Flourens	ablation experiment
equipotential		

Matching

52. Brought phrenology to the United States.

a. Franz Gall

53. Coined the term, agnosia.

b. Carl Wernicke

54. Believed that loss of brain function was related to extent of damage, not location of damage.

c. Sigmund Freud

55. Identified the first specific neuroanatomical correlate to a cognitive function.

d. Johann Spurzheim

56. He "mapped" the cerebral cortex.

e. Pierre Flourens

57. Localized speech comprehension in the brain.

f. Paul Broca

True/False

58. _____	Franz Gall believed that there was a part of the brain that was responsible for friendliness.
59. _____	Gall explained personality differences in the context of varying childhood experiences.
60. _____	Craniology was the study of brain function as it related to brain size.

5

61._____ The theory that individual intellectual abilities functioned separately of one another was called faculty psychology.

62._____ Localization theory held that specific locations on the cerebral cortex accounted for specific brain functions.

63._____ The theory of phrenology held that brain size was relatively unimportant when considering an individual's cognitive abilities.

64._____ Mechanical phrenology equipment measured bumps and indentations of the human skull in order to determine psychological characteristics.

65._____ Franz Gall's theory of phrenology is widely used today.

66._____ Phrenology held that there were measurable gender and cultural differences in the size of different areas of the brain.

67._____ Today scientists have lost interest in studying the physical characteristics of individual brains.

68._____ The United States attempted to prove that abnormalities existed in the brains of Nazi leaders.

69._____ The Nazis attempted to show that skulls of "inferior" individuals exhibited biological abnormalities.

70._____ Today, it is widely known that violent individuals suffer from identifiable brain damage.

71._____ In 1861 Paul Broca identified a region of the left frontal lobe as implicated in speech.

72._____ Aphasia is a disorder directly impacting speech and memory.

73._____ Paul Broca was the first to show that there was a relationship between brain anatomy and cognitive function.

74._____ Paul Broca based his conclusions regarding the localization of expressive speech on a single case study.

75._____ Monsieur Leborgne's only neurological problem was the loss of expressive speech.

76._____ The brains of Albert Einstein, Jeffrey Dahmer, and Paul Broca have been preserved.

77._____ Paul Broca's findings met the criteria of double-dissociation.

78._____ Paul Broca's conclusions continue to hold up today.

79._____ Carl Wernicke disproved Paul Broca's expressive language theories.

80._____ The localization of speech comprehension was studied by Carl Wernicke.

81._____ Fluent aphasia refers to the inability to make sense when talking.

82._____ Carl Wernicke's work began to dispel the notion of localization because, coupled with Broca's theories, it showed that two distinct areas of the brain were used for a single cognitive ability (speech).

83._____ Sigmund Freud was a neurologist prior to becoming a psychoanalyst.

84._____ Sigmund Freud explained the flaws in both Broca's and Wernicke's theories.

85._____   Agnosia is the inability to speak.

86._____   Sigmund Freud's first area of research was an area of the brainstem, the medulla.

87._____   Sigmund Freud's first book, which was on aphasia, was a best-seller and widely accepted among neurologists of the time.

88._____   Sigmund Freud believed that, in the future, all behavior would be able to be explained via organic processes.

89._____   Pierre Flourens was a proponent of localization theory.

90._____   An ablation experiment is one in which a part of the brain is removed.

91._____   With the ablation experiment, Flourens showed that location of ablated brain tissue was more important than the amount removed.

92._____   Pierre Flourens described brain tissue as equipotential, meaning that remaining brain tissue can compensate for that which is removed.

93._____   Pierre Flourens proved that humans only use 10% of their brains.

Localization versus Equipotentiality

Key Terms, Concepts, and Theorists

Pierre Marie	Hermann Munk	mind-blindness	Joseph Babinski
anosognosia	Karl Lashley	mass action	

Sentence Completion

94.   The ability to see an object but be unable to comprehend its significance is called
_____.

95.   An inability to recognize that you have a specific disorder is called _____.

96.   _____ studied the brains of Broca's patients and determined that the amount of brain damage present caused the inability to speak, as opposed to the location of the lesion.

97.   The principle of _____ notes that the mass of removed brain tissue is directly proportional to behavioral/cognitive dysfunction.

98.   _____ performed experiments by producing mind-blindness.

99.   _____ performed experiments very similar to those of Pierre Flourens.

100.   The founder of neurology was _____.

Integrated Theories of Brain Function

Key Terms, Concepts and Theorists

Hughlings Jackson	Alexander Luria	functional systems
pluripotentiality		

101._____ Hughlings Jackson believed that humans have a distinct speech center.

102._____ Hughlings Jackson examined the notion that higher cognitive processes are made up of simpler skills.

103._____ According to Hughlings Jackson, a single behavior can exist on several levels within the nervous system.

104._____ Hughlings Jackson believed that different areas of the brain rarely interacted with one another.

105._____ Alexander Luria disagreed vehemently with the ideas of Hughlings Jackson.

106._____ Alexander Luria proposed that three units or functions of the brain operated independently of one another.

107._____ Alexander Luria believed only in localization theory.

108._____ According to Alexander Luria, a functional system is composed of all areas of the brain required to complete a behavior.

109._____ Pluripotentiality is the theory that each area of the brain has five distinct functions.

110._____ Using the idea of Alexander Luria's functional systems, there exists some plasticity or compensation for a given ability, following damage to a given system or unit.

111._____ According to Alexander Luria's theories, there is no way to recover from a brain injury.

Modern Neuropsychology

Key Terms, Concepts and Theorists

Lobotomy	Walter Freeman	Ward Halstead	Hans-Leukas Teuber
Henry Hecaen	Arthur Benton	Oliver Zangwill	Norman Geschwind
Muriel Lezak	Halstead-Reitan Neuropsychological Test Battery		

Matching

112.	Developed objective measures for assessing functioning of the right hemisphere.	a.	Henry Hecaen
113.	Founded the first neuropsychology laboratory.	b.	Oliver Zangwill
114.	Published the classic text <u>Neuropsychological Assessment.</u>	c.	Norman Geschwind
115.	Founded the field of behavioral neurology.	d.	Walter Freeman
116.	Credited with being the first to use the term "neuropsychology" in a national forum.	e.	Arthur Benton
117.	Known predominantly for his use of lobotomies as treatment for patients.	f.	Hans-Leukas Teuber
118.	Founded the journal <u>Neuropsychologia.</u>	g.	Muriel Lezak
119.	Evaluated patients with traumatic brain injuries (TBI) during World War II.	h.	Ward Halstead

True False

120._____ A lobotomy involves the removal of brain tissue.

121._____ In the 1950s lobotomy patients were first anesthetized using electroconvulsive shock.

122._____ Some lobotomies took as little as 15 minutes to perform.

123._____ Electroconvulsive shock induces a seizure in patients.

124._____ The lobotomy was shown to cure schizophrenia in 90% of patients.

125._____ The Halstead-Reitan Neuropsychological Test Battery is an objective way in which to assess brain functioning.

126._____ Henry Hecaen proved the right hemisphere of the brain does relatively little.

127._____ Oliver Zangwill showed that the brains of left-handers are organized in exactly the same way as those of right-handers.

128._____ 1990-2000 was the decade of the brain.

129._____ There are three main professional organizations for neuropsychologists: International Neuropsychological Society (INS), National Academy of Neuropsychology (NAN), and the Division of Clinical Neuropsychology (#40) of the American Psychological Association (APA).

130._____ Currently, there are no certification boards for neuropsychologists.

131._____ Political changes in health care are impacting the field of neuropsychology.

132._____ The future of neuropsychology is an exciting one.

Post-Test
Multiple Choice

1. What type of professional is a trained psychologist who studies brain and behavior relationships?

    a. neurologist
    b. neuropsychologist
    c. neuropsychiatrist
    d. neuroscientist

2. According to the theory of vitalism, the following is true:

    a. the brain is the only vital determinant in human behavior.
    b. the brain is viewed as a machine.
    c. the brain is irrelevant since psychic phenomena are responsible for behavior.
    d. the brain in neurologically impaired individuals is controlled by spirits.

3. Trephination is:

    a. the ancient science of neuropsychology.
    b. the practice of removing the entire skull in order to preserve the brain.
    c. a surgical operation designed to remove a portion of the skull.
    d. a means to improve cognition by eliminating unwanted brain tissue.

4. Trephination was probably performed in order to:

    a. study the functioning of the human brain.
    b. treat neurological disorders.
    c. perform religious rituals.
    d. induct pledges into ancient fraternities.

5. Heraclitus is famous for recognizing that:

    a. the brain is responsible for human behavior as opposed to the heart.
    b. the mind is a vast entity which is difficult to understand.
    c. the answer my friend is blowing in the wind.
    d. the brain is constructed of four main lobes.

6. Who was one of the first people to indicate that the brain is responsible for cognitive reasoning?

    a. Leonardo da Vinci
    b. Rene Descartes
    c. Galen
    d. Pythagoras

7. What theory denotes the idea that the brain is responsible for all behavior?

    a.   the Pythagorian theorem
    b.   the brain hypothesis
    c.   vitalism
    d.   all of the above

8. Who was the first person to realize that the brain served lateralizing functions?

    a.   Hippocrates
    b.   Andreas Vesalius
    c.   George Washington
    d.   Aristotle

9. In 400 B.C., the brain was not physically studied because:

    a.   physicians lacked the proper surgical instruments.
    b.   researchers were more concerned with the mechanics of the human hand.
    c.   dissection of the human body was not permitted.
    d.   there were no satisfactory methods of documenting findings.

10. Plato divided the human soul into three parts: appetite, reason and temper. He hypothesized that the seat of reason was in the brain. This was because:

    a.   Plato believed that his own rational thoughts originated in his head and thus hypothesized the brain as the location of reason.
    b.   He noted the profound reasoning deficits of individuals with known brain damage.
    c.   He secretly performed human experiments geared to understand brain function.
    d.   Plato felt that reason was in the organ closest to the heavens.

11. Aristotle disagreed with Plato and believed that _____ was responsible for cognition.

    a.   the liver
    b.   the heart
    c.   the kidneys
    d.   the intestines

12. During the 3rd and 4th centuries B.C., Egyptian scientists learned a great deal about the human nervous system by:

    a.   reading scrolls in the library of Alexandria.
    b.   performing autopsies on individuals who died suspiciously.
    c.   improving neurosurgical techniques.
    d.   performing public dissections.

13. The ventricular localization hypothesis, which surmised that mental processes were located in the cerebral ventricles, came to be known as:

    a. the cell doctrine.
    b. the cardiac hypothesis.
    c. the brain hypothesis.
    d. materialism.

14. Leonardo da Vinci sketched a representation of what neural structure?

    a. the frontal lobes.
    b. the ventricles.
    c. the pituitary gland.
    d. the brain stem.

15. The function of cerebral spinal fluid is currently thought to be:

    a. the enhancement of higher cognitive processes.
    b. the facilitation of memory.
    c. the coordination of motor movements.
    d. the disposal of waste products.

16. Galen, a Roman physician, studied brain anatomy and function through his job as:

    a. mortician.
    b. gladiator surgeon.
    c. pediatrician.
    d. research scientist.

17. Galen hypothesized that the brain was actually a large clot of:

    a. blood.
    b. bile.
    c. phlegm.
    d. mucus.

18. The concept of humors was introduced by:

    a. Galen
    b. Leonardo da Vinci
    c. Rene Descartes
    d. Plato

19. Albertus Magnus was a German Dominican monk who hypothesized that:

    a.   the brain is inhabited by spirits who motivate behavior.
    b.   behavior is a complex act influenced by the interaction of many brain structures.
    c.   the study of neuroanatomy would lead to understanding the meaning of life.
    d.   the brain and behavior are directed by quality of blood circulating in the body at any given time.

20. Who is accredited with performing the first systematic human dissections and providing accurate drawings of anatomical structures?

    a.   Aristotle
    b.   Galen
    c.   Pythagoras
    d.   Andreas Vesalius

21. According to Rene Descartes, mental processes originated from the:

    a.   pineal gland.
    b.   cerebral ventricles.
    c.   heart.
    d.   pituitary gland.

22. Rene Descartes is considered the father of dualism. Dualism is:

    a.   a theory which states that there are two distinct halves of the brain which work separately of one another.
    b.   a theory which states that the mind and body are separate entities which interact with one another.
    c.   a theory which focuses on the relationship between black bile and yellow bile.
    d.   a theory which emphasizes the power of the church over scientific matters.

23. Thomas Willis, best known for his research on blood circulation in the brain, thought that mental faculties:

    a.   were a result of the interaction of the frontal lobes and occipital lobes.
    b.   were a myth propagated to dispel strong religious beliefs.
    c.   were present only in individuals with large brains.
    d.   were located in the corpus striatum.

24. Giovanni Lancisi disagreed with Willis and believed that the location of mental functions was to be found in:

    a.   the pineal gland.
    b.   the cerebral ventricles.
    c.   the corpus callosum.
    d.   the frontal lobes.

25. The Atharva-Veda, an Indian medical document written in 700 B.C. proposed that:

    a.   the brain was the center of the soul.
    b.   the soul and the brain were interconnected.
    c.   the soul was non-material and immortal.
    d.   the soul existed only so long as the brain survived.

26. Treatment of the mentally ill in Arab countries in the middle ages was characterized by:

    a.   an ancient form of electroconvulsive therapy.
    b.   humane and equal treatment for all.
    c.   life-long institutionalization in locked facilities.
    d.   family shame.

27. Franz Gall is well-known for his "science" of:

    a.   neuropsychology.
    b.   phrenology.
    c.   computerized tomography.
    d.   cartography.

28. Franz Gall believed that mental faculties were:

    a.   innate.
    b.   nurtured throughout the life-span.
    c.   diminished by toxic substances.
    d.   all of the above.

29. Franz Gall proposed the idea that mental faculties could be determined by:

    a.   recording reaction time following novel sounds.
    b.   taking a white blood cell count.
    c.   measuring the size of bumps and indentations of the skull.
    d.   weighing the brain post-mortem.

30. Franz Gall formulated the basis of what theory?

    a.   pluripotentiality
    b.   equipotentiatility
    c.   objective neuropsychological measurement
    d.   localization

31. Franz Gall hypothesized correctly that what parts of the brain were the most intellectual parts?

    a.   frontal lobes
    b.   occipital lobes
    c.   temporal lobes
    d.   parietal lobes

32. Which of the following did Franz Gall claim to be able to measure through phrenology?

    a.   friendship
    b.   combativeness
    c.   destructiveness
    d.   parental love
    e.   all of the above

33. Currently, phrenology is:

    a.   believed to be completely inaccurate.
    b.   still practiced widely.
    c.   used only in conjunction with other techniques.
    d.   none of the above.

34. Phrenology in the United States was:

    a.   immediately detected as a farce.
    b.   of little interest to American scientists.
    c.   popular.
    d.   Phrenology was never introduced to the United States.

35. Franz Gall's student was:

    a.   Sigmund Freud.
    b.   Johann Spruzheim.
    c.   Paul Broca.
    d.   Carl Wernicke.

36. Franz Gall believed that there were significant differences between the brains of:

    a.   men and women.
    b.   different racial groups.
    c.   both a and b.
    d.   none of the above.

37. In the United States, what famous murderer's brain has been preserved for research?

    a.   Ted Bundy
    b.   Jack the Ripper
    c.   The Son of Sam
    d.   Jeffrey Dahmer

38. Analysis of the brains of geniuses and criminals has shown that:

    a.   there are consistent and definitive differences in each type of brain.
    b.   there are absolutely no differences.
    c.   there is no conclusive evidence upon which conclusions may be drawn.
    d.   criminal brains show obvious pathology.

39. Robert Ley's brain was proven to:

    a.   have obvious pathology, explaining the atrocious behavior of the Nazis.
    b.   have no blatant pathology.
    c.   be missing major structures related to conscience.
    d.   both a and c.

40. Paul Broca is most famous for:

    a.   localizing expressive speech.
    b.   localizing receptive speech.
    c.   determining a circuit for all aspects of speech.
    d.   discovering a new neuroanatomical structure.

41. Aphasia refers to:

    a.   lacking the ability to move any part of the face.
    b.   a disruption in speech.
    c.   the inability to coordinate muscle movements.
    d.   differences between the right and left hemispheres of the brain.

42. Paul Broca based his historical conclusions on:

    a.   elaborate empirical research.
    b.   the objective measurement of expressive speech.
    c.   hundreds of brain dissections.
    d.   case studies.

43. It is probable that the most famous patient of Paul Broca's, Monsier Leborgne had:

    a.   damage only to "Broca's Area."
    b.   had diffuse damage thus confounding Broca's conclusions.
    c.   was subsequently found to have no brain damage at all.
    d.   none of the above.

44. In order to attribute a specific function to a specific neuroanatomical site, what must be true?

    a.   That specific function is impaired after damage to the site.
    b.   That specific function is enhanced following electrical stimulation.
    c.   That specific function does not become impaired following damage to another site.
    d.   Both a and c.

45. Carl Wernicke is most famous for:

    a.   localizing expressive speech.
    b.   localizing receptive speech.
    c.   determining a circuit for all aspects of speech.
    d.   discovering a new neuroanatomical structure.

46. If a patient sounds as if they are speaking in an unknown foreign language this may be explained by that fact that they are experiencing:

    a.   agnosia.
    b.   fluent aphasia.
    c.   multiple personality disorder.
    d.   an aneurysm.

47. Wernicke inadvertently showed that:

    a.   language could not be localized.
    b.   research of the structures of the human brain was impossible.
    c.   Broca was completely inaccurate in his conclusions.
    d.   none of the above.

48. Prior to developing his theory of psychoanalysis, Sigmund Freud was:

    a.   a neuroscientist.
    b.   a shoe salesman.
    c.   a psychologist.
    d.   a neurologist.

49. Sigmund Freud criticized the theories of:

    a.   Galen and Hippocrates.
    b.   Broca and Wernicke.
    c.   Ley and Spurzheim.
    d.   Vesalius and Gall.

50. Sigmund Freud contended that:

    a.   language was represented by a complex interchange of neurons.
    b.   there was a specific identifiable lesion for each different aphasia.
    c.   there was no way in which to adequately study aphasia except for dream analysis.
    d.   language was represented in the right hemisphere.

51. Sigmund Freud published papers on what brain structure?

    a.   the frontal lobes
    b.   the pineal gland
    c.   the medulla
    d.   the corpus striatum

52. Sigmund Freud researched which of the following topics?

    a.   visual field deficits
    b.   the brainstem
    c.   hemianopsia
    d.   all of the above

53. Pierre Flourens utilized _____ as a method of investigation into brain function

    a.   the case study
    b.   the lobotomy
    c.   electroconvulsive shock
    d.   the ablation experiment

54. Through his experiments Pierre Flourens supported the theory of:

    a.   pluripotentiality
    b.   localization
    c.   equipotentiality
    d.   phrenology

55. Flourens suggested that _____ of the brain is actually used.

    a.   100%
    b.   50%
    c.   10%
    d.   0% (in a small number of college professors)

56. In Hermann Munk's experiments, he conditioned dogs to associate the shape of a triangle with fear. After the teaching trials, he lesioned the association cortex of the dogs. What was the result?

    a.   The dogs showed no changes.
    b.   The dogs were no longer fearful of the triangular shape due to a process called mind-blindness.
    c.   The dogs became fearful of all objects due to a process called mind-blindness.
    d.   One of the dogs bit Hermann Munk who ceased his experimentation.

57. The term, anosognosia, refers to:

    a.   the inability to speak.
    b.   the inability to understand speech.
    c.   unawareness that one has a certain disorder.
    d.   the inability to see or hear.

58. Who introduced the term, anosognosia?

    a.   Sigmund Freud
    b.   Hermann Munk
    c.   Aristotle
    d.   Joseph Babinski

59. Karl Lashley performed ablation experiments on:

    a.   birds.
    b.   dogs.
    c.   humans.
    d.   rats.

60. Karl Lashley concluded from his experiments that:

    a.   the location of the ablated material is the most important determinant for degree of impairment.
    b.   the technique used to ablate brain tissue is the most important determinant for degree of impairment.
    c.   the amount of tissue ablated is the most important determinant for degree of impairment.
    d.   the age of the test subject is the most important determinant for degree of impairment.

61. Karl Lashley's famous principle is called:

    a.   mind-blindness
    b.   mass action
    c.   anosognosia
    d.   vitalism

62. Karl Lashley believed that:

    a.   each part of the brain has more than one function.
    b.   each part of the brain has exactly three functions.
    c.   each part of the brain has one function.
    d.   over half of neuroanatomical structures have no functions.

63. Hughlings Jackson believed that:

    a.   the loss of a certain cognitive ability can be attributed to the loss of more basic abilities.
    b.   the loss of a certain cognitive ability can be attributed to the destruction of localized brain tissue.
    c.   the loss of a certain cognitive ability is unrelated to brain damage.
    d.   the loss of a certain cognitive ability can be attributed to the ablation of brain tissue only in the left hemisphere.

64. Hughlings Jackson believed that:

    a.   all areas of the brain interact with one another.
    b.   different parts of the brain act independently of others.
    c.   one part of the brain interacts and mediates for all others.
    d.   the left hemisphere does not communicate with the right hemisphere.

65. Alexander Luria developed a theory of three functional units, composed of:

    a.   the brain stem, spinal cord and frontal lobes.
    b.   the brain stem, posterior areas of the cortex and frontal lobes.
    c.   the spinal cord, frontal lobes and corpus striatum.
    d.   the frontal lobes, prefrontal lobes and Broca's area.

66. According to Alexander Luria, these three functional units are involved in:

    a.   conscious behavior.
    b.   unconscious behavior.
    c.   involuntary reflexes.
    d.   all behavior.

67. How much of the brain would you hypothesize Alexander Luria to believe we use at any given time? (Even though you are hypothesizing, there is a right answer.)

    a.   100%
    b.   75%
    c.   50%
    d.   10%

68. A functional system, according to Alexander Luria is:

    a.   a neurological representation of an involuntary response.
    b.   a neurological representation of a conscious response.
    c.   a neurological representation of language.
    d.   all of the above.

69. Alexander Luria's work supports the theory of:

    a.   localization
    b.   equipotentiality
    c.   pluripotentiality
    d.   materialism

70. According to Alexander Luria, following brain trauma, what is likely to occur?

    a.   Following brain trauma, neurons will continue to die and the individual will become more impaired.
    b.   Following brain trauma, an alternative functional system may be able to compensate for some or all of the impairment.
    c.   Following brain trauma, the entire functional system which included the damaged tissue will fail.
    d.   Following brain trauma, new neurons will grow.

71. Who were the first people to operate on the human frontal lobes in an effort to treat mental illness?

    a.   Freud and Gall
    b.   Moniz and Lima
    c.   Freeman and Watts
    d.   Jackson and Luria

72. What was the procedure called, which included severing neural connections to the frontal lobes?

    a.   temporal lobectomy
    b.   frontal lobotomy
    c.   frontal lobectomy
    d.   electroconvulsive shock therapy

73. Which of the following is a characteristic of a lobotomy performed by Freeman?

    a.   Electroconvulsive shock was used to anesthetize the patient prior to the lobotomy.
    b.   The procedure was done in the psychiatrist's office.
    c.   A leucotome was pushed through the orbital cavity and into the brain.
    d.   All of the above.

74. What mental illness was treated by the frontal lobotomy more than any other?

    a.   Depression
    b.   Multiple Personality Disorder
    c.   Antisocial Personality Disorder
    d.   Schizophrenia

75. Ward Halstead is attributed with:

    a.   founding the first neuropsychology laboratory.
    b.   development of an objective means of assessing brain function.
    c.   development of the Halstead-Reitan Neuropsychological Test Battery.
    d.   all of the above.

76. Who is the first person credited for using the term "neuropsychology" in a national forum?

    a.   Sigmund Freud
    b.   Alexander Luria
    c.   Ward Halstead
    d.   Hans-Leukas Teuber

77. Henry Hecaen is credited with:

    a.   writing Neuropsychological Assessment.
    b.   studying the right hemisphere of the brain.
    c.   founding the National Academy of Neuropsychology.
    d.   all of the above.

78. Arthur Benton is credited with:

    a.   founding the journal, Neuropsychologia.
    b.   studying the right hemisphere of the brain.
    c.   founding the first neuropsychology laboratory in the United States.
    d.   all of the above.

79. Who showed that left and right-handers may have different dominant cerebral hemispheres?

    a.   Arthur Benton
    b.   Alexander Luria
    c.   Norman Geschwind
    d.   Oliver Zangwill

80. Who is famous for the idea that behavioral impairment is a result of damage to brain pathways?

    a.   Oliver Zangwill
    b.   Norman Geschwind
    c.   Hughlings Jackson
    d.   Muriel Lezak

81. Muriel Lezak is well-known for:

    a.   developing the first neuropsychological test battery.
    b.   writing <u>Neuropsychological Assessment.</u>
    c.   opposing the use of neuropsychological tests.
    d.   none of the above.

82. The last three decades have been characterized by what developments in the field of neuropsychology?

    a.   Formation of professional organizations for neuropsychologists.
    b.   Founding of many different journals in the field of neuropsychology.
    c.   Increase in the recognition of neuropsychology as a field of psychology.
    d.   All of the above.

83. It is hypothesized that in the future:

    a.   Neuropsychologists will no longer be needed.
    b.   There will be biological explanations for mental illnesses.
    c.   Genetic explanations of behavior will disappear.
    d.   Means of protecting the brain from injury will decrease.

Essay Questions

1.   What is trephination and how does it relate to current medical practices?

2.   Discuss the contributions of Paul Broca and Carl Wernicke to neuropsychology.

3.   In one paragraph, argue against the statement that humans only use 10% of their brains, integrating theories from this chapter.

Answer Key

Chapter Exercises

1. Neurosurgeon (p.4)
2. Neurons (p.5)
3. Neuroscientist (p.4)
4. Vitalism (p.5)
5. Neuropsychologist (p.4)
6. Neuropsychiatrist (p.4)
7. Neurologist (p.4)
8. Materialism (p.5)
9. Psychologist (p.4)
10. k (p.11)
11. i (p.14)
12. d (p.8)
13. g (p.8)
14. h (p.11)
15. a (p.10)
16. c (p.13)
17. f (p.9)
18. e (p.8)
19. j (p.8)
20. b (p.13)
21. False (p.5)
22. False (p.5)
23. True (p.6)
24. True (p.7)
25. True (p.7)
26. True (p.8)
27. False (p.8)
28. False (p.8)
29. True (p.8)
30. False (p.8)
31. True (p.8)
32. True (p.8)
33. False (p.8)
34. True (p.9)
35. False (p.9)
36. True (p.9)
37. False (p.9)
38. True (p.9)
39. True (p.10)
40. True (p.10)
41. False (p.11)
42. True (p.11)
43. True (p.11)

44. False (p.13)
45. True (p.11)
46. False (p.11)
47. False (p.13)
48. False (p.13)
49. False (p.14)
50. False (p.14)
51. True (p.14)
52. d (p.16)
53. c (p.22)
54. e (p.23)
55. f (p.18)
56. a (p.15)
57. b (p.20)
58. True (p.15)
59. False (p.15)
60. True (p.15)
61. True (p.15)
62. True (p.16)
63. False (p.16)
64. True (p.16)
65. False (p.16)
66. True (p.17)
67. False (p.17)
68. True (p.19)
69. True (p.19)
70. False (p.19)
71. True (p.18)
72. False (p.19)
73. True (p.19)
74. True (p.20)
75. False (p.21)
76. True (pp.17,21)
77. False (p.20)
78. True (p.20)
79. False (p.20)
80. True (p.20)
81. True (p.20)
82. True (p.21)
83. True (p.21)
84. True (p.21)
85. False (p.22)
86. True (p.23)
87. False (p.23)
88. True (p.23)
89. False (p.22)

90. True (p.22)
91. False (p.22)
92. True (p.22)
93. False (p.22)
94. mind-blindness (p.24)
95. anosognosia (p.24)
96. Pierre Marie (p.23)
97. mass action (p.24)
98. Hermann Munk (p.24)
99. Karl Lashley (p.24)
100. Joseph Babinski (p.24)
101. False (p.24)
102. True (p.24)
103. True (p.25)
104. False (p.25)
105. False (p.25)
106. False (p.26)
107. False (p.26)
108. True (p.26)
109. False (p.26)
110. True (p.26)
111. False (p.26)
112. e (p.31)
113. h (p.27)
114. g (p.32)
115. c (p.31)
116. f (p.30)
117. d (p.27)
118. a (p.31)
119. b (p.31)
120. False (p.29)
121. True (p.29)
122. True (p.29)
123. True (p.28)
124. False (p.30)
125. True (p.30)
126. False (p.31)
127. False (p.31)
128. True (p.32)
129. True (p.32)
130. False (p.32)
131. True (p.33)
132. True

Post-Test

Multiple Choice

1.	B (p.4)	46.	B (p.20)
2.	C (p.5)	47.	A (p.21)
3.	C (p.5)	48.	D (p.21)
4.	B (p.7)	49.	B (p.21)
5.	B (p.8)	50.	A (p.22)
6.	D (p.8)	51.	C (p.23)
7.	B (p.8)	52.	D (p.23)
8.	A (p.8)	53.	D (p.22)
9.	C (p.8)	54.	C (p.22)
10.	D (p.8)	55.	C (p.22)
11.	B (p.8)	56.	B (p.24)
12.	D (p.9)	57.	C (p.24)
13.	A (p.9)	58.	D (p.24)
14.	B (p.9)	59.	D (p.24)
15.	D (p.9)	60.	C (p.24)
16.	B (p.10)	61.	B (p.24)
17.	C (p.10)	62.	A (p.24)
18.	A (p.11)	63.	A (p.25)
19.	B (p.11)	64.	A (p.25)
20.	D (p.11)	65.	B (p.25)
21.	A (p.11)	66.	D (p.26)
22.	B (p.13)	67.	A (p.26)
23.	D (p.13)	68.	D (p.26)
24.	C (p.14)	69.	C (p.26)
25.	C (p.14)	70.	B (p.26)
26.	B (p.14)	71.	B (p.26)
27.	B (p.16)	72.	B (p.28)
28.	A (p.15)	73.	D (p.29)
29.	C (p.16)	74.	D (p.30)
30.	D (p.16)	75.	D (pp.27,30)
31.	A (p.16)	76.	D (p.30)
32.	E (p.16)	77.	B (p.31)
33.	A (p.17)	78.	B (p.31)
34.	C (p.16)	79.	D (p.31)
35.	B (p.16)	80.	B (p.31)
36.	C (p.17)	81.	B (p.31)
37.	D (p.17)	82.	D (pp.32,33)
38.	C (p.17)	83.	B (p.33)
39.	B (p.19)		
40.	A (p.18)		
41.	B (p.18)		
42.	D (p.18)		
43.	B (p.21)		
44.	D (p.20)		
45.	B (p.20)		

Chapter 2

The Functioning Brain
A Closer Look at Neurons

Chapter Outline

Overview

The human brain is made up of billions of neurons that form exceedingly complex structures. The number of interconnections is mind-boggling and to understand the neurological organization of the brain is a daunting task. Brain scientists have only begun to connect the structural hardware, the neurons, neuronal systems, and brain structures, with the software of behavior, thought, and emotions. In this chapter we outline the function of a single neuron and how neurons communicate with each other. The neuron can be studied as a universe unto its own. Neurons exchange information with each other through action potentials analogous to simple yes/no messages. All human behavioral events originate from this basic process mediated by interconnections and fiber systems in different areas of the brain. Thus, it is important for the neuropsychology student to learn as much as is possible about these interconnections of the brain, before learning about brain-behavior relationships. Different topics like the neuron's ability to regenerate are emphasized in this chapter in order to give a brief review of the central nervous system and to provide basic terminology. We review neuronal structures and their function, describe the supporting cells within the brain, and summarize the most well known neurotransmitters.

Learning Objectives

- To learn the anatomical structure and function of the neuron.
- To learn how neurons communicate with each other and how such communication can result in behavior or the absence of behavior.
- To understand the major groups of neurotransmitters found in the brain and how they influence neuronal communication.
- To obtain an appreciation of the limitations of neurons.

Neurons and Supporting Cells: The Central Nervous System

Key Terms and Concepts

gray matter	dendrites	Purkinje Cell	Pyramidal Cell
axon	myelin sheath	white matter	oligodendrocytes
Schwann Cells	nodes of Ranvier	multiple sclerosis	terminal buttons
synapse	multipolar neuron	bipolar neuron	
monopolar neuron	interneuron	motor neuron	
sensory neuron	tracts	pathways	
fibers	nerves	intracerebral fibers	
intercerebral fibers	nuclei	ganglia	
glia	astrocytes	blood brain barrier	

True/False

1._____   Neurons act independently of other neurons.

2._____   There are approximately one billion neurons in the cerebral cortex.

3._____   Neurons communicate with one another via an electrochemical impulse.

4._____   Humans regenerate neurons annually.

5._____   Paralysis gives evidence that neurons in the central nervous system do not regenerate.

6._____   The structure of the neuron is specialized to send and receive electrochemical signals.

7._____   Cell bodies are white, thus the term white matter is used when referring to areas of the brain dense in cell bodies.

8._____   Protein synthesis occurs in the axon as well as the cell body.

9._____   Dendrites deliver chemical messages to neurons.

10._____   Purkinje cells are found in the cerebellar cortex.

11._____   Pyramidal cells are found in the hippocampus.

12._____   Dendrites are longer than axons.

13._____   The axon's function is to transmit electochemical information.

14._____   The myelin sheath serves to slow down axonal transmission.

15._____   Myelin is white in color, giving rise to the term white matter.

16._____   Myelin functions as a sort of insulation.

17._____   In the central nervous system the myelin sheath is formed by oligodendrocytes.

18._____   Schwann cells form the myelin sheath in the peripheral nervous system.

19._____   Nodes of Ranvier are naturally occurring gaps in the myelin sheath.

20._____   Myelination is completed by birth in humans.

21._____   Two-year olds may not be able to successfully achieve toilet training due to insufficient myelination of axons.

22._____   Fast axonal conduction serves an evolutionary purpose in allowing us to respond quickly in dangerous situations.

23._____   Because of the incredibly long distances that neural impulses had to travel in dinosaurs, they had an additional brain located in the pelvis to compensate.

24._____   Multiple Sclerosis (MS) is the result of the demyelination of axons.

25._____   MS is most likely to be noticed when individuals are in their 70's or 80's.

26._____   MS occurs equally in all geographical locations.

27._____   Symptoms accompanying MS are the direct result of impaired neuronal transmission.

28._____   There is no cure for MS.

29._____   Terminal buttons are located at the end of the axon and are also called axon terminals.

30._____   Neurochemical information is transmitted from one neuron to another across the synapse.

31._____   The terminal button is post-synaptic.

32._____   As with axonal transmission, signals traveling across the synapse are electrical.

33._____   Multipolar neurons have two axons.

34._____   Bipolar neurons have one axon which sends information in either direction.

35._____   A monopolar neuron has one axon.

36._____   An interneuron has three axons which integrate neural activity within a specific brain region.

37._____   Motor neurons affect muscles and glands.

38._____   Sensory neurons respond only to light.

39._____   Most neurons are interneurons.

40._____   In the central nervous system bundles of myelinated axons are called pathways, fibers, tracts, and white matter.

41._____   In the peripheral nervous system bundles of myelinated axons are called tracts.

42._____   Intracerebral fibers connect structures in the two cerebral hemispheres.

43._____   Intercerebral fibers connect regions within one hemisphere.

44._____   White matter is typically found on the surface of the cerebral cortex.

45._____   In the central nervous system clusters of gray cell bodies are called ganglia.

46._____   In the peripheral nervous system clusters of gray cell bodies are called nuclei.

47._____   Nuclei are generally not thought to play a role in functional behavior.

48._____   There are many more nerve cells than supporting cells in the human brain.

49._____   Support cells are directly involved in the electrical transmission of nerve impulses.

50._____   Glia cells surround neurons and buffer them from other neurons.

51._____   Glia cells control the oxygen supply of neurons and remove "dead" nerve cells.

52._____   An astrocyte is a type of glia cell.

53._____   One of the functions of the astrocyte is to decrease swelling of neurons following a traumatic brain injury.

54._____   The swelling of astrocytes following a traumatic brain injury can result in a coma.

55._____   Blood flows directly to neurons.

56._____   Astrocytes make up part of the blood-brain barrier.

57._____   Oligodendrocytes and Schwann cells are types of glia cells.

58._____   Schwann cells are able to myelinate several segments of an axon simultaneously.

Labeling

Identify each of these structures of the neuron:

a.   axon
b.   cell body
c.   nucleus
d.   myelin sheath
e.   dendrites

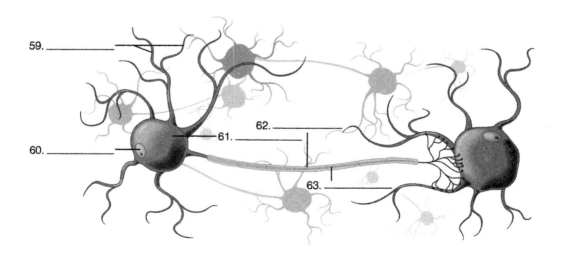

Communication Within a Neuron: The Neural Impulse

<u>Key Terms and Concepts</u>

resting potential	membrane potential	ions
sodium-potassium pump	action potential	depolarization
refractory period	disinhibition	seizure
Electroconvulsive shock therapy	electroencephalogram	

<u>Matching</u>

64.	ions	a.	It is the same as membrane potential.
65.	electroencephalogram	b.	It results in the firing of the neuron.
66.	refractory period	c.	A transport system which exchanges sodium and potassium.
67.	resting potential	d.	A result of the loss of inhibitory neurons.
68.	membrane potential	e.	A slight chemical imbalance between the inner and outer surfaces of the neural membrane when the neuron is inactive.
69.	seizure	f.	Monitors the brain's electrical activity.
70.	depolarization	g.	Induces a seizure to improve depression.
71.	action potential	h.	During this period, the neuron cannot fire.
72.	disinhibition	i.	An "electrical storm" in the brain.
73.	sodium-potassium pump	j.	Sodium ions pass through the membrane and reduce its voltage.
74.	Electroconvulsive Therapy (ECT)	k.	An electrically charged molecule.

Communication Among Neurons

reductionism	synaptic knobs	synaptic vesicles
receptor sites	excitatory postsynaptic potential	neurotransmitters
biogenic amines	inhibitory postsynaptic potential	amino acids
peptides	acetylcholine	muscarinic
nicotinic	striatum	reticular activating system
basal forebrain	hippocampus	nuclear basalis of Meynert
serotonin	raphe nuclei	norepinephrine
locus ceruleus	substantia nigra	dopamine
glutamate	gamma-amino butyric acid	endorphins

True/False

75._____ Reductionists believe that there are distinct neuroanatomical correlates for every human behavior.

76._____ Most neurons are present in the human fetus by the fifth month.

77._____ By middle age, humans lose thousands of neuronal connections a day.

78._____ Neurons are physically connected to one another.

79._____ A single, simple human behavior requires the communication of millions of neurons.

80._____ While learning about neuropsychology, you are developing new connections among your own neurons.

81._____ Synaptic knobs or buttons have direct contact with the postsynpatic neuron.

82._____ The space separating two neurons is called the synaptic cleft.

83._____ The synaptic cleft is so distinct that it is easily observed by the human eye.

84._____ Synaptic vesicles exist within the synaptic cleft.

85._____ Neurotransmitters are found within the synaptic vesicle.

86._____ Different neurotransmitters have their own specific receptor sites on the postsynaptic neuron.

87._____ The symmetrical synapse is involved in inhibitory functions.

88._____ The asymmetrical synapse is involved in excitatory functions.

89._____ Terminal buttons are only found on dendrites.

90._____ The synapse consists of the postsynaptic membrane, the presynaptic membrane and the synaptic cleft.

91._____ The neural impulse stimulates the release of neurotransmitters.

92._____ Once a neurotransmitter has been released, all of the neurotransmitter molecules readily bind to the postsynaptic neuron.

93._____ Once a neurotransmitter binds with the receptor site, either a postsynaptic excitation or inhibition is stimulated in the receiving neuron.

94._____ The act of the binding of a neurotransmitter can result in the depolarization of the postsynaptic neuron.

95._____ The depolarization of the postsynaptic neuron is referred to as inhibitory postsynaptic potential.

96._____ The hyperpolarization of the postsynaptic neuron is referred to as excitatory postsynaptic potential.

97._____ Neurotransmitters come in different shapes and sizes.

98._____ Neuropeptides are smaller than biogenic amines.

99._____ There are over 100 different types of neuropeptides.

100._____ The amino acids consist of acetylcholine and serotonin.

101._____ Acetylcholine (ACh) plays a role in attention and memory.

102._____ Acetylcholine's method of action is well-understood.

103._____ One of the complications associated with ACh is that choline cannot cross the blood-brain barrier.

104._____ ACh can bind to more than one postsynaptic receptor site.

105._____ Two main receptor subtypes for ACh are muscarinic and nicotinic.

106._____ The distribution of ACh in the brain is specific and limited.

107._____ ACh neurons or cholinergic neurons located in the striatum influence motor functioning.

108._____ ACh impacts the reticular activating system and subsequently influences sleep patterns.

109._____ Decreased levels of ACh in the basal forebrain are associated with increased levels of wakefulness.

110._____ The hippocampus is thought to be associated with memory.

111._____ Individuals suffering from Alzheimer's Disease have inordinantly high levels of ACh in the nucleus basalis of Meynert.

112._____ Scopolamine has a positive impact on memory.

113._____ Clinical trials including manipulation of ACh levels in Alzheimer's patients have been promising.

114._____ The dopamine system originates within the raphe nuclei.

115._____ Serotonin is believed to play a large role in mood, emotions and sleep.

116._____ Increased levels of serotonin have been linked to depression.

117._____ Norepinephrine originates within the locus ceruleus.

118._____ Norepinephrine is the most prominent neurotransmitter implicated in schizophrenia.

119._____ Most dopamine is found in the substantia nigra.

120._____ 90% of all synapses in the central nervous system are receptive to the amino acid, gamma-amino butyric acid (GABA).

121._____ GABA is a prominent inhibitory neurotransmitter.

122._____ A peptide is a short chain of amino acids.

123._____ Endorphins are an example of a peptide.

Labeling

Identify each of these structures/events of synaptic transmission.

a.   neurotransmitter molecules
b.   axon
c.   synaptic cleft
d.   receptor sites
e.   terminal button
f.   neural impulse
g.   postsynaptic membrane

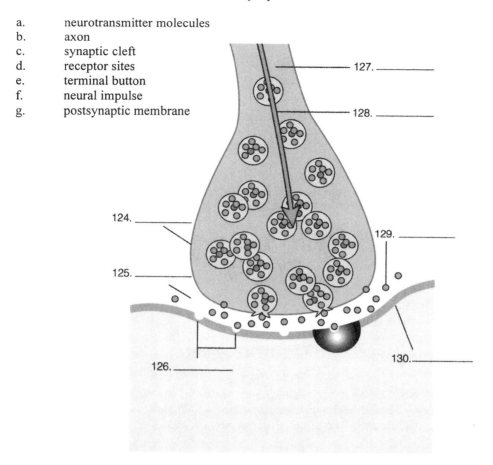

124. _____
125. _____
126. _____
127. _____
128. _____
129. _____
130. _____

The Regeneration of Neurons

True/False

131._____   Regenerative capacity of damaged neurons in the peripheral nervous system is poor.

132._____   Regenerative capacity of damaged neurons in the central nervous system is good.

133._____   Paraplegia results from injury to neurons in the spinal cord.

134._____   Humans regenerate neurons every 20 years.

135._____   Some songbirds form new neurons in relation to seasonal changes.

Post-Test
Multiple Choice

1. In the human central nervous system, what percentage of cells are neurons?

    a. 25%
    b. 33%
    c. 50%
    d. 85%

2. Which region of the human central nervous system contains the most neurons?

    a. Association cortex.
    b. Cerebral cortex.
    c. Cerebellum.
    d. Spinal cord.

3. In Greek, glia translates into:

    a. glue.
    b. little brain.
    c. cell.
    d. There is no comprehensible translation.

4. All neurons consist of which of the following structures?

    a. Cell body, dendrites, lucites, and axon.
    b. Nucleus, dendrites, ketones, and axon.
    c. Cell body, dendrites, terminal buttons, and ketones.
    d. Cell body, dendrites, terminal buttons, and axon.

5. Neurons communicate with each other via:

    a. the cellular membrane.
    b. the blood-brain barrier.
    c. electrochemical transmission.
    d. digital phones.

6. The gap between two neurons is called:

    a. a node of Ranvier.
    b. a synapse.
    c. a neuronal break.
    d. a critical juncture.

7. In the central nervous system, neurons:

    a. regenerate regularly, particularly after some kind of trauma.
    b. reorganize themselves methodically to compensate for damaged cells.
    c. can be regenerated with the proper medication and neuropsychological treatment.
    d. do not regenerate.

8. Cell bodies are:

    a. gray.
    b. red.
    c. white.
    d. blue.

9. Generally, neurons have how many dendrites?

    a. At least 10.
    b. Hundreds.
    c. Thousands.
    d. Millions.

10. Purkinje cells are found in the:

    a. cerebral cortex.
    b. cerebellar cortex.
    c. association cortex.
    d. spinal cord.

11. The axon:

    a. transmits electrochemical information.
    b. receives electrochemical information.
    c. interprets electrochemical information.
    d. none of the above.

12. The myelin sheath:

    a. is implicated in Multiple Sclerosis.
    b. is white in color.
    c. increases the speed of axonal transmission.
    d. all of the above.

13. In the central nervous system, the myelin sheath is formed by:

      a.   Schwann cells.
      b.   nodes of Ranvier.
      c.   oligodendrocytes.
      d.   dendrites.

14. Which of the following statements is true regarding myelination?

      a.   Myelination is completed by birth in humans.
      b.   Myelination of axons results in successful toilet training in humans.
      c.   Failure of axons to become myelinated in the first years of life causes Multiple Sclerosis.
      d.   Myelination causes neural messages to slow down giving the brain time to interpret all incoming stimuli.

15. Dinosaurs required an additional brain in their pelvis because:

      a.   their large size required additional neurons for processes such as memory and spatial reasoning.
      b.   compensation was required for the distance in which messages had to travel along axons.
      c.   compensation was required for the lack of terminal buttons which had not yet evolved.
      d.   this development enhanced the reproductive process.

16. Multiple Sclerosis is first noticed between the ages of:

      a.   10-20.
      b.   20-40.
      c.   40-60.
      d.   60-80.

17. Which of the following are symptoms of Multiple Sclerosis?

      a.   Blindness.
      b.   Tremors.
      c.   Paraplegia.
      d.   All of the above.

18. The terminal button is:

      a.   presynaptic.
      b.   postsynaptic.
      c.   located in the synapse.
      d.   present only in Schwann cells.

19. The synapse is:

    a.   a space across which chemical messages are sent.
    b.   a space across which electrical messages are sent.
    c.   a space across which chemical and electrical messages are sent.
    d.   none of the above.

20. _____ neurons have more than two axons.

    a.   Unipolar neurons
    b.   Bipolar neurons
    c.   Monopolar neurons
    d.   Multipolar neurons

21. The majority of neurons are:

    a.   sensory neurons.
    b.   motor neurons.
    c.   unipolar neurons.
    d.   interneurons.

22. Collections of axons in the central nervous system are referred to as:

    a.   tracts.
    b.   fibers.
    c.   white matter.
    d.   all of the above.

23. Collections of axons in the peripheral nervous system are referred to as:

    a.   neurons.
    b.   nerves.
    c.   pathways.
    d.   gray matter.

24. Association fibers which connect regions within one cerebral hemisphere are called:

    a.   intercerebral.
    b.   projection.
    c.   intracerebral.
    d.   nerves.

25. In which of the following would gray matter not be found?

    a.   Spinal cord.
    b.   Cerebral cortex.
    c.   Axons.
    d.   Thalamus.

26. Gray cell bodies in the central nervous system are called:

    a.   ganglia.
    b.   neurons.
    c.   nuclei.
    d.   nerves.

27. Gray cell bodies in the peripheral nervous system are called:

    a.   ganglia.
    b.   neurons.
    c.   nuclei.
    d.   nerves.

28. Which of the following is true with regards to support cells?

    a.   Support cells are directly implicated in the transmission of neural messages.
    b.   Support cells transport nutrients for storage in neurons.
    c.   Support cells outnumber nerve cells.
    d.   Support cells provide nutrients with the exception of oxygen to neurons.

29. Glia cells:

    a.   control the oxygen supply to neurons.
    b.   assist in the transmission of nerve impulses.
    c.   are not implicated in brain tumors.
    d.   none of the above.

30. Astrocytes:

    a.   are found in white matter.
    b.   have one primary function (i.e., regulate ion balance).
    c.   are not implicated in coma after brain injury.
    d.   none of the above.

31. Which of the following would not be transferable across the blood-brain barrier?

    a.   Oxygen.
    b.   Water.
    c.   Carbon dioxide.
    d.   Electrically charged molecules.

32. A membrane potential exists when the neuron is:

    a.   inactive.
    b.   firing.
    c.   depolarizing.
    d.   in a refractory period.

33. Ions are:

    a.   implicated only in the depolarization of the neuron.
    b.   required for communication to occur between neurons.
    c.   integral in the regeneration of neurons.
    d.   something with which your high school chemistry teacher tortured you endlessly.

34. When the neuron is not firing, which ions are located outside of the neuron?

    a.   Sodium.
    b.   Potassium.
    c.   Calcium.
    d.   Chloride.

35. The sodium-potassium pump:

    a.   pumps sodium out of the cell because it is naturally attracted to the inside of the neuron.
    b.   pumps sodium into the cell in order to maintain equal electrical charges between the inside and outside of the neuron.
    c.   pumps an equal amount of sodium and potassium in and out of the cell in order for the neuron to fire.
    d.   is a passive system which requires the expenditure of little cellular energy.

36. A rapid influx of sodium ions into the neuron results in:

    a.   a membrane potential.
    b.   an action potential.
    c.   destruction of the sodium-potassium pump.
    d.   disinhibition.

37. Which of the following statements is true?

    a.   Neuronal firing can be halted at varying stages following depolarization.
    b.   When in the proper circumstances, a neuron can fire following sub-threshold stimulation.
    c.   Timing and sequence of neural impulses are random.
    d.   Neurons fire in an all-or-none fashion.

38. During the refractory period:

    a.   the neuron cannot fire.
    b.   the neuron can fire but only with increased stimulation.
    c.   the neuron is in a vulnerable state which makes it more vulnerable to neurologic injury.
    d.   None of the above.

39. The loss of inhibitory neurons may result in:

    a.   impulsiveness.
    b.   crying.
    c.   hypersexuality.
    d.   All of the above.

40. Which of the following statements is true regarding seizures?

    a.   Seizures are not caused by tumors.
    b.   Seizures may result in alterations in mood.
    c.   Seizures are the result of increased chemical activity in the brain.
    d.   None of the above.

41. Novocaine:

    a.   prevents sodium ions from entering the neuron.
    b.   facilitates sodium ions in entering the neuron.
    c.   prevents potassium ions from entering the neuron.
    d.   facilitates potassium ions in entering the neuron.

42. Lithium:

    a.   is a well understood mood stabilizer commonly used in the treatment of bipolar disorder.
    b.   may replace sodium in crossing the neuronal membrane thus impacting brain activity and subsequently mood.
    c.   is known to coordinate the exchange of sodium and potassium, subsequently stabilizing mood.
    d.   None of the above.

43. Which of the following statements regarding Electroconvulsive Therapy (ECT) is true?

    a.   ECT induces a seizure.
    b.   ECT is a treatment used today.
    c.   ECT is an effective cure for depression.
    d.   All of the above.

44. When is an individual considered dead?

    a.   When the lungs cease to function.
    b.   When the brain stops firing.
    c.   When the heart stops beating.
    d.   When a medical examiner says so.

45. Reductionism is closely associated with what theory:

      a.   Localization.
      b.   The Cell Doctrine.
      c.   The Cardiac Hypothesis.
      d.   Vitalism.

46. Which of the following may interfere with neuronal development in the fetus?

      a.   Maternal smoking.
      b.   Exposure to alcohol.
      c.   Exposure to drugs.
      d.   All of the above

47. Which of the following statements is true regarding synaptic knobs?

      a.   Synaptic knobs are in direct contact with the postsynaptic membrane in order to facilitate communcation.
      b.   Synaptic vesicles are found within the synaptic knob.
      c.   Synaptic knobs are only found on axons.
      d.   Each neuron has one synaptic knob.

48. Synaptic vesicles:

      a.   are found in the synaptic cleft.
      b.   provide nutrients to the neuron.
      c.   contain neurotransmitters.
      d.   have to be regenerated following each neural impulse.

49. Receptor sites:

      a.   operate in a first-come first-served basis.
      b.   operate in a one size fits all basis.
      c.   treat each neurotransmitter equally.
      d.   None of the above.

50. Once a neurotransmitter has been released:

      a.   it is possible that none will bind to the postsynaptic membrane.
      b.   it may seek out neurons, which are not in the vicinity of the point of release.
      c.   it may be recycled by the presynaptic cell.
      d.   All of the above.

51. An excitatory postsynaptic potential occurs when:

    a.   the cell is depolarized.
    b.   the cell is hyperpolarized.
    c.   neurotransmitters miss their designated receptor sites and bind unintentionally to other postsynaptic cells.
    d.   neurotransmitters are recycled back into their presynaptic cell creating an excess of molecules in that cell.

52. _____ is an example of a biogenic amine.

    a.   Serotonin
    b.   GABA
    c.   Oxytocin
    d.   Aspartate

53. Which of the following statements is true of neurotransmitters?

    a.   Each neurotransmitter has a distinct shape and size requiring a specialized receptor site.
    b.   Receptor sites are fluctuating and depending on neuronal needs at a specified time may accommodate different neurotransmitters.
    c.   Receptor sites can accommodate a variety of neurotransmitters at any given time.
    d.   All receptor sites can accommodate any neurotransmitter.

54. Acetylcholine is implicated in:

    a.   spatial reasoning.
    b.   attention.
    c.   problem solving.
    d.   schizophrenia.

55. Which of the following does not provide choline (which is required for the synthesis of ACh)?

    a.   Liver.
    b.   Egg yolks.
    c.   Vegetables.
    d.   Pop-tarts.

56. What are the two main types of ACh post-synaptic receptor sites?

    a.   Muscarinic and striatal.
    b.   Muscarinic and cholinergic.
    c.   Muscarinic and nicotinic.
    d.   Muscarinic and dopaminergic.

57. Increased levels of ACh are associated with:

      a.   impaired motor functioning.
      b.   fatigue.
      c.   hallucinations.
      d.   memory.

58. Serotonin originates in the:

      a.   striatum.
      b.   raphe nucleus.
      c.   substantia nigra.
      d.   reticular activating system.

59. Serotonin pathways project to:

      a.   the cerebellum.
      b.   the limbic system.
      c.   spinal cord.
      d.   All of the above.

60. Serotonin has been linked to:

      a.   depressed mood.
      b.   hallucinations.
      c.   manic behavior.
      d.   Multiple Personality Disorder.

61. Norepinephrine originates in the:

      a.   raphe nucleus.
      b.   substantia nigra.
      c.   locus ceruleus.
      d.   cerebellum.

62. Dopamine has been implicated in:

      a.   schizophrenia.
      b.   pedophilia.
      c.   Post Traumatic Stress Disorder.
      d.   delirium.

63. Dopamine is a(n):

      a.   amino acid.
      b.   peptide.
      c.   indolamine.
      d.   catecholamine.

64. The loss of GABA in the basal ganglia may attribute to the debilitating symptoms of what disease?

    a.   Parkinson's Disease.
    b.   Huntington's Disease.
    c.   Alzheimer's Disease.
    d.   Schizophrenia.

65. Peptides are present in:

    a.   the hypothalamus, spinal cord and cerebellum.
    b.   the cortex, thalamus and spinal cord.
    c.   the thalamus, cerebellum and cortex.
    d.   the cerebellum, spinal cord and amygdala.

66. The presence of opiate receptors in the brain indicates that:

    a.   humans are naturally prone to drug use.
    b.   an opiate neurotransmitter is created naturally by the brain.
    c.   drug use, if done correctly, could be beneficial to humans.
    d.   None of the above.

67. Once neurons in the central nervous system are damaged, which of the following is true?

    a.   Neurons spontaneously regenerate.
    b.   The brain naturally eliminates dead cells to clear room for new ones.
    c.   No new neurons are formed.
    d.   Neurons respecialize and take over jobs of damaged cells.

68. Healing after a neurologic injury may be attributed to:

    a.   regeneration of neurons.
    b.   reduction of the swelling of brain tissue.
    c.   regeneration of neurons and reduction of the swelling of brain tissue.
    d.   brain surgery to replace dead brain cells.

69. In male songbirds:

    a.   neurons regenerate according to the season.
    b.   neurons get larger increasing the size of various brain structures during different mating rituals.
    c.   neurons are reassigned in order for mating rituals to be successfully completed.
    d.   no seasonal changes are noted in brain structures.

Essay Questions

1. Discuss the neurological basis of Multiple Sclerosis (MS) and how it is exhibited with regards to symptomatology.

2. Discuss the complexities of nuclei in the context of their functional importance.

3. Describe the events involved in neuronal communication starting with a neuron in its resting state to the binding of the neurotransmitter on the postsynaptic membrane.

Answer Key

Chapter Exercises

1. False (p.41)
2. False (p.41)
3. True (p.41)
4. False (p.42)
5. True (p.42)
6. True (p.42)
7. False (p.42)
8. False (p.42)
9. True (p.42)
10. True (p.43)
11. False (p.43)
12. False (p.43)
13. True (p.43)
14. False (p.44)
15. True (p.44)
16. True (p.44)
17. True (p.44)
18. True (p.44)
19. True (p.44)
20. False (p.45)
21. True (p.45)
22. True (p.45)
23. True (p.45)
24. True (p.45)
25. False (p.45)
26. False (p.45)
27. True (p.45)
28. True (p.45)
29. True (p.45)
30. True (p.45)
31. False (p.46)
32. False (p.46)
33. False (p.47)
34. False (p.47)
35. True (p.47)
36. False (p.47)
37. True (p.47)
38. False (p.47)
39. True (p.47)
40. True (p.47)
41. False (p.47)
42. False (p.47)
43. False (p.47)
44. False (p.47)
45. False (p.47)
46. False (p.48)
47. False (p.48)
48. False (p.48)
49. False (p.48)
50. True (p.48)
51. True (p.48)
52. True (p.48)
53. False (p.48)
54. True (p.49)
55. False (p.49)
56. True (p.49)
57. True (p.49)
58. False (p.49)
59. e (p.42)
60. c (p.42)
61. b (p.42)
62. d (p.42)
63. a (p.42)
64. k (p.49)
65. f (p.52)
66. h (p.51)
67. a (p.49)
68. e (p.49)
69. i (p.52)
70. j (p.50)
71. b (p.50)
72. d (p.51)
73. c (p.50)
74. g (p.52)
75. True (p.53)
76. False (p.53)
77. True (p.53)
78. False (p.53)
79. True (p.53)
80. True (p.53)
81. False (p.54)
82. True (p.54)
83. False (p.54)
84. False (p.54)
85. True (p.54)
86. True (p.54)
87. True (p.54)
88. False (p.54)
89. False (p.54)
90. True (p.54)
91. True (p.54)
92. False (p.54)
93. True (p.54)
94. True (p.54)
95. False (p.54)
96. False (p.54)
97. True (pp.56,57)
98. False (pp.56,57)
99. False (p.57)
100. False (p.57)
101. True (p.57)
102. False (p.57)
103. False (p.57)
104. True (p.57)
105. True (p.57)
106. False (p.58)
107. True (p.58)
108. True (p.59)
109. False (p.59)
110. True (p.59)
111. False (p.59)
112. False (p.59)
113. False (p.59)
114. False (p.59)
115. True (p.59)
116. False (p.59)
117. True (p.59)
118. False (pp.59,60)
119. True (p.59)
120. False (p.60)
121. True (p.60)
122. True (p.60)
123. True (p.60)
124. e (p.56)
125. c (p.56)
126. d (p.56)
127. b (p.56)
128. f (p.56)
129. a (p.56)
130. g (p.56)
131. False (p.60)
132. False (p.61)
133. True (p.62)
134. False (p.61)
135. True (p.61)

Post-Test

Multiple Choice

1. B (p.41)
2. C (p.41)
3. A (p.41)
4. D (p.41)
5. C (p.41)
6. B (p.41)
7. D (p.42)
8. A (p.42)
9. C (p.42)
10. B (p.43)
11. A (p.43)
12. D (pp.44,45)
13. C (p.44)
14. B (p.45)
15. B (p.45)
16. B (p.45)
17. D (p.45)
18. A (p.46)
19. A (p.46)
20. D (p.47)
21. D (p.47)
22. D (p.47)
23. B (p.47)
24. C (p.47)
25. C (p.47)
26. C (p.47)
27. A (p.48)
28. C (p.48)
29. A (p.48)
30. D (pp.48,49)
31. D (p.49)
32. A (p.49)
33. B (p.49)
34. A (p.50)
35. A (p.50)

36. B (p.50)
37. D (pp.50,51)
38. A (p.51)
39. D (p.51)
40. B (p.52)
41. A (p.52)
42. B (p.52)
43. D (p.52)
44. B (p.52)
45. A (p.53)
46. D (p.53)
47. B (p.54)
48. C (p.54)
49. D (pp.54,57)
50. D (p.54)
51. A (p.54)
52. A (p.57)
53. A (p.57)
54. B (p.57)
55. D (p.57)
56. C (p.57)
57. D (p.59)
58. B (p.59)
59. D (p.59)
60. A (p.59)
61. C (p.59)
62. A (p.60)
63. D (p.57)
64. B (p.60)
65. C (p.60)
66. B (p.60)
67. C (p.61)
68. B (p.62)
69. A (p.61)

Chapter 3

The Functioning Brain
Functional Neuroanatomy

Chapter Outline

Overview
Learning Objectives
Organization of the Nervous System
Peripheral Nervous System (PNS)
Central Nervous System (CNS)
Brain
> Anatomical Terms of Relationship

Spinal Cord
Gross Anatomy: Protection and Sustenance of the Brain
Skull
Meninges
Ventricular System
Vascular System
Arteries Supplying the Brain
The Circle of Willis
Cerebral Arteries
Venous System
Principle Divisions of the Brain
Brain Stem and Cerebellum
Lower Brain Stem
Cranial Nerves
Reticular Formation
Upper Brain Stem: Diencephalon
> Hypothalamus

Thalamus
Cerebellum
Telencephalon
Basal Ganglia
Limbic System
Corpus Callosum
The Cerebral Hemispheres
> Asymmetry, Lateralization and Dominance
> Neuropsychological and Behavioral Cerebral Differences

Post-Test

Answer Key

Overview

Novices look at the brain as an anatomical object. In contrast, neuropsychologists examine it as a functioning organ of interconnected systems. Thus, neuroanatomy is best understood within a conceptual framework of structure-function relationships. In this chapter the major structures and functions of the brain are reviewed. This anatomy lesson is important for a variety of reasons. It is important to understand the functional aspects of the brain as they relate to brain anatomy. However, knowledge of brain structures, in-and-of-itself, is not very useful to neuropsychologists. The material covered in this chapter is not intended as a detailed review of the content often covered in courses on neuroscience, or sensory-motor systems, but rather it constitutes an illustrated account of the functional anatomy of the major components of the nervous system. The structures reviewed here represent the important geographical features on which the various processing systems of the brain depend. This chapter is intended as a stepping stone for the next chapters related to functional systems, and indeed the entire book. The structures presented here will be integrated and developed further in examinations of functional systems and neuropsychological disorders. In the first section of this chapter a general overview of the major components of the nervous system is presented. The necessary terminology for a common orientation to the geographical locations of structures is also introduced. Following this, structural features important for the protection and sustenance of the brain are presented. Next, principle divisions of the brain are organized in an inferior to superior bottom-up fashion, from lower, evolutionarily older structures to higher-order structures.

Learning Objectives

- To know the basic organization of the human nervous system.
- To learn the principal functional structures of the brain and how they relate to each other.
- To be able to identify the principal divisions of the brain.

Organization of the Nervous System

Key Terms and Concepts

peripheral nervous system	central nervous system	somatic nervous system
autonomic nervous system	brain	spinal cord
cranial nerves	afferent	efferent
sympathetic division	parasympathetic division	meninges
brain stem	telencephalon	cerebellum
horizontal plane	coronal plane	sagittal plane
anterior	posterior	inferior
superior	medial	lateral
rostral	caudal	proximal
distal	dorsal	ventral
ipsalateral	contralateral	

1._____   The nervous system is divided into two parts; the peripheral and central nervous systems.
2._____   The central nervous system is divided into two parts; the somatic and autonomic nervous systems.
3._____   The autonomic system is divided into two parts; the sympathetic and parasympathetic systems.
4._____   The central nervous system consists of the brain and spinal cord.

5._____   Cranial nerves run through the spinal cord assisting in the transmission of sensory and motor information.
6._____   The autonomic nervous system consists of afferent and efferent nerves.

7._____   Afferent nerves carry motor signals from the central nervous system to muscles.

8._____   Efferent nerves carry messages from the sense organs to the central nervous system.
9._____   Cranial nerves synapse directly with the brain.

10._____   The sympathetic division of the autonomic nervous system prepares the body to respond to a stressful event.
11._____   The parasympathetic division of the autonomic nervous system is associated with relaxed states.
12._____   The skull and spine exist to protect the central nervous system.

13._____   Meninges are types of neurons found in the cranial nerves.

14._____   Cerebrospinal fluid serves to protect the brain.

15._____   The brainstem is located at the top of the spinal cord.

16._____   The telencephalon contains the cerebellum.

17._____   The horizontal plane corresponds to the x axis.

18._____   The coronal plane shows the brain as it would be viewed from the side.

19._____   The sagittal plane shows the brain as it would be viewed from the side.

20.   Away from the center.   a.   anterior

21.   On the same side.   b.   posterior

22.   Towards the bottom.   c.   inferior

23.   Towards the belly.   d.   superior

24.   Towards the rear.   e.   medial

25.   Towards the back or tail.   f.   lateral

26.   Near the center.   g.   rostral

27.   Towards the side.   h.   caudal

28.   Towards the back.   i.   proximal

29.   Towards the middle.   j.   distal

30.   Towards the front.   k.   dorsal

31.   Towards the head.   l.   ventral

32.   On the opposite side.   m.   ipsalateral

33.   Towards the top.   n.   contralateral

Gross Anatomy: Protection and Sustenance of the Brain

Key Terms and Concepts

ventricular system
foramen
arachnoid membrane
epidural space
meningitis
cerebral aqueduct
foramena of Luschka
hydrocephalus
aortic arch
cerebrovascular accident
middle cerebral artery
posterior communicating artery

vascular system
foramen magnum
subarachnoid space
subdural space
ventricles
choroid plexus
superior sagittal sinus
internal carotid arteries
basilar artery
Circle of Willis
anterior communicating artery

fossae
fontanelles
dura mater
subdural hematoma
foramen of Monro
foramen of Magendie
arachnoid granulations
vertebral arteries
posterior cerebral artery
anterior cerebral artery

34._____   Meninges represent a protective pad between the brain and the skull.

35._____   The ventricular and vascular systems of the central nervous system are not known to perform a protective role.

36._____   The cranial plates of the skull got their names from the corresponding lobes of the brain.

37._____   Fossae serve to hold the brain in place.

38._____   Foramina allow for the passage of nerves and blood vessels through the base of the skull.

39._____   The spinal cord passes through the foramen magnum.

40._____   The brain reaches its adult weight by age one year.

41._____   Fontanelles are abnormal openings in the newborn skull.

42._____   The skull is smooth in its interior.

43._____   The three meningeal membranes from the inside out are the dura mater, the arachnoid membrane, and the pia mater.

44._____   The pia mater covers the subarachnoid space.

45._____   The dura mater consists of two layers.

46._____   Between the two dural layers is the subdural space.

47._____   Bleeding in the subdural space is referred to as a subdural hematoma.

48._____   The meninges play a direct role in several cognitive functions.

49._____   Meningitis is the inflammation of the meninges caused by either bacterial or viral infection.

Labeling

Identify each of these parts of the ventricular system:

a. lateral ventricles
b. third ventricle
c. fourth ventricle
d. cerebral or Sylvanian aqueduct
e. central canal of the spinal cord

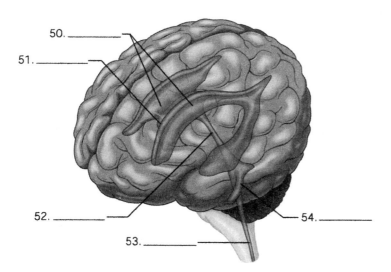

50. _____
51. _____
52. _____
53. _____
54. _____

True/False

55. _____ The choroid plexus secretes cerebrospinal fluid.

56. _____ Humans produce about 24 ounces of cerebrospinal fluid each day.

57. _____ Cerebrospinal fluid is recirculated every 24 hours.

58. _____ Cerebrospinal fluid serves to buffer the brain and remove its waste products.

59. _____ Ventricles have a direct role in cognitive processes.

60. _____ An increase in cerebrospinal fluid and subsequent increase in intracranial pressure results in hydrocephalus.

<u>Labeling</u>

Identify each of the major arteries of the brain:

a. Anterior cerebral artery
b. Anterior communicating artery
c. Anterior inferior cerebellar artery
d. Anterior spinal artery
e. Basilar artery
f. Internal carotid artery
g. Labyrinthine artery
h. Middle cerebral artery
i. Pontine arteries
j. Posterior cerebral artery
k. Posterior communicating artery
l. Posterior inferior cerebellar artery
m. Superior cerebellar artery
n. Vertebral artery

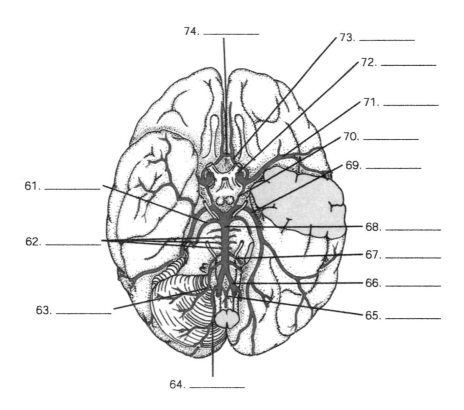

True/False

75._____   The internal carotid arteries supply the posterior portion of the brain.

76._____   The two vertebral arteries form the basilar artery at the brainstem.

77._____   The Circle of Willis allows for some redundancy among blood vessels and blood supply to various areas of the brain.

78._____   The left and right anterior cerebral arteries are connected by the posterior communicating artery.

Principle Divisions of the Brain

Key Terms and Concepts

forebrain	prosencephalon	midbrain
rhombencephalon	telencephalon	diencephalon
mesencephalon	metencephalon	mylencephalon

Matching

79.	Consists of the tectum and tegmentum.	a.	forebrain
80.	Consists of the thalamus and the hypothalamus.	b.	prosencephalon
81.	Consists of the cerebral cortex and corpus callosum.	c.	midbrain
82.	Consists of the medulla oblongata.	d.	rhombencephalon
83.	Synonymous for forebrain.	e.	telencephalon
84.	Synonymous for hindbrain.	f.	diencephalon
85.	Consists of the pons.	g.	mesencephalon
86.	Synonymous for midbrain.	h.	metencephalon
87.	Can be subdivided into the telencephalon and diencephalon.	i.	mylencephalon

Brain Stem and Cerebellum

Key Terms and Concepts

medulla oblongata	pons	decussate
cerebellar peduncles	tectum	tegmentum
inferior colliculi	superior colliculi	cranial nerves
reticular formation	hypothalamus	thalamus
ventral posterolateral nuclei	ventral posteromedial nuclei	lateral geniculate body
medial geniculate body	ventral lateral nuclei	ventral intermedial nuclei
medial dorsal nucleus	cerebellum	vermis

True/False

88. _____ The four parts of the brain stem are the medulla oblongata, pons, midbrain, and cerebellum.

89. _____ The medulla contains myelinated tracts which carry messages between the brain and spinal cord.

90. _____ Decussation occurs in the cerebellum, and transmission of information is subsequently switched from one side of the body to the contralateral side of the brain.

91. _____ Cerebellar peduncles run through the pons.

92. _____ The midbrain is made up of the tectum and tegmentum.

93. _____ The pons has a role in balance, vision, and auditory processing.

94. _____ The inferior colliculi serve as an important center for the auditory pathway.

95. _____ Bats have proportionally smaller inferior colliculi than humans.

Matching: Match each cranial nerve to its respective number.

96.	I		a.	Facial
97.	II		b.	Trochlear
98.	III		c.	Hypoglossal
99.	IV		d.	Olfactory
100.	V		e.	Statoacoustic
101.	VI		f.	Oculomotor
102.	VII		g.	Vagus
103.	VIII		h.	Accessory
104.	IX		i.	Optic
105.	X		j.	Trigeminal
106.	XI		k.	Glossopharyngeal
107.	XII		l.	Abducens

True/False

108._____ The reticular formation is mainly responsible for higher order complex cognitive functioning.

109._____ Coma is linked to a deficit in the reticular activating system.

110._____ The diencephalon is also known as the midbrain.

111._____ The diencephalon consists of the thalamus and hypothalamus.

112._____ The thalamus regulates thirst, appetite, digestion, sleep, body temperature, and sex drive.

113._____ The hypothalamus facilitates normal development of secondary sex characteristics.

114._____ There is a separate thalamus in each cerebral hemisphere.

115._____ With the exception of olfaction, the thalamus acts as a relay system for the senses.

116._____ The cerebellum contains 25% of all of the neurons in the brain.

117._____ The cerebellum is implicated in the coordination of motor and sensory information.

Labeling

Identify each of the major structures of the brain:

a. Central canal of the spinal cord
b. Cerebellum
c. Cerebral cortex
d. Cingulate gyrus
e. Corpus callosum
f. Frontal lobe
g. Hypothalamus
h. Medulla oblongata
i. Midbrain
j. Nucleus accumbens
k. Occipital lobe
l. Parietal lobe
m. Pituitary gland
n. Pons
o. Spinal cord
p. Superior and inferior colliculi
q. Thalamus
r. Tissue dividing lateral ventricles

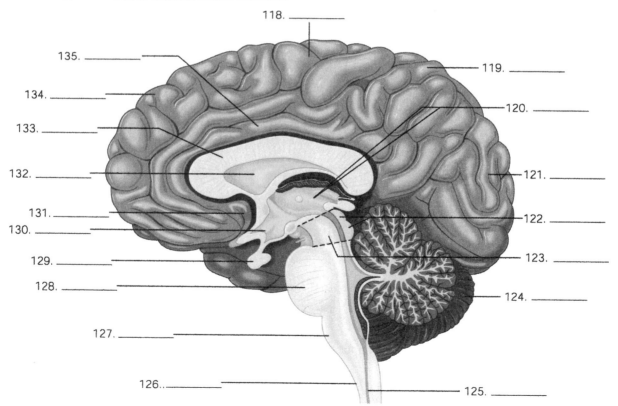

Telencephalon: Basal Ganglia

corpus callosum	basal forebrain	subcortical
basal ganglia	basal nuclei	caudate nucleus
putamen	striatum	substantia nigra
extrapyramidal motor system	pyramidal system	tardive dyskinesia

Sentence Completion

136.   The _____ are also referred to as the basal ganglia.

137.   _____ refers to anything below the cortex.

138.   Through the nigro-striatal system, the _____ plays a role in basal ganglia functioning.

139.   A medication side effect resulting in unwanted motor movements is known as _____.

140.   The _____ and _____ are the two major structures of the basal ganglia.

141.   The caudate nucleus, putamen, and anterior limb of the internal capsule are usually referred to as the _____.

142.   The _____ is a bundle of fibers which connects the two cerebral hemispheres.

143.   The _____ is responsible for stereotyped postural and reflexive motor activity.

144.   _____ are a collection of nuclei of the telencephalon which are implicated in the initiation of movement.

145.   The _____, a motor system, originates in the cerebral cortex.

146.   The _____ is interconnected with limbic system structures and surrounds the inferior tip of the frontal horn.

Telencephalon: Limbic System

Key Terms and Concepts

limbic system	rhinencephalon	cingulate gyrus
parahippocampal gyrus	hippocampal formation	fornix
mamillary bodies	amygdala	septum
basolateral circuit	Papez circuit	
Wernicke-Korsakoff's Syndrome		

147._____   Paul Broca coined the term, limbic.

148._____   The limbic system was initially believed to be involved primarily with sex.

149._____   The rhinencephalon has also been called the smell brain.

150._____   James Papez is credited with describing the limbic system.

151._____   The limbic system is believed to be involved in emotional processing and is not involved with cognitive functions.

152._____   The limbic system is made up of the amygdala, hippocampus, parahippocampal gyrus, cingulate gyrus, fornix, septum, and olfactory bulbs.

153._____   There are no limbic structures in reptiles, such as the crocodile.

154._____   The function of the basolateral circuit is emotional processing.

155._____   Limbic system dysfunction has been attributed to behavioral problems, memory problems, and sexual dysfunction.

156._____   Wernicke-Korsakoff's Syndrome is most often observed in individuals with Alzheimer's disease.

157._____   Vitamin B1 deficiencies cause lesions of the posterior hypothalamus.

Telencephalon: Corpus Callosum

Key Terms and Concepts

longitudinal fissure	cingulum	cingulate gyrus
anterior commissure	hippocampal commissure	

True/False

158._____   The corpus callosum is a bundle of dendrites.

159._____   The corpus callosum is located within the longitudinal fissure.

160._____   The cingulum is located within the cingulate gyrus.

161._____   The corpus callosum provides the only means for information to cross from one hemisphere to another.

162._____   The anterior commissure and hippocampal commissure are involved with the exchange of information from one hemisphere to another.

163._____   Severing of the corpus callosum results in death.

Telencephalon: Cerebral Hemispheres

cerebral hemispheres	cerebrum	sulci
gyri	lateral fissure	central sulcus
occipital notch	Brodmann's areas	somatosensory cortex
primary motor cortex	sensory association areas	prefrontal cortex
hemispheric asymmetry	lateralization	dominance
Sylvian fissure	Heschel's gyrus	planum temporale

Sentence Completion

164.   The _____ is one of the boundaries separating the parietal and occipital lobes.

165.   The _____ is often larger in the left hemisphere and is implicated in speech comprehension.

166.   The surface of each cerebral hemisphere folds in upon itself creating grooves called _____.

167.   The _____, a part of the parietal lobe, are involved with the processing of sensory information.

168.   The morphological and physiological differences between the right and left cerebral hemispheres are referred to as _____.

169.   The frontal and parietal lobes are separated from the temporal lobe by the _____.

170.   The _____ is responsible for the reception of primary tactile sensation from the body.

171.   The _____ separates the frontal from the temporal and parietal lobes.

172.   The _____ is referred to as the executive of the brain.

173.   _____ and _____ refer to the differences in functional specialization between the right and left cerebral hemispheres.

174.   Irregularly shaped ridges between sulci on the surface of the cerebral hemispheres are called _____.

175.   _____ is also known as the primary auditory cortex and is often larger in the right hemisphere than the left.

176.   The _____ are made up of the frontal, parietal, occipital, and temporal lobes.

177.   The _____ is made up of the right and left cerebral hemispheres.

178. The human brain has been divided into 52 _____.

179. The _____, a part of the frontal lobe, is partially responsible for the initiation, activation and performance of motor activity.

180. The frontal and parietal lobes are separated by the _____.

Post-Test
Multiple Choice

1. The nervous system is divided into two parts. These are:

    e. the brain and spinal cord.
    f. the peripheral and central nervous systems.
    g. the somatic and autonomic nervous systems.
    h. the jittery and anxious nervous systems.

2. The peripheral nervous system is comprised of the:

    a. brain and spinal cord.
    b. cranial nerves.
    c. somatic and autonomic nervous systems.
    d. telencephalon.

3. The autonomic nervous system is comprised of the:

    a. brain and spinal cord.
    b. sympathetic and parasympathetic systems.
    c. cranial nerves.
    d. cerebellum.

4. Which of the following statements is true regarding the somatic nervous system?

    a. The somatic nervous system is composed of the sympathetic and parasympathetic systems.
    b. The somatic nervous system prepares the body for "fight" or "flight."
    c. The main role of the somatic nervous system is the neural control of internal organs.
    d. The somatic nervous system communicates via afferent and efferent nerves.

5. Which of the following is an example of sympathetic activity?

    a. Decreased blood flow.
    b. Increased sweating.
    c. Increased sexual arousal.
    d. Understanding a friend's problems really well.

6. The central nervous system is protected by:

    a. the skull.
    b. cerebrospinal fluid.
    c. meninges.
    d. All of the above.

7. Which of the following planes refers to the view if one was to look at the brain from above?

    a.   Horizontal.
    b.   Coronal.
    c.   Sagittal.
    d.   Medial.

8. Which of the following planes refers to the view if one was to look at the brain from the side?

    a.   Horizontal.
    b.   Coronal.
    c.   Sagittal.
    d.   Medial.

9. Which of the following directions means towards the bottom, or below?

    a.   Anterior.
    b.   Posterior.
    c.   Inferior.
    d.   Superior.

10. Which of the following directions means towards the side, or away from the midline?

    a.   Medial.
    b.   Lateral.
    c.   Rostral.
    d.   Caudal.

11. Which of the following directions means near the trunk or center, or close to the origin of attachment?

    a.   Proximal.
    b.   Distal.
    c.   Dorsal.
    d.   Ventral.

12. How many levels of the spinal cord are there?

    a.   10
    b.   16
    c.   21
    d.   31

13. Which of the following statements is true of the spinal cord?

    a.   The spinal cord is not protected by meninges like the skull.
    b.   At each level of the spinal cord are pairs of afferent and efferent fibers.
    c.   White matter makes up the inside of the spinal cord while gray matter is located on the exterior.
    d.   The spinal cord is composed only of motor neurons.

14. What is the term for the ridges found in the base of the skull, which hold the brain in place?

    a.   Fossae.
    b.   Foramina.
    c.   Meninges.
    d.   Fontanelles.

15. What is the term for the openings in the base of the skull which provide passage for nerves and blood vessels?

    a.   Fossae.
    b.   Foramina.
    c.   Meninges.
    d.   Fontanelles.

16. What is the term for the openings between the bony plates in newborn skulls, which allow for the increasing size of the developing brain?

    a.   Fossae.
    b.   Foramina.
    c.   Meninges.
    d.   Fontanelles.

17. The meninges consist of which of the following?

    a.   Arachnoid membrane, subarachnoid space, and subdural space.
    b.   Arachnoid membrane, epidural space, and pia mater.
    c.   Arachnoid membrane, dura mater, and subarachnoid space.
    d.   Arachnoid membrane, dura mater, and pia mater.

18. Which of the following is a role of the meninges?

    a.   Improve cognition by increasing neuronal transmission.
    b.   Protect the brain and spinal cord.
    c.   Enhance executive functions.
    d.   Facilitate memory.

19. Which of the following is a symptom of meningitis?

     a.   Fever.
     b.   Stiff neck.
     c.   Headache.
     d.   All of the above.

20. Which of the ventricles is the largest?

     a.   Lateral ventricle.
     b.   Third ventricle.
     c.   Fourth ventricle.
     d.   They are all the same size.

21. Which of the following connects the lateral ventricles to the third ventricle?

     a.   Foramen magnum.
     b.   Foramen of Monro.
     c.   Foramen of Magendie.
     d.   Foramen of Luschka.

22. Which of the following is true of cerebrospinal fluid?

     a.   Cerebrospinal fluid is secreted by the pia mater.
     b.   Cerebrospinal fluid circulates through the ventricles only.
     c.   Approximately 900 ml of cerebrospinal fluid is produced by adults each day.
     d.   Cerebrospinal fluid is recirculated every 6-7 hours.

23. Which of the following may result from increased intracranial pressure?

     a.   Meningitis.
     b.   Hydocephalus.
     c.   Subdural hematoma.
     d.   None of the above.

24. Which of the following statements is false?

     a.   The two vertebral arteries join together to form the basilar artery.
     b.   The internal carotid arteries supply the posterior portions of the brain and the vertebral arteries supply the anterior portions.
     c.   The basilar artery divides into the left and right posterior cerebral arteries.
     d.   The Circle of Willis allows for some redundancy among blood vessels, and subsequently blood supply to various regions of the brain.

25. Which of the following statements is true?

    a.   Arachnoid granulations decline in adulthood.
    b.   Arterial blood supply is not composed of a right and left system.
    c.   The venous system is not composed of a right and left system.
    d.   The structure of the venous system minimizes the spread of infectious agents between cerebral hemispheres.

26. Which of the following is synonymous for rhombencephalon?

    a.   Forebrain.
    b.   Midbrain.
    c.   Hindbrain.
    d.   Endbrain.

27. Decussation occurs in the:

    a.   tegmentum.
    b.   medulla.
    c.   superior colliculi.
    d.   midbrain.

28. The lower brain stem is implicated in:

    a.   auditory processing.
    b.   control of movement.
    c.   arousal level.
    d.   All of the above.

29. Which of the following statements is true?

    a.   The superior colliculi contain important reflex centers for auditory information.
    b.   Bats have enlarged superior colliculi.
    c.   The inferior colliculi contain important reflex centers for visual information.
    d.   Tracts in the superior and inferior colliculi influence the movement of the neck and head in response to visual and auditory information.

30. Which of the following cranial nerves is responsible for smell?

    a.   I.
    b.   III.
    c.   V.
    d.   VIII.

31. Which of the following cranial nerves is responsible for motor movements, specifically of the shoulder and head?

    a.   Oculomotor.
    b.   Abducens.
    c.   Vagus.
    d.   Accessory.

32. Which of the following cranial nerves is responsible for the parasympathetic nerves to the heart and viscera?

    a.   I.
    b.   IV.
    c.   X.
    d.   XII.

33. One role of the reticular formation is:

    a.   the integration of higher cognitive functions.
    b.   the consolidation of memory.
    c.   the coordination of motor movements.
    d.   regulating sleep and wakefulness.

34. Which of the following might indicate a deficit in the reticular activating system?

    a.   Coma.
    b.   Distractibility.
    c.   Respiratory problems.
    d.   All of the above.

35. Which of the following statements is true?

    a.   The pituitary gland is controlled by the thalamus.
    b.   The hypothalamus is implicated in the proper development of secondary sex characteristics.
    c.   The hypothalamus acts independently of the thalamus.
    d.   Behavioral disorders have not been associated with the hypothalamus.

36. The word thalamus literally means:

    a.   beneath.
    b.   seahorse.
    c.   bridal chamber.
    d.   almond.

37. Which of the following statements is true?

    a.   The thalamus consists mostly of white matter.
    b.   The thalamus has an integral role in the processing of sensory information.
    c.   There are three thalamic nuclei.
    d.   The thalamus is the major sensory relay for the olfactory system.

38. The lateral geniculate body:

    a.   receives input from the optic tract.
    b.   receives input from somatosensory relay neurons.
    c.   receives input from the auditory relay nuclei.
    d.   receives input from the cerebellum.

39. Which of the following might be observed following a thalamic lesion?

    a.   Defects in facial recognition.
    b.   Defects in the perception of music.
    c.   Defects in spatial ability.
    d.   All of the above.

40. The cerebellum contains _____ of all of the neurons in the brain.

    a.   10%
    b.   25%
    c.   50%
    d.   75%

41. Which of the following might result following a lesion of the cerebellum?

    a.   Verbal memory deficits.
    b.   Defects of visual-spatial ability.
    c.   Impairment in balance.
    d.   Disruption of the sleep-wake cycle.

42. The telencephalon is also referred to as the:

    a.   endbrain.
    b.   midbrain.
    c.   hindbrain.
    d.   birdbrain.

43. The two cerebral hemispheres of the telencephalon are connected by the:

    a.   corpus striatum.
    b.   corpus callosum.
    c.   cerebellum.
    d.   hypothalamus.

44. Which of the following is implicated in the initiation of movement?

    a.   Corpus callosum.
    b.   Cerebellum.
    c.   Papez circuit.
    d.   Basal ganglia.

45. Which of the following are considered part of the basal ganglia?

    a.   Amygdala.
    b.   Thalamus.
    c.   Putamen.
    d.   None of the above.

46. Which of the following is believed to be a role of the basal ganglia?

    a.   The basal ganglia play an integrative role between visual centers, balance centers, and muscles and joints.
    b.   The basal ganglia act as a relay station.
    c.   The basal ganglia regulate planning and initiating motor behavior.
    d.   All of the above.

47. Tardive dyskinesia can be a consequence of taking some antipsychotic medications. Which motor system is implicated in this disorder?

    a.   The voluntary motor system.
    b.   The pyramidal motor system.
    c.   The extrapyramidal motor system.
    d.   The integrative motor system.

48. Who coined the term "limbic"?

    a.   Broca.
    b.   Wernicke.
    c.   Papez.
    d.   Luria.

49. Initially the primary role of the limbic lobe was believed to be in:

    a.   vision.
    b.   tactile sensation.
    c.   olfaction.
    d.   emotion.

50. Papez hypothesized that the limbic system was involved in:

    a.   vision.
    b.   tactile sensation.
    c.   olfaction.
    d.   emotion.

51. Which of the following is a part of the limbic system?

    a.   Cerebral cortex.
    b.   Hippocampus.
    c.   Cerebellum.
    d.   Corpus callosum.

52. Which of the following structures is believed to be primarily responsible for integrating and organizing autonomic processes related to the emotional expression of behavior?

    a.   Thalamus.
    b.   Hypothalamus.
    c.   Mamillary bodies.
    d.   Cingulate gyrus.

53. Which of the following structures is believed to be primarily responsible for the acquisition of memories?

    a.   Hypothalamus.
    b.   Fornix.
    c.   Hippocampus.
    d.   Amygdala.

54. Which of the following structures is believed to be primarily responsible for the conditioning of fear?

    a.   Thalamus.
    b.   Hippocampus.
    c.   Hypothalamus.
    d.   Amygdala.

55. Alcoholics may exhibit a severe disorder of memory called:

    a.   Huntington's disease.
    b.   Wernicke-Korsakoff's Syndrome.
    c.   Asperger's Syndrome.
    d.   Fetal Alcohol Syndrome.

56. The corpus callosum is made up of:

    a.   nuclei.
    b.   gray matter.
    c.   axons.
    d.   Nacho Cheese Doritos.

57. Which of the following allows for the transmission of information from one hemisphere to another?

    a.   Corpus callosum.
    b.   Anterior commissure.
    c.   Hippocampal commissure.
    d.   All of the above.

58. With regards to evolution, how old are the cerebral hemispheres?

    a.   50,000-100,000 years old.
    b.   500,000 to one million years old.
    c.   One to three million years old.
    d.   One billion years old.

59. The largest structure in the brain is the:

    a.   cerebrum.
    b.   cerebellum.
    c.   corpus callosum.
    d.   thalamus.

60. Grooves in the surface of the cortex are called:

    a.   gyri.
    b.   sulci.
    c.   abnormal.
    d.   lobes.

61. Ridges on the surface of the cortex are called:

    a.   gyri.
    b.   sulci.
    c.   abnormal.
    d.   lobes.

62. Which of the following covers the surface of the cerebral hemispheres?

    a.   Fibers.
    b.   White matter.
    c.   Axons.
    d.   Gray matter.

63. Who divided the cortical surface into 52 functional areas?

    a.   Gall.
    b.   Brodmann.
    c.   Papez.
    d.   Broca.

64. Broca's area corresponds to Area:

    a.   1.
    b.   14.
    c.   44.
    d.   51.

65. The somatosensory cortex is located on the:

    a.   posterior aspect of the parietal lobes.
    b.   anterior aspect of the parietal lobes.
    c.   frontal lobes.
    d.   temporal lobes.

66. The primary motor cortex is located on the:

    a.   posterior aspect of the parietal lobes.
    b.   anterior aspect of the parietal lobes.
    c.   frontal lobes.
    d.   temporal lobes.

67. Visual processing is associated with the:

    a.   frontal lobes.
    b.   temporal lobes.
    c.   parietal lobes.
    d.   occipital lobes.

68. Auditory processing is associated with the:

    a.   frontal lobes.
    b.   temporal lobes.
    c.   parietal lobes.
    d.   occipital lobes.

69. Which of the following is responsible for organizing, controlling, and managing socially appropriate behavior?

   a. prefrontal cortex.
   b. sensory association areas.
   c. primary somatosensory cortex.
   d. your parents.

For questions 70 – 76 please answer either a. Right hemisphere. or b. Left hemisphere.

70. Has the greatest density.

71. Is larger.

72. Has a smaller Heschel's gyrus.

73. Has a smaller planum temporale.

74. The Sylvian fissure has a steeper slope.

75. Usually dominant for visual-spatial processing.

76. Usually dominant for verbal abilities.

Essay Questions

1. Discuss the protective roles of the meninges, skull, cerebrospinal fluid, and vascular system.

2. Identify and discuss the roles of the four parts of the brain stem.

3. An individual with severe intractible epilepsy undergoes a corpus callosotomy (i.e., the corpus callosum is surgically severed). Following the surgery he is asked by the neuropsychologist to show how to make a phone call. The patient picks up the phone with his right hand and his left hand immediately hangs up the phone. Using the information you have about the brain and specifically the corpus callosum, why was the patient unable to complete the phone call?

Answer Key

Chapter Exercises

1. True (p.65)
2. False (p.66)
3. True (p.66)
4. True (p.66)
5. False (p.67)
6. False (p.67)
7. False (p.67)
8. False (p.67)
9. True (p.67)
10. True (p.67)
11. True (p.67)
12. True (p.67)
13. False (p.67)
14. True (p.67)
15. True (p.68)
16. False (p.94)
17. True (p.68)
18. False (p.68)
19. True (p.68)
20. j (p.68)
21. m (p.68)
22. c (p.68)
23. l (p.68)
24. h (p.68)
25. b (p.68)
26. i (p.68)
27. f (p.68)
28. k (p.68)
29. e (p.68)
30. a (p.68)
31. g (p.68)
32. n (p.68)
33. d (p.68)
34. True (p.70)
35. False (p.70)
36. False (p.70)
37. True (p.70)
38. True (p.70)
39. True (p.70)
40. False (p.71)
41. False (p.71)
42. False (p.71)
43. False (p.71)
44. False (p.71)
45. True (p.71)
46. False (p.71)
47. True (p.71)
48. False (p.71)
49. True (p.71)
50. Lateral ventricles (p.75)
51. Third ventricle (p.75)
52. Cerebral or Sylvanian aqueduct (p.75)
53. Central canal of the spinal cord (p.75)
54. Fourth ventricle (p.75)
55. True (p.73)
56. False (p.73)
57. False (p.74)
58. True (pp.74,75)
59. False (p.75)
60. True (p.75)
61. Superior cerebellar artery (p.78)
62. Pontine arteries (p.78)
63. Anterior inferior cerebellar artery (p.78)
64. Posterior inferior cerebellar artery (p.78)
65. Anterior spinal artery (p.78)
66. Vertebral artery (p.78)
67. Labyrinthine artery (p.78)
68. Basilar artery (p.78)
69. Posterior cerebral artery (p.78)
70. Posterior communicating artery (p.78)
71. Middle cerebral artery (p.78)
72. Internal carotid artery (p.78)
73. Anterior cerebral artery (p.78)
74. Anterior communicating artery (p.78)
75. False (p.77)
76. True (p.77)
77. True (p.77)
78. False (p.77)
79. c (p.83)
80. f (p.82)
81. e (pp.99,100)
82. i (p.82)
83. b (p.79)
84. d (p.79)
85. h (p.82)
86. g (p.79)
87. a (p.88)
88. False (p.82)
89. True (p.83)
90. False (p.82)

91. True (p.83)
92. True (p.83)
93. True (p.84)
94. True (p.84)
95. False (p.84)
96. d (p.87)
97. i (p.87)
98. f (p.87)
99. b (p.87)
100. j (p.87)
101. l (p.87)
102. a (p.87)
103. e (p.87)
104. k (p.87)
105. g (p.87)
106. h (p.87)
107. c (p.87)
108. False (p.85)
109. True (p.85)
110. False (p.88)
111. True (p.88)
112. False (pp.88,89)
113. True (pp.88,89)
114. False (p.90)
115. True (p.92)
116. False (p.92)
117. True (p.94)
118. Cerebral cortex (p.84)
119. Parietal lobe (p.84)
120. Thalamus (p.84)
121. Occipital lobe (p.84)
122. Superior and inferior colliculi (p.84)
123. Midbrain (p.84)
124. Cerebellum (p.84)
125. Central canal of spinal cord (p.84)
126. Spinal cord (p.84)
127. Medulla oblongata (p.84)
128. Pons (p.84)
129. Pituitary gland (p.84)
130. Hypothalamus (p.84)
131. Nucleus accumbens (p.84)
132. Tissue dividing lateral ventricles (p.84)
133. Corpus callosum (p.84)
134. Frontal lobe (p.84)
135. Cingulate gyrus (p.84)
136. basal nuclei (p.94)
137. Subcortical (p.94)
138. substantia nigra (p.96)
139. tardive dyskinesia (p.97)

140. caudate nucleus, putamen (p.96)
141. striatum (p.96)
142. corpus callosum (p.94)
143. extrapyramidal motor system (p.96)
144. Basal ganglia (p.94)
145. pyramidal motor system (p.96)
146. basal forebrain (p.94)
147. True (p.97)
148. False (p.97)
149. True (p.97)
150. True (p.97)
151. False (p.97)
152. True (p.97)
153. False (p.97)
154. True (p.97)
155. True (p.98)
156. False (p.99)
157. True (p.99)
158. False (p.99)
159. True (p.99)
160. True (p.99)
161. False (p.99)
162. True (p.99)
163. False (p.100)
164. occipital notch (pp.100,101)
165. planum temporale (p.108)
166. sulci (p.100)
167. sensory association areas (p.105)
168. hemispheric asymmetry (p.106)
169. lateral fissure (p.100)
170. somatosensory cortex (p.104)
171. Sylvian fissure (p.107)
172. prefrontal cortex (p.105)
173. Dominance and lateralization (p.106)
174. gyri (p.100)
175. Heschel's gryus (p.108)
176. cerebral hemispheres (p.100)
177. cerebrum (p.100)
178. Brodmann's areas (p.101)
179. primary motor cortex (p.104)
180. central sulcus (p.100)

Post-Test

Multiple Choice

1. B (p.65)
2. C (p.66)
3. B (p.66)
4. D (p.67)
5. B (p.67)
6. D (p.67)
7. A (p.68)
8. C (p.68)
9. C (p.68)
10. B (p.68)
11. A (p.68)
12. D (p.69)
13. B (p.69)
14. A (p.70)
15. B (p.70)
16. D (p.71)
17. D (p.71)
18. B (p.71)
19. D (p.71)
20. A (p.72)
21. B (p.72)
22. D (pp.73,74)
23. B (p.75)
24. B (p.77)
25. C (p.79)
26. C (p.79)
27. B (p.83)
28. D (p.84)
29. D (p.84)
30. A (p.87)
31. D (p.87)
32. C (p.87)
33. D (p.85)
34. D (p.85)
35. B (p.88)
36. C (p.90)

37. B (pp.91,92)
38. A (p.92)
39. D (p.92)
40. C (p.92)
41. C (p.94)
42. A (p.94)
43. B (p.94)
44. D (p.94)
45. C (p.96)
46. D (p.96)
47. C (pp.96,97)
48. A (p.97)
49. C (p.97)
50. D (p.97)
51. B (p.97)
52. B (pp.97,98)
53. C (p.98)
54. D (p.98)
55. B (p.99)
56. C (p.99)
57. D (p.99)
58. C (p.100)
59. A (p.100)
60. B (p.100)
61. A (p.100)
62. D (p.100)
63. B (p.101)
64. C (p.101)
65. B (p.104)
66. C (p.104)
67. D (p.105)
68. B (p.105)
69. A (p.105)
70. B (p.107)
71. A (p.107)
72. B (p.107)
73. A (p.107)
74. A (p.107)
75. A (p.107)
76. B (p.107)

Chapter 4

The Functioning Brain
Sensory-Perceptual and Motor Systems

Chapter Outline

Overview

Sensation is the window to the world. The range of what humans can detect is unique to our species and becomes the raw material of our perceptions and the "stuff" of our experiences. Information comes in fragments and requires the central processor of the brain to literally "make sense" of the outside environment. Sensory receptor cells throughout the body detect numerous stimuli, including sight, sound, pressure, pain, chemical irritation, smell, and taste, to name a few. We hear with our ears and see with our eyes, but if photoreceptor cells were on our hands we would see with our fingers. Some sensory systems are very complex. For example, the visual system uses two primary systems (i.e., rods and cones). From the primary sensory cortices where information is first labeled, it is then sorted and relayed to the secondary sensory processing areas. Secondary areas may process only specific qualities of sensory information in a parallel manner, such as we have seen with the "what" and "where" visual streams. In other systems a distributed "map-like" representation may remain. As processing moves into tertiary or association areas dense reciprocal interconnections both within and between sensory modalities are evident. Language and visual-perceptual processing are examples representing the highest level of processing emerging from individual sensory systems. The motor system involves both cortical and subcortical areas of processing. Some of the coordination and planning of movement takes place in the subcortical areas of the cerebellum and the basal ganglia. Planning, sequencing, and motivational aspects of behavior are augmented by the three secondary cortical motor areas. The primary motor cortex, or motor homunculus, is topographically mapped and responsible for managing the fine details of movement. It is difficult to imagine the variety of behavioral oddities that disorders of specific sensory and motor systems can present with. While these disorders can be connected to specific sensory modalities it will be evident to the neuropsychology student that most afflictions do not stay within the bounds of a single cognitive system.

Learning Objectives

- To learn the anatomical correlates of the sensory-perceptual and motor systems of the brain.
- To be able to differentiate between primary and higher order processing of the visual and auditory systems.
- To appreciate the uniqueness of the chemical perceptual system as it relates to the sense of tasting and smelling.

Key Terms and Concepts

transduction	receptor cells	agnosia	visual agnosia
tactile agnosia	astereognosis		

Sentence Completion

1. The inability to recognize objects and/or people is known as _____.

2. _____ is synonymous with tactile agnosia.

3. The inability to recognize objects by touch is known as _____.

4. Environmental stimuli activate specific _____ so that information may be processed by the brain.

5. Energy undergoes the process of _____ after receptor cells are activated by various environment stimuli.

6. The inability to recognize something by sight is known as a _____.

Somatosensory Processing

Key Terms, Concepts and Scientists

somatosensory system   proprioception
mechanical receptors   chemoreceptors
proprioceptors   ascending spinal-thalamic tract
dorsal column medial lemniscal pathway   medical lemniscus
somatopical organization   Wilder Penfield
finger agnosia   paresthesia
peripheral neuropathy   phantom limb pain
tactile extinction   kinesthetic sense

True/False

7._____   The somatosensory system includes both internal and external sensory stimulation.
8._____   The ability to accurately perceive where your body is in your extra-personal space is known as proprioception.
9._____   There are ten types of receptor cells found on the skin.

10._____   Mechanical receptors respond to various chemicals on the surface of the skin and to mucous membranes.
11._____   Thermoreceptors respond to heat and cold.

12._____   Nocioceptors are present in the brain.

13._____   Sensory information is carried to the ipsilateral hemisphere from the point of origin.
14._____   The ascending spinal-thalamic tract carries sensory information related to pain and temperature and runs parallel to the spinal cord.
15._____   Information regarding touch and vibration is carried via the dorsal column medial lemniscal pathway.
16._____   The dorsal column medical lemniscal pathway is the means for the transduction of information regarding facial stimulation.
17._____   The primary somatosensory cortex is located in the frontal lobe.

18._____   The sensory humunculus represents somatopic organization of the primary somatosensory cortex.
19._____   Wilder Penfield mapped motor functions by electrically stimulating the cortex.

20._____ Paresthesia refers to the sensation of "pins and needles."

21._____ Phantom limb pain refers to the belief that one has an extra arm or leg that causes chronic pain.

22._____ The kinesthetic sense of one's own body is supplied by vision, vestibular organs, and proprioceptive sense.

23._____ 70% of amputees experience phantom limb pain.

24._____ Individuals with visual and/or auditory phantoms are considered psychotic.

25._____ Re-mapping of the somatosensory cortex or the relay station of the thalamus may occur following an amputation.

Chemical Senses

Key Terms and Concepts

papillae	aguesia	dysguesia	phantoguesia
hypoguesia	olfaction	anosmia	dysosmia
phantosmia	hyposmia		

Matching

26. _____ is diminished taste sensitivity.

27. _____ is a distortion of taste sensation.

28. Taste receptor cells are located on _____ on the tongue.

29. _____ is diminished smell sensation.

30. _____ is the distortion of smell sensation.

31. The oldest sensory system is that of _____.

32. The inability to recognize tastes is known as _____.

33. _____ is a complete loss of smell.

34. Experiencing hallucinatory smells is known as _____.

35. Experiencing hallucinatory tastes is known as _____.

Labeling

Identify each of these structures of the primary sensory and motor cortices:

a. Central sulcus
b. Frontal lobe
c. Occipital lobe
d. Parietal lobe
e. Primary auditory cortex
f. Primary olfactory cortex
g. Primary motor cortex
h. Primary somatosensory cortex
i. Primary visual cortex
j. Temporal lobe

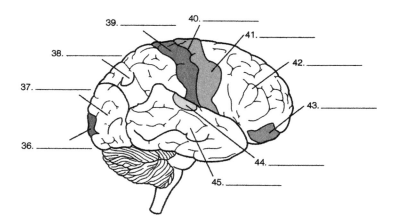

Visual Processing

decussate	anopsia	homonymous hemianopsia
secondary association	prestriate cortex	achromatopsia
akinetopsia	visual object agnosia	prosopagnosia
apperceptive visual agnosia	associative visual agnosia	Ballint's syndrome
neglect		

True/False

46._____   One fourth of the entire cortex is devoted to visual-perceptual processing.

47._____   There is a "master processor" which integrates all visual information.

48._____   Spatial location, object recognition, and form interpretation are processed by the same visual area.

49._____   Cones detect wavelengths of color.

50._____   Rods detect shades of gray and are active in low-light and night time conditions.

51._____   The primary route of visual processing includes the optic nerve, optic chiasm, thalamus, and occipital lobes.

52._____   Decussation occurs at the optic chiasm.

53._____   An anopsia refers to a visual difficulty.

54._____   Homonymous hemianopsia refers to a rare form of complete blindness.

55._____   In instances of homonymous hemianopsia there are specific malfunctions of the eye.

56._____   Hemorrhage, tumor, and acquired brain trauma are all potential causes of homonymous hemianopsia.

57._____   The primary visual cortex corresponds to Brodmann's area 17.

58._____   The secondary association cortex corresponds to Brodmann's areas 18 and 19.

59._____   Area V2 is a visual preprocessing area, which assembles and maps information.

60._____   Area V3 codes aspects of color.

61._____   Area V5 contains visual motion detector cells.

62._____   Achromatopsia refers to the complete loss of ability to detect color and is related to damage in Area V4.

63._____   Akinetopsia refers to the inability to identify objects in motion.

64._____ The ventral processing stream is specialized for higher aspects of visual object recognition.

65._____ The left hemisphere is involved when an individual is processing strings of letters.

66._____ The right hemisphere is involved when an individual is perceiving objects and faces.

67._____ The dorsal processing stream is specialized for the visual localization of objects in space.

68._____ Apraxia refers to a specific type of language deficit.

69._____ The term agnosia was coined by Paul Broca.

70._____ Visual object agnosia refers to the inability to recognize objects.

71._____ Prosopagnosia refers to the inability to detect some colors.

72._____ People with visual agnosias are blind.

73._____ The essential difficulty in associative visual agnosia is object perception.

74._____ The essential difficulty in apperceptive visual agnosia is assigning meaning to an object.

75._____ The most common site of damage in apperceptive agnosia is the parietal-occipital area of the right hemisphere.

76._____ An individual with Ballint's syndrome may misreach for objects and exhibit a left-sided neglect.

77._____ Generally, it is believed that the right hemisphere assigns meaning whereas the left hemisphere is responsible for the global aspects of perceptual integration.

78._____ Unilateral neglect is also known as contralesional neglect, hemineglect, visuospatial agnosia, hemispatial agnosia, visuospatial inattention, and hemispatial inattention.

79._____ An individual experiencing neglect may believe that the left-sided part of their body does not belong to them.

80._____ Neglect may be caused by a right parietal stroke.

81._____ Neglect is synonymous with attentional deficits.

82._____ Neglect is the result of a visual acuity deficit.

83._____ Right-sided neglect is more common than left-sided neglect.

Labeling

Identify each of these structures of visual pathways:

a. Lateral geniculate nucleus of the thalamus
b. Optic chiasm
c. Optic nerve
d. Retina
e. Superior colliculus
f. Visual cortex

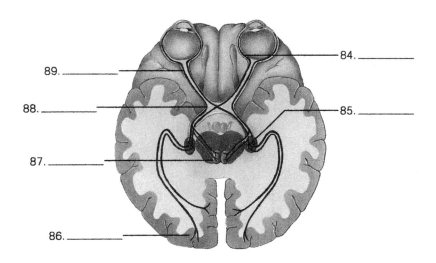

Auditory and Language Processing

Key Terms and Concepts

Wernicke's area	receptive aphasia	Wernicke's aphasia
frontal operculum	Broca's area	aphasia
dysarthria	speech apraxia	fluent aphasia
confluent aphasia	expressive aphasia	Broca's aphasia
anomia	articulation	word salad
paragrammatism	extended paraphasia	conduction aphasia
phonemic paraphasia	transcortical motor aphasia	transcortical sensory aphasia
anomic aphasia	global aphasia	synthesthesia

90._____   Auditory receptors are located in the cochlea.

91._____   The auditory nerve projects contralaterally to the cochlear nuclei of the medulla.

92._____   The auditory system allows each cerebral hemisphere to receive input from both ears.

93._____   Heschel's gyrus corresponds to Brodmann's area 21.

94._____   The tonopic map reflects the layout of auditory frequency ranges mapped onto the cochlea.

95._____   The primary auditory cortex is known as Wernicke's area.

96._____   Wernicke's area is located on the superior temporal gyrus.

97._____   Wernicke's aphasia refers to the inability to decipher spoken words.

98._____   The frontal operculum is thought to play a role in the recognition of sounds.

99._____   Broca's area is associated with the mediation of speech fluency and the grammatical and syntactical arrangement of words.

100._____   There is no neuroanatomical link between Wernicke's and Broca's areas.

101._____   The right hemisphere is dominant for speech.

102._____   The left hemisphere is dominant for speech prosody.

103._____   Bilateral representation of speech is present in more women than men.

104._____   Impairments in the comprehension or expression of spoken, written, or gestured language may be referred to generally as aphasia.

105._____   Aphasia may be caused by paralysis of the vocal apparatus.

106._____   Mutism is a type of aphasia.

107._____   Broken or halted speech may indicate a nonfluent aphasia.

108._____   Receptive aphasia implies a disorder of speech output.

109._____   Damage to the angular gyrus is often associated with disorders of writing.

110._____   In Broca's aphasia, verbal comprehension is typically somewhat preserved.

111._____   Anomia refers to word finding difficulties.

112._____   Broca's aphasia may present as a word salad.

113._____ Running speech which may sound like a foreign language is referred to as extended paraphasia.

114._____ Transcortical motor aphasia refers to difficulties in repeating words and sentences.

115._____ The ability to repeat phrases and sentences, but with the inability to comprehend spoken language is referred to as transcortical sensory aphasia.

116._____ A global aphasia refers to a condition in which all areas of speech functioning are negatively impacted.

Motor Systems

<u>Key Terms and Concepts</u>

primary motor cortex	secondary motor cortex	supplementary motor area
premotor area	cingulate motor area	parietal lobes
dorsolateral prefrontal cortex	dissociation	apraxia
dyspraxia	dysarthria	dyskinesia
tremors	striatal complex	Tourette's syndrome

<u>Sentence Completion</u>

117. The _____ plays a role in motor planning and sequencing, as well as movement readiness.

118. Uncontrolled involuntary motor movements are also referred to as _____.

119. A disorder which is characterized by facial and bodily tics and repetitive verbal utterances is known as _____.

120. The _____ is located in Brodmann's area 6.

121. Adequate motor strength in the absence of the ability to perform voluntary actions refers to _____ or _____.

122. The _____ is partially responsible for perceptual-motor learning and adaptation.

123. The _____ is located in the precentral gyrus, anterior to the central sulcus.

124. The supplementary motor area, premotor area, and cingulate motor area are structures within the _____.

125. Initiation of motor behavior and executive programming for movement originates in the _____.

126. A _____, or separation, exists between the functional contributions of the primary motor cortex and the supplementary motor area.

127.   Occurring either in a resting state or with intentional movements, _____ include the involuntary shaking of a limb.

128.   The posterior areas of the _____ contribute to the coordination of spatial mapping and motor coordination.

129.   The _____ is probably involved in the emotional and motivational aspects of motor movement.

130.   _____ refers to a difficulty in formulating words because of a motor control deficit.

Post-Test
Multiple Choice

1. What is it called when an individual is unable to recognize a familiar person?

   a.   Visual agnosia.
   b.   Tactile agnosia.
   c.   Astereognosis.
   d.   None of the above.

2. The sensation of the position of one's own body in extra-personal space is referred to as:

   a.   astereognosis.
   b.   agnosia.
   c.   proprioception.
   d.   None of the above.

3. Which of the following transduces energy from vibrations?

   a.   Mechanical receptors.
   b.   Nocioreceptors.
   c.   Proprioceptors.
   d.   Thermoreceptors.

4. Which of the following carries information related to pain and temperature and runs parallel to the spinal cord?

   a.   Dorsal column medial lemniscal pathway.
   b.   Ascending spinal-thalamic tract.
   c.   Primary somatosensory cortex.
   d.   Medial lemniscus.

5. Who attempted to map the cortex through the use of electrical stimulation?

   a.   Walter Freeman.
   b.   Franz Gall.
   c.   Wilder Penfield.
   d.   Dr. Frankenstein.

6. The secondary somatosensory cortex corresponds to Brodmann's areas:

   a.   1 and 2.
   b.   3 and 5.
   c.   5 and 7.
   d.   42 and 44.

7. In the case of right parietal damage, which of the following might be true?

    a.   An individual is likely to report increased sensation in the left hand.
    b.   An individual is likely to report increased sensation in the left hand when it is touched simultaneously with the right.
    c.   An individual is likely to report no sensation in the left hand when it is touched simultaneously with the right.
    d.   An individual is likely to report decreased sensation in the right hand.

8. Which of the following refers to a crawling, burning, or tingling sensation?

    a.   Paresthesia.
    b.   Peripheral neuropathy.
    c.   Finger agnosia.
    d.   Proprioceptive disorder.

9. Which of the following medical conditions is most likely to result in phantom limb pain?

    a.   Schizophrenia.
    b.   Amputation.
    c.   Hypertension.
    d.   Chronic lower back pain.

10. What percentage of individuals undergoing amputation is expected to experience phantom limb pain?

    a.   10%
    b.   30%
    c.   50%
    d.   70%

11. What might account for the phenomenon of the phantom limb?

    a.   Individuals who undergo amputation or who are born without limbs are at a higher risk of developing a psychosis.
    b.   Healthy neurons reorganize themselves to take over an area of the brain, which is no longer being served by the body.
    c.   New neurons are formed to compensate for the missing part of the body.
    d.   Phantom limb pain is a proprioceptive disorder.

12. Taste receptors are replaced every _____ days.

    a.   Two.
    b.   Five.
    c.   Ten.
    d.   Twenty-eight.

13. Which cranial nerves are implicated in taste?

      a.   I, VII, and IX.
      b.   II, IX, and X.
      c.   VII, IX, and X.
      d.   I, II, and III.

14. Which of the following neuroanatomical structures responds directly to the sweetness of food?

      a.   Frontal lobe.
      b.   Hippocampus.
      c.   Hypothalamus.
      d.   Caudate nucleus.

15. Which of the following indicates a distorted taste sensation?

      a.   Aguesia.
      b.   Dysguesia.
      c.   Hypoguesia.
      d.   Phantoguesia.

16. Which of the following indicates a complete loss of taste?

      a.   Aguesia.
      b.   Dysguesia.
      c.   Hypoguesia.
      d.   Phantoguesia.

17. The olfactory epithelium is replaced every _____.

      a.   10 minutes.
      b.   10 hours.
      c.   24 hours.
      d.   28 days.

18. Which cranial nerves are implicated in olfaction?

      a.   I, II, and III.
      b.   I, V, and X.
      c.   I, IV, and V.
      d.   I only.

19. Which of the following statements is true regarding olfactory neurons?

    a.   Like all other neurons, olfactory neurons do not regenerate.
    b.   Olfactory receptors synapse with olfactory neurons beneath the epithelial layer.
    c.   The olfactory system provides an easy means for some diseases to travel to the brain.
    d.   Olfactory neurons are well-protected and rarely damaged during traumatic brain injuries.

20. Olfaction proceeds to the _____ and _____ prior to reaching the thalamus.

    a.   amygdala, hippocampus
    b.   caudate nucleus, hippocampus
    c.   amygdala, hypothalamus
    d.   caudate nucleus, hypothalamus

21. Smell is tied strongly to:

    a.   emotional intelligence.
    b.   emotional memory.
    c.   social skills.
    d.   socio-emotional functioning.

22. Which of the following refers to diminished smell sensation?

    a.   Anosmia.
    b.   Dysosmia.
    c.   Phantosmia.
    d.   Hyposmia.

23. Which of the following refers to the experience of a hallucinatory smell?

    a.   Anosmia.
    b.   Dysosmia.
    c.   Phantosmia.
    d.   Hyposmia.

24. How much of the cerebral cortex is dedicated to visual processing?

    a.   10%
    b.   25%
    c.   50%
    d.   75%

25. Which of the following statements is true?

    a.   Rods detect wavelengths of color.
    b.   Cones detect wavelengths of color.
    c.   Cones are attuned to shades of gray.
    d.   Both rods and cones are attuned to shades of gray.

26. Where does visual information decussate in the brain?

    a.   Medulla.
    b.   Pons.
    c.   Optic nerve.
    d.   Optic chiasm.

27. Homonymous hemianopsia refers to:

    a.   blindness in one eye.
    b.   blindness in one visual field in one eye.
    c.   blindness in one visual field in both eyes.
    d.   blindness in both eyes.

28. Which area contains the retinotopic map?

    a.   V1.
    b.   V2.
    c.   V3.
    d.   V4.

29. Which area is selective for the electromagnetic wavelengths of color?

    a.   V1.
    b.   V2.
    c.   V3.
    d.   V4.

30. Damage to V4 is most likely to result in:

    a.   complete blindness.
    b.   homonymous hemianopsia.
    c.   achromatopsia.
    d.   akinetopsia.

31. Which of the following is specialized for visual object recognition?

    a.   Dorsal processing stream.
    b.   Ventral processing stream.
    c.   Dorsal column medial lemniscal pathway.
    d.   Ascending spinal-thalamic tract.

32. Which of the following is specialized to detect the visual localization of objects in space?

    a.   Dorsal processing stream.
    b.   Ventral processing stream.
    c.   Dorsal column medial lemniscal pathway.
    d.   Ascending spinal-thalamic tract.

33. Damage to the dorsal processing stream would most likely result in which of the following problems?

    a.   Apperceptive agnosia.
    b.   Associative agnosia.
    c.   Right-left discrimination problems.
    d.   All of the above.

34. Which of the following refers to the inability to recognize people by their faces?

    a.   Apraxia.
    b.   Visual object agnosia.
    c.   Prosopagnosia.
    d.   Proprioception.

35. Which of the following indicates a deficit in object perception or synthesis?

    a.   Apraxia.
    b.   Aphasia.
    c.   Apperceptive agnosia.
    d.   Associative agnosia.

36. Which of the following indicates a deficit in the loss of knowledge of the semantic meaning of objects?

    a.   Apraxia.
    b.   Aphasia.
    c.   Apperceptive agnosia.
    d.   Associative agnosia.

37. Which of the following might result in an apperceptive agnosia?

    a.   Cardiac arrest.
    b.   Carbon monoxide poisoning.
    c.   Mercury intoxication.
    d.   All of the above.

38. A symptom of Ballint's syndrome is:

    a.   visual agnosia.
    b.   misreaching for objects.
    c.   left-sided neglect.
    d.   All of the above.

39. Damage to which of the following neuroanatomical sites is most likely to result in unilateral neglect?

    a.   Right frontal-temporal lobe.
    b.   Right temporal-parietal lobe.
    c.   Right parietal-occipital lobe.
    d.   Right temporal-occipital lobe.

40. Which of the following might indicate a neglect syndrome?

    a.   An individual is paralyzed on the left side.
    b.   An individual has a difficult time reading due to blindness in the left eye.
    c.   An individual does not read the left side of any pages in a book.
    d.   An individual loses motivation to maintain good personal hygiene.

41. Which of the following statements is true regarding neglect?

    a.   Individuals with neglect are neither consciously nor unconsciously aware of stimuli in their left side of space.
    b.   Galvanic skin conductance and evoked potentials failed to show that individuals with neglect unconsciously recognize stimuli presented to the left side.
    c.   Individuals with neglect may be unconsciously aware of both the presence and the meaning of stimuli presented to their left side.
    d.   None of the above.

42. Which of the following statements is true regarding the auditory system?

    a.   Auditory information is projected ipsilaterally.
    b.   Auditory information is projected contralaterally.
    c.   Auditory information is projected both ipsilaterally and contralaterally.
    d.   All of the above.

43. The primary auditory cortex is located in the _____.

    a.   frontal lobe.
    b.   temporal lobe.
    c.   parietal lobe.
    d.   occipital lobe.

44. The secondary auditory processing area is also known as _____.

    a.   Broca's area.
    b.   Wernicke's area.
    c.   Heschel's gyrus.
    d.   None of the above.

45. The inability to decipher spoken words is known as:

    a.   expressive aphasia.
    b.   Broca's aphasia.
    c.   Wernicke's aphasia.
    d.   dysarthria.

46. Which of the following might result from right hemisphere damage?

    a.   Loss of the ability to decipher spoken language.
    b.   No changes in harmonic ability.
    c.   Loss of the nuances of humor.
    d.   No changes in sound discrimination.

47. The frontal operculum is also known as:

    a.   Broca's area.
    b.   Wernicke's area.
    c.   Heschel's gyrus.
    d.   None of the above.

48. Wernicke's area and Broca's area are connected by the:

    a.   corpus callosum.
    b.   anterior commissure.
    c.   arcuate fasiculus.
    d.   frontal operculum.

49. Aphasia may be exhibited by:

    a.   the impairment of the ability to speak.
    b.   the impairment of the ability to comprehend language.
    c.   the impairment of the ability to read and/or write.
    d.   All of the above.

50. Word-finding difficulties are also referred to as:

    a.   apraxia.
    b.   aphasia.
    c.   anomia.
    d.   articulation.

51. The word salad is more formally known as:

    a.   Broca's aphasia.
    b.   paragrammatism.
    c.   anomia.
    d.   apraxia.

52. _____ is significant for phonemic paraphasias.

    a.   Transcortical sensory aphasia
    b.   Global aphasia
    c.   Conduction aphasia
    d.   Anomic aphasia

53. _____ is significant for dysfunction in all aspects of speech functioning.

    a.   Transcortical sensory aphasia
    b.   Global aphasia
    c.   Conduction aphasia
    d.   Anomic aphasic

54. A "melding" of sensory experiences is also known as:

    a.   transcortical sensory aphasia.
    b.   synthesthesia.
    c.   paragrammatism.
    d.   None of the above.

55. Which of the following organizes and sequences the timing of movement?

    a.   Primary motor cortex.
    b.   Supplemental motor area.
    c.   Premotor area.
    d.   Cingulate motor area.

56. Which of the following is located next to the supplemental motor area in Brodmann's area 6?

    a.   Primary motor cortex.
    b.   Dorsolateral prefrontal cortex.
    c.   Premotor area.
    d.   Cingulate motor area.

57. Which of the following plays a role in the emotional and motivational aspects of movement?

    a.   Primary motor cortex.
    b.   Supplemental motor area.
    c.   Premotor area.
    d.   Cingulate motor area.

58. Uncontrolled involuntary motor movement is referred to as:

    a.   apraxia.
    b.   dysarthria.
    c.   dyskinesia.
    d.   tremor.

59. Which of the following coordinates reflex action, times movement, and aids in the maintenance of balance and posture?

    a.   Striatal complex.
    b.   Supplemental motor area.
    c.   Primary motor cortex.
    d.   Cerebellum.

60. Which of the following statements is true regarding Tourette's syndrome?

    a.   Tourette's syndrome occurs in 3% of the population.
    b.   Tourette's syndrome is most likely to be observed in females.
    c.   Tourette's syndrome is most likely to be observed in right-handers.
    d.   Tourette's syndrome is usually evident by age 10 years.

Essay Questions

1.   Compare and contrast apperceptive and associative agnosias.

2.   What are some possible explanations for why neglect syndromes are almost always left-sided?

3.   Relate the various types of aphasia both from a behavioral and a neuroanatomical point of view.

Answer Key

Chapter Exercises

1. agnosia (p.113)
2. Astereognosis (p.114)
3. tactile agnosia (p.114)
4. receptor cells (p.113)
5. transduction (p.113)
6. visual agnosia (p.114)
7. True (p.114)
8. True (p.114)
9. False (p.114)
10. False (p.114)
11. True (p.114)
12. False (pp.114,115)
13. False (p.115)
14. True (p.115)
15. True (p.115)
16. False (p.115)
17. False (p.115)
18. True (p.115)
19. True (p.115)
20. True (p.119)
21. False (p.117)
22. True (p.116)
23. True (p.120)
24. False (p.120)
25. True (p.121)
26. Hypoguesia (p.122)
27. Dysguesia (p.122)
28. papillae (p.119)
29. Hyposmia (p.125)
30. Dysosmia (p.125)
31. olfaction (p.123)
32. aguesia (p.122)
33. Anosmia (p.125)
34. phantosmia (p.125)
35. phantoguesia (p.122)
36. Primary visual cortex (p.113)
37. Occipital lobe (p.113)
38. Parietal lobe (p.113)
39. Primary somatosensory cortex (p.113)
40. Central sulcus (p.113)
41. Primary motor cortex (p.113)
42. Frontal lobe (p.113)
43. Primary olfactory cortex (p.113)
44. Primary auditory cortex (p.113)
45. Temporal lobe (p.113)
46. True (p.125)
47. False (p.125)
48. False (p.125)
49. True (p.126)
50. True (p.126)
51. True (p.126)
52. True (p.126)
53. True (p.126)
54. False (p.126)
55. False (p.126)
56. True (p.126)
57. True (p.127)
58. True (p.127)
59. True (p.127)
60. False (p.129)
61. True (p.129)
62. True (p.129)
63. True (p.129)
64. True (p.130)
65. True (p.130)
66. True (p.130)
67. True (p.130)
68. False (p.130)
69. False (p.130)
70. True (p.130)
71. False (pp.130,131)
72. False (p.131)
73. False (p.131)
74. False (p.131)
75. True (p.131)
76. False (p.133)
77. True (p.133)
78. True (p.134)
79. True (p.134)
80. True (p.134)
81. False (p.135)
82. False (p.135)
83. False (p.137)
84. Retina (p.127)
85. Lateral geniculate nucleus of the thalamus (p.127)
86. Visual cortex (p.127)
87. Superior colliculus (p.127)
88. Optic chiasm (p.127)

89. Optic nerve (p.127)
90. True (p.139)
91. False (p.139)
92. True (p.139)
93. False (p.139)
94. True (p.140)
95. False (p.141)
96. True (p.141)
97. True (p.141)
98. False (p.141)
99. True (p.141)
100. False (p.141)
101. False (p.142)
102. False (p.143)
103. True (p.143)
104. True (p.143)
105. False (p.143)
106. False (p.143)
107. True (p.144)
108. False (p.144)
109. True (p.144)
110. True (p.144)
111. True (p.145)
112. False (p.145)
113. True (p.145)
114. False (p.147)
115. True (p.147)
116. True (p.148)
117. premotor area (p.151)
118. dyskinesia (p.152)
119. Tourette's syndrome (p.153)
120. supplementary motor area (p.150)
121. apraxia or dyspraxia (pp.151,152)
122. striatal complex (p.152)
123. primary motor cortex (p.150)
124. secondary motor cortex (pp.150,151)
125. dorsolateral prefrontal cortex (p.151)
126. dissociation (p.150)
127. tremors (p.152)
128. parietal lobes (p.151)
129. cingulate motor area (p.151)
130. Dysarthria (p.152)

Post-Test

Multiple Choice

1. A (p.114)
2. C (p.114)
3. A (p.114)
4. B (p.115)
5. C (p.115)
6. C (p.115)
7. C (p.115)
8. A (p.119)
9. B (p.120)
10. D (p.120)
11. B (pp.120,121)
12. C (p.119)
13. C (p.121)
14. C (p.121)
15. B (p.122)
16. A (p.122)
17. A (p.123)
18. D (p.123)
19. C (p.123)
20. A (p.123)
21. B (p.125)
22. D (p.125)
23. C (p.125)
24. B (p.125)
25. B (p.126)
26. D (p.126)
27. C (p.126)
28. A (p.127)
29. D (p.129)
30. C (p.129)

31. B (p.130)
32. A (p.130)
33. C (p.130)
34. C (pp.130,131)
35. C (p.131)
36. D (p.131)
37. D (p.131)
38. D (p.133)
39. C (p.134)
40. C (p.134)
41. C (p.137)
42. C (p.139)
43. B (p.139)
44. B (p.141)
45. C (p.141)
46. C (p.141)
47. A (p.141)
48. C (p.141)
49. D (p.143)
50. C (p.145)
51. B (p.145)
52. C (p.146)
53. B (p.148)
54. B (p.146)
55. B (p.150)
56. C (p.151)
57. D (p.151)
58. C (p.152)
59. D (p.152)
60. D (p.153)

Chapter 5

The Functioning Brain
Higher Functional Systems

Chapter Outline

Overview

This chapter summarizes the highest level of brain integration known as higher functional systems that are not sensory modality specific and include memory, attention, and executive functioning, as well as emotional processes and consciousness. Such systems are also referred to as "higher order" because, evolutionarily, the expression in humans is complex and highly integrated, and does not depend on any one sensory or motor modality. These management systems of human thinking are important because they allow us to focus on what is important, to remember, to prioritize for action, to reflect, to self-regulate, and to problem solve. For each system the chapter outlines and discusses the conceptual organization of the system, as well as known structure/function relationships. Many of the processes of these systems operate automatically or unconsciously without apparent verbal awareness. Many of the "unconscious" processes are controlled by subcortical brain regions. The more explicit, and therefore more seemingly conscious aspects of higher order processing are represented in the cortical areas, most notably the frontal lobes. It is important for the neuropsychology student to understand these higher order processes of the brain since they are the cornerstone of cognitive neuropsychology and our human experience. In addition, an understanding of higher functional systems will provide a foundation for the clinical syndromes presented later in the text.

Learning Objectives

- To conceptualize the higher functional systems of attention and memory.
- To understand the neuropsychology of executive functions and their relationship to brain anatomy.
- To appreciate the brain organization as it relates to anatomical correlates of consciousness and emotions.

Memory Systems

Key Terms and Concepts

anterograde amnesia	retrograde amnesia	short-term memory
long-term memory	remote memory	declarative memory
procedural memory	implicit memory	implicit priming
semantic memory	episodic memory	working memory
central executive	articulatory phonological loop	visual-spatial sketch pad

1.	working memory	a.	Type of memory which has a theoretically unlimited capacity for information and may be permanent.
2.	retrograde amnesia	b.	Type of memory which uses aspects of attention and executive functioning and coordinates the temporary storage of information so that it can be processed.
3.	semantic memory	c.	Prior learning, though unconscious, which positively impacts memory for skill acquisition.
4.	implicit priming	d.	This is also referred to as an attention controlling system.
5.	central executive	e.	Loss of the ability to learn new information following a neurological event.
6.	procedural memory	f.	Type of memory which has the capacity for 7 +/- 2 bits of information.
7.	visual-spatial sketch pad	g.	Memory for autobiographical information.
8.	anterograde amnesia	h.	Memory for long-past events.
9.	long-term memory	i.	This stores verbally based information.
10.	implicit memory	j.	Loss of the ability to recall memories which occurred prior to a neurological event.
11.	short-term memory	k.	Performance memory, such as for various motor skills.
12.	declarative memory	l.	Memory for specific information or facts.
13.	remote memory	m.	This stores visual and spatial information.
14.	articulatory phonological loop	n.	Conscious awareness is not always required for this type of memory.
15.	episodic memory	o.	Type of memory which is accessible to conscious awareness and able to be verbalized.

Attention

<u>Key Terms and Concepts</u>

focused attention   alternate attention   divided attention
sustained attention

16._____   Attention is considered to be a single-faceted neuropsychological concept.

17._____   The reticular activating system is considered integral in cortical arousal.

18._____   The frontal lobes are attributed to directing attentional resources.

19._____   The basal ganglia are indicated in the selection of sensory information to be processed.

20._____   Focused attention refers to the ability to concentrate.

21._____   Alternate attention refers to the tendency for humans to revert to altered states of arousal throughout any given day.

22._____   Divided attention refers to the ability to allocate various attentional resources to different simultaneous tasks.

23._____   Sustained attention refers to the ability to maintain attention over a period of time.

24._____   The posterior parietal lobe is thought to modulate sustained visual attention.

25._____   The frontal cortex is thought to have a role in divided attention.

26._____   Dopamine is considered the most important neurotransmitter with regards to maintaining alertness and attention.

27._____   Alzheimer's disease, head trauma and schizophrenia can have adverse consequences with regards to attention.

Executive Functioning

Key Terms and Concepts

executive functioning   frontal lobes

True/False

28._____   Frontal lobe damage results in primary sensory disorders.

29._____   Executive functions are related to managing, structuring, and directing behavior.

30._____   A deficit in executive functioning may be reflected in the inability to problem solve.

31._____   The prefrontal cortex is generally not implicated in the ability to evaluate our own actions.

32._____   The prefrontal cortex is implicated in working memory.

33._____   The frontal lobes are involved in our ability to handle novel situations.

34._____   The frontal lobes are strongly activated when we are faced with routine situations.

35._____   There are differences between the frontal lobes of males and females.

36._____   Frontal lobe injury may result in the inability to make safe choices.

37._____   Injuries to the frontal lobes are not known to alter an individual's personality.

38._____   Injuries to the frontal lobes can result in impulsive behavior.

39._____   The first documented case of frontal lobe damage was that of Phineas Gage, who became impulsive, obstinate, disinhibited and unable to follow through with plans.

Consciousness

Key Terms and Concepts

mind   brain   binding problem

True/False

40._____   Consciousness has been widely and objectively studied in the field of neuropsychology.

41._____   Consciousness can be conceptualized as a level of awareness, a state of mental alertness, or as an "inner self."

42._____   The ability to describe internal experiences is integral to measuring individual consciousness.

43._____   Consciousness is regularly altered by biological and cosmic rhythms.

44._____   Individuals who have had their corpus callosum severed (i.e., split-brain patients) develop two distinct realities or levels of consciousness.

45._____   Within all human beings there are brain and body processes which are unavailable to conscious experience.

46._____   Biofeedback can make some previously unconscious physiological mechanisms in the body available to modification by the conscious mind.

47._____   It is widely accepted, as Descartes suggested, that the pineal gland is the center of consciousness in the human brain.

48._____   The experience of consciousness is partially accounted for via the sensory systems (i.e., vision, audition, proprioception, olfaction, and taste).

49._____   The reticular activating system has a clear role in human consciousness.

50._____   The cerebellum has a clearly identified role in human consciousness.

51._____   The binding problem refers to the way in which the brain is able to create one definable conscious experience at any given moment in time.

52._____   The larger the cortex of any given organism, the smaller the capacity for self-awareness.

53._____   Individual concepts are stored on a single-cellular level within different cortices.

54._____   The neocortex is not believed to play a role in the evaluation of experiences.

55. _____	Neurons which fire together in bursts may be a partial explanation to the binding problem and to human consciousness.
56. _____	Brain waves may play a role in the binding problem and in the unification of conscious experience.
57. _____	The thalamus may operate as the "integrator" of conscious experience.
58. _____	Scientists continue to search for the one neuroanatomical structure implicated in consciousness.

Emotional Processing

Key Terms and Concepts

James-Lange theory   Cannon-Bard theory   primary emotions
secondary emotions

True/False

59. _____	Emotional intelligence refers to the ability to understand emotions and mood in one's self and in others and to utilize that information effectively.
60. _____	The James-Lange theory postulates that emotions are experienced in reaction to a stimulus and then our bodies react with physical experiences, such as a racing heart.
61. _____	The Cannon-Bard theory pronounced that conscious emotional experience in humans could not be separated from physical sensation.
62. _____	Our thoughts can influence our emotions.
63. _____	There is one discrete emotional system in the brain.
64. _____	Primary emotions are processed through the limbic system.
65. _____	Anger is an example of a primary emotion.
66. _____	It is well-known that the conscious perception of an emotional situation always precedes the emotional response.
67. _____	Conditioning of the fear response occurs on a subcortical level.
68. _____	The amygdala is not thought to play a role in the fear response.
69. _____	Secondary emotions are processed primarily through the limbic system.
70. _____	Disgust and surprise are examples of secondary emotions.
71. _____	Secondary emotions may also be referred to as social emotions.
72. _____	The left side of the human face is more emotionally expressive than the right because the right hemisphere of the brain is dominant for emotional expression.

73._____   It is theorized that various emotions are controlled by different hemispheres of the brain.

74._____   Posed smiles (for photographs, for example) appear to be controlled by subcortical limbic system structures.

Post-Test
Multiple Choice

1.   Memory can be negatively impacted by:

 a.   a dementia.
 b.   anoxia.
 c.   traumatic brain injury.
 d.   all of the above.

2.   A neurological injury would be most likely to cause which of the following scenarios?

 a.   An individual is unable to remember his/her name.
 b.   An individual forgets all aspects of his/her personal life but continues to recall learned facts and skills.
 c.   An individual is unable to learn new information.
 d.   An individual forgets to do a neuropsychology assignment and suddenly recalls that he/she was abducted by aliens and was unable to complete it.

3.   Anterograde amnesia is:

 a.   the inability to learn new information following a neurological trauma.
 b.   the inability to recall information prior to a neurological trauma.
 c.   the inability to learn new information and recall information prior to a neurological trauma.
 d.   none of the above.

4.   Retrograde amnesia is:

 a.   the inability to learn new information following a neurological trauma.
 b.   the inability to recall information prior to a neurological trauma.
 c.   the inability to learn new information and recall information prior to a neurological trauma.
 d.   none of the above.

5.   In the case of N. A. an injury was sustained to the left dorsomedial nucleus of the thalamus, which resulted in:

 a.   severe retrograde and anterograde amnesia.
 b.   severe anterograde amnesia.
 c.   severe retrograde amnesia.
 d.   complete loss of memory.

6.   Which of the following statements is true regarding short-term memory?

        a.   Information is stored for only approximately 5 minutes.
        b.   There is a capacity for unlimited storage in short-term memory.
        c.   Short-term memory and sensory memory are synonymous.
        d.   Information can be held in short-term memory assuming a strategy such as
                rehearsal is utilized to keep it there.

7.   Which of the following statements is true regarding long-term memory?

        a.   Storage in long-term memory is thought to be permanent.
        b.   Long-term memory is not typically a complaint of individuals with neurological
                impairment.
        c.   Long-term memory has a large but probably limited storage capacity.
        d.   None of the above.

8.   Evidence supporting separate neurological systems for short-term and long-term memory
        could be:

        a.   a lesion in a specific area of the brain impairs both short and long-term memory.
        b.   a lesion in one area of the brain impairs long-term memory but not short-term
                memory.
        c.   a lesion in one area of the brain does not impair any type of memory.
        d.   All of the above.

9.   An example of a remote memory would be:

        a.   the information you retain to take your next examination in this class.
        b.   what you had for dinner last night.
        c.   that ridiculous hair piece your professor was wearing last week.
        d.   the surprise party you had on your 8th birthday.

10.   An example of a procedural memory is:

        a.   your tennis forehand.
        b.   the specific regions of the brain implicated in memory.
        c.   your high school graduation.
        d.   your phone number.

11.   An example of a semantic memory is:

        a.   your tennis forehand.
        b.   the specific regions of the brain implicated in memory.
        c.   your high school graduation.
        d.   your first date.

12. Explicit memory is to implicit memory as declarative memory is to:

    a.   sensory memory.
    b.   procedural memory.
    c.   semantic memory.
    d.   working memory.

13. What is the function of the declarative memory system?

    a.   To provide temporary storage of information so that it can be utilized later.
    b.   To coordinate information from all of the sensory systems for storage in the brain's memory center.
    c.   To process information for storage in the brain.
    d.   None of the above.

14. What are the three major areas of the brain implicated in declarative memory?

    a.   Frontal lobes, medial temporal lobes and basal forebrain.
    b.   Frontal lobes, diencephalon and basal forebrain.
    c.   Occipital lobes, diencephalon and basal forebrain.
    d.   Medial temporal lobes, diencephalon and basal forebrain.

15. What happened to H. M. after having his hippocampus and surrounding areas removed bilaterally?

    a.   He was no longer able to remember who he was.
    b.   His IQ dropped significantly and he was no longer able to form new memories.
    c.   He experienced a significant anterograde amnesia.
    d.   His memory improved.

16. Within the diencephalon, which structures are believed to be implicated in declarative memory?

    a.   Dorsal medial nucleus of the thalamus and mammilary bodies.
    b.   Dorsal medial nucleus of the thalamus and hippocampus.
    c.   Dorsal medial nucleus of the thalamus and amygdala.
    d.   Mammilary bodies and hippocampus.

17. Which of the following is not a basal forebrain structure implicated in declarative memory?

    a.   Nucleus basalis of Meynert.
    b.   Broca's area.
    c.   Substantia innominata.
    d.   Medial septal nucleus.

18.   Memory is best described as:

        a.   integrated communication between various systems.
        b.   a localized function.
        c.   interaction between two distinct areas of the brain.
        d.   a system independent of other cognitive functions.

19.   The route of information through the Papez circuit is:

        a.   cingulate gyrus, parahippocampal gyrus, brain stem, hippocampus, mammilary
                bodies, and back to the cingulate gyrus.
        b.   cingulate gyrus, parahippocampal gyrus, hippocampus, fornix, mammillary
                bodies, anterior nucleus of the thalamus, and back to the cingulate gyrus.
        c.   cingulate gyrus, parahippocampal gyrus, hippocampus, basalis of Meynert,
                anterior nucleus of the thalamus, and back to the cingulate gyrus.
        d.   "the leg bone's connected to the hip bone...."

20.   What is considered the most crucial anatomical structure implicated in memory?

        a.   Cingulate gyrus.
        b.   Thalamus.
        c.   Hypothalamus.
        d.   Hippocampus.

21.   Which of the following is not considered a part of declarative memory?

        a.   Procedural memory.
        b.   Implicit memory.
        c.   Habit memory.
        d.   All of the above.

22.   Implicit memories are:

        a.   reflected by conscious awareness of requirements to complete a specific skill.
        b.   synonymous with semantic memories.
        c.   influenced by prior experience without conscious awareness.
        d.   always preceded by implicit priming.

23.   An example of procedural learning is:

        a.   memorization of a recipe.
        b.   a proper golf swing.
        c.   using this study guide as a means to retain information.
        d.   paying someone to write your papers for you.

24.   Organisms with no hippocampus:

     a.   are unable to exhibit any type of learning.
     b.   are able to consciously recall information with an excessive amount of rehearsal.
     c.   are able to learn simple stimulus-response associations.
     d.   do not exist.

25.   Which of the following statements is true regarding working memory?

     a.   Information can be stored in working memory indefinitely.
     b.   Working memory is an integrated system, which also incorporates attention and executive functions.
     c.   Working memory is a static process, designed to temporarily store information until it can be integrated into short-term memory.
     d.   Working memory is localized to the hippocampus.

26.   The central executive:

     a.   is a part of working memory.
     b.   is thought to be lacking in Alzheimer's disease.
     c.   controls attention.
     d.   all of the above.

27.   The purpose of the articulatory phonological loop is to:

     a.   promote speech in the absence of verbal memory.
     b.   accelerate the transmission of neurochemicals in order to improve verbal memory.
     c.   store verbally based information.
     d.   improve language skills in the right hemisphere of the brain.

28.   The visual-spatial sketch pad:

     a.   is associated with the left hemisphere of the brain.
     b.   is designed to promote visual-spatial abilities in the absence of visual memory.
     c.   is important in the acquisition of vocabulary.
     d.   is linked to frontal lobe executive processes.

29.   Which of the following is a definition of attention?

     a.   A general level of alertness.
     b.   The ability to focus mental effort.
     c.   The ability to target processing within a specific sensory modality.
     d.   All of the above.

30.   Which of the following neuroanatomical structures are primarily implicated in attention?

a.   Reticular activating system, hippocampus, and posterior parietal lobes.
b.   Reticular activating system, hippocampus, posterior parietal lobes, and frontal lobes.
c.   Reticular activating system, cingulate gyrus, hippocampus, posterior parietal lobes, and frontal lobes.
d.   Reticular activating system, posterior parietal lobes, cingulate gyrus, and frontal lobes.

31.   Which of the following plays a role in anticipatory responding?

a.   Basal ganglia.
b.   Cingulate gyrus.
c.   Reticular activating system.
d.   Posterior parietal lobes.

32.   Effortful processing or concentration is also referred to as:

a.   alternate attention.
b.   focused attention.
c.   divided attention.
d.   sustained attention.

33.   The ability to allocate attention to different stimuli simultaneously is referred to as:

a.   alternate attention.
b.   focused attention.
c.   divided attention.
d.   sustained attention.

34.   Within the posterior parietal lobe attentional system, the superior colliculus is believed to:

a.   direct the eyes from one position to another.
b.   mediate conscious attention to spatial targets.
c.   filter sensory information for processing.
d.   none of the above.

35.   Within the posterior parietal lobe attentional system, the pulvinar of the thalamus is believed to:

a.   direct the eyes from one position to another.
b.   mediate conscious attention to spatial targets.
c.   filter sensory information for processing.
d.   none of the above.

36.   Which of the following tasks is influenced by the frontal lobes?

  a.   Shifting of attentional set.
  b.   Sustained attention.
  c.   Attentional planning.
  d.   All of the above.

37.   Which is an important neurotransmitter required to maintain alertness and attention?

  a.   Serotonin.
  b.   Dopamine.
  c.   Acetylcholine.
  d.   Norepinephrine.

38.   Which of the following is a psychiatric disorder, which negatively impacts attention?

  a.   Multiple Sclerosis.
  b.   Depression.
  c.   Hyperthyroidism.
  d.   Epilepsy.

39.   Which of the following are thought to be components of executive functioning?

  a.   Planning and problem solving.
  b.   Mental flexibility.
  c.   Self-monitoring.
  d.   All of the above.

40.   Females are more likely to:

  a.   utilize the left prefrontal system for context-dependent selection bias.
  b.   utilize the right prefrontal system for context-independent selection bias.
  c.   exhibit significant lateralization between left and right prefrontal systems.
  d.   exhibit less lateralization than males between the left and right prefrontal systems.

41.   Frontal lobe injury is most likely to result in:

  a.   memory deficits.
  b.   language impairment.
  c.   difficulties solving problems.
  d.   sensory-perceptual deficits.

42.   Personality changes in an individual with frontal lobe damage may be a reflection of:

  a.   impulsivity, poor social judgment, and disinhibition.
  b.   impulsivity, memory problems and poor social judgment.
  c.   impulsivity, loss of the ability to form abstractions, and speech impairment.
  d.   impulsivity, poor social judgment and motor deficits.

43. Phineas Gage was:

   a. a frontal lobe researcher who pioneered the idea of executive functioning.
   b. the first documented case of frontal lobe damage.
   c. the first survivor of a frontal lobe injury.
   d. a phrenologist.

44. Consciousness:

   a. is an objectively measurable phenomenon.
   b. implies a certain level of awareness.
   c. does not vary widely among human beings.
   d. does not require the ability to express the experience verbally.

45. Which of the following can influence level of consciousness?

   a. The sun.
   b. Drugs.
   c. Food.
   d. All of the above.

46. Which of the following is true of split-brain patients?

   a. Split-brain patients develop two personalities, which maintain two different conscious experiences.
   b. Split-brain patients exhibit no neuropsychological sequelae following the brain surgery (corpus callosotomy).
   c. Split-brain patients continue to exhibit one unified conscious experience.
   d. None of the above.

47. The role that the reticular activating system displays in consciousness is:

   a. the integration of sensory information which is then sent to the cortex and limbic system for simultaneous processing.
   b. the maintenance of alertness.
   c. the integration of sensory information for higher order processing.
   d. the binding of fragments of information in order to create a unified conscious experience.

48. The binding problem refers to:

   a. difficulties that individual neurons display in binding to one another in an effort to improve neuronal communication and enhance conscious experience.
   b. how the brain creates various conscious experiences at any given time for the same event.
   c. how the brain is able to process an almost unlimited stream of information and interpret it meaningfully without conscious experience.
   d. how the brain creates one conscious experience at any given time.

49.   A partial solution to the binding problems lies in the fact that:

        a.   neurons in the visual cortex fire in bursts.
        b.   brain waves are unrelated to the integration of information.
        c.   hard-wired spatial patterns of neurons act as a prime binding mechanism.
        d.   the thalamus appears to play no role in the binding problem indicating that
                subcortical structures play a secondary role in consciousness.

50.   Which of the following statements is true regarding the thalamus?

        a.   Communication with the thalamus is one-way.
        b.   Sensory and motor systems are routed around the thalamus.
        c.   The thalamus integrates information from all areas of the brain.
        d.   The thalamus is not implicated in seizure disorders.

51.   Which of the following neuroanatomical structures is not implicated in consciousness?

        a.   Thalamus.
        b.   Cerebellum.
        c.   Reticular Activating System.
        d.   Frontal Lobes.

52.   The James-Lange theory of emotion states:

        a.   that emotion creates the physical reaction experienced in any given
                circumstance.
        b.   that conscious emotional experience can be separated from the physical reaction.
        c.   that emotion is experienced as a result of a physical reaction.
        d.   that the physical reaction to any emotional experience can be consciously
                manipulated.

53.   The cerebral cortex allows humans to:

        a.   respond with fear to an immediately threatening situation.
        b.   think about a situation and experience an emotion related to that situation.
        c.   initiate a startle response.
        d.   None of the above.

54.   Which of the following is a primary emotion?

        a.   Joy.
        b.   Shame.
        c.   Anxiety.
        d.   Pride.

55. Which of the following neuroanatomical structures is primarily implicated in fear?

   a. Thalamus.
   b. Hippocampus.
   c. Hypothalamus.
   d. Amygdala.

56. Which of the following is an example of a secondary emotion?

   a. Surprise.
   b. Embarrassment.
   c. Anger.
   d. Disgust.

57. Which of the following statements is true regarding primary and secondary emotions?

   a. Primary and secondary emotions are both eventually processed through the limbic system.
   b. Social learning is required for the experience of primary emotions.
   c. Both primary and secondary emotions require higher cortical processing.
   d. Primary and secondary emotions travel the same route via sensory systems to the limbic system.

Essay Questions

1. Compare and contrast short and long-term memory.

2. Discuss the roles of the frontal lobes in relation to executive functioning.

3. Describe two neurological explanations of consciousness.

Answer Key

Chapter Exercises

1. b (pp.169,170)
2. j (p.158)
3. l (p.161)
4. c (p.167)
5. d (p.170)
6. k (pp.160,161)
7. m (p.170)
8. e (p.158)
9. a (p.158)
10. n (p.166)
11. f (p.158)
12. o (pp.160,161)
13. h (p.160)
14. i (p.170)
15. g (p.161)
16. False (p.170)
17. True (p.172)
18. True (p.172)
19. True (p.172)
20. True (p.173)
21. False (p.173)
22. True (p.173)
23. True (p.173)
24. True (p.173)
25. True (p.173)
26. False (p.174)
27. True (p.175)
28. False (p.175)
29. True (p.175)
30. True (p.175)
31. False (p.177)
32. True (p.177)
33. True (p.177)
34. False (p.177)
35. True (p.177)
36. True (p.177)
37. False (p.178)
38. True (p.178)
39. True (p.179)
40. False (p.178)
41. True (pp.179,180)
42. True (p.180)
43. True (p.180)
44. False (p.180)
45. True (p.180)
46. True (p.181)
47. False (p.181)
48. True (p.181)
49. True (p.181)
50. False (p.181)
51. True (p.181)
52. False (p.181)
53. False (p.182)
54. False (p.182)
55. True (p.182)
56. True (p.182)
57. True (p.182)
58. False (p.183)
59. True (p.184)
60. False (p.185)
61. False (p.185)
62. True (p.185)
63. False (p.185)
64. True (p.185)
65. True (p.185)
66. False (p.185)
67. True (p.186)
68. False (p.186)
69. False (p.186)
70. False (pp.185,186)
71. True (p.186)
72. True (p.186)
73. True (pp.186,187)
74. False (p.187)

Post-Test

1. D (p.158)
2. C (p.158)
3. A (p.158)
4. B (p.158)
5. A (p.159)
6. D (p.158)
7. A (p.158)
8. B (pp.159,160)
9. D (p.160)
10. A (pp.160,161)
11. B (pp.160,161)
12. B (p.161)
13. C (p.161)
14. D (p.161)
15. C (pp.161,163)
16. A (p.163)
17. B (p.163)
18. A (p.163)
19. B (p.163)
20. D (p.166)
21. D (p.166)
22. C (p.166)
23. B (pp.166,167)
24. C (p.167)
25. B (p.169)
26. D (p.170)
27. C (p.170)
28. D (p.170)
29. D (p.170)
30. D (p.172)
31. C (p.172)
32. B (p.173)
33. C (p.173)
34. A (p.173)
35. C (p.173)
36. D (p.173)
37. D (p.174)
38. B (p.175)
39. D (p.175)
40. D (p.177)
41. C (p.177)
42. A (p.178)
43. B (p.179)
44. B (pp.178,180)
45. D (p.180)
46. C (p.180)
47. B (p.181)
48. D (p.181)
49. A (p.182)
50. C (pp.182,183)
51. B (pp.182,183)
52. C (p.185)
53. B (p.185)
54. A (p.185)
55. D (p.186)
56. B (p.186)
57. A (pp.185,186)

Chapter 6

The Functioning Brain
Methods of Investigating the Brain

Chapter Outline

Magnetic Imaging Procedures
> Magnetic Resonance Imaging (MRI)
>> Technique
>> Clinical Use
>> Functional MRI (fMRI)
> Magnetoencephalogram (MEG)

Cerebrospinal Fluid Studies: Lumbar Puncture

Behavioral Examinations
> Neurological Exam
> Neuropsychological Evaluation

New Advances in Imaging Techniques: Mapping the Brain
> Subtraction Procedures
> Image Analysis and Quantification (3-D)
> Future Directions

Post-Test

Answer Key

Overview

In the past it was impossible for scientists to examine the living brain. As a result many suggested that the brain was not the province of psychologists. Over the last 100 years, however, there has been an explosion in technology that has allowed for the precise imaging of the brain. With the advent of technologies like Computer Transaxial Tomography (CT) and Magnetic Resonance Imaging (MRI), the visualization of specific and detailed brain structures has become possible. The most recent development in imaging technology has been in the integration of different evaluation modalities such as MRI with electroencephalography (EEG) in order to obtain a more complete picture of the brain. This includes new technology that allows for the interfacing of multiple and quantitative analysis of brain images using different examination methods. Also, computer modeling has allowed for the three-dimensional viewing of brain structures and brain pathology. These recent advances in neuroimaging dramatically changed how scientists have been investigating neural correlates of human behavior. As a result, the neuropsychologist's role in diagnosis has been reduced somewhat, although behavioral techniques remain the primary approach in the diagnosis of disorders like early stages of dementia or attention deficit disorder. In this chapter we summarize the major technological methods of examining the brain. The neuropsychology student should understand how each procedure works and what the advantages and disadvantages for each procedure are. This information is important as these technologies play an important role in the understanding of brain-behavior relationships and disease processes. In fact, one of the most exciting advances in the imaging of the living brain has been the collaboration between different disciplines including biomedical engineers, psychiatrists, neurologists, neurosurgeons, and neuropsychologists to differentiate between the normal and malfunctioning brain.

Learning Objectives

- To be able to list the advantages and disadvantages of the major imaging techniques of the brain.
- To be able to discuss the differences of MRI, EEG, and PET.
- To understand the role of the neuropsychologist in the context of modern methods of investigating the brain.

Neurohistology Techniques

Key Terms, Concepts, and Scientists

Camillo Golgi	Golgi stain	Franz Nissl
Nissl stain	myelin staining	horseradish peroxidase

True/False

1._____ The electron microscope made it possible to analyze synaptic contacts between individual neurons.

2._____ Camillo Golgi was a nineteenth century Peruvian neurologist.

3._____ Golgi used silver chromate to stain dead neurons.

4._____   The Golgi method is now outdated and is not useful to researchers or clinicians.

5._____   One drawback to the Golgi stain was that it did not allow for the visualization of the inner structures of the neuron.

6._____   Franz Nissl was a nineteenth century German histologist.

7._____   Nissl used dyes, which were used for dyeing cloth to stain the inner structures of neurons and central nervous system cells.

8._____   The Nissl methods are no longer in use today.

9._____   In addition to other neural structures, the Nissl methods stain the axon of the neuron.

10._____   The Golgi method is useful for examining dendrites and axons.

11._____   Myelin staining targets myelinated axons.

12._____   Horseradish peroxidase is used as a means to chart the course of neuronal messages.

Radiological Procedures

<u>Key Terms, Concepts and Scientists</u>

Wilhelm Conrad von Roentgen
air encephalogram
computerized transaxial tomography
hyperdensity
femorocerebral angiography
Carotid Sodium Amobarbital Injection

X-ray
Pneumoencephalography
hypo-density
angiography
digital subtraction angiography

Matching

13. Radiographic visualization of the fluid-containing structures of the brain.

a. Wilhelm Conrad von Roentgen

14. This method is particularly effective for visualizing arterial, capillary, and venous phases of cerebral blood circulation.

b. X-rays

15. Permits an anatomical image of the brain based on multiple X-ray images.

c. air encephalogram

16. Used to examine the blood supply to and from the brain.

d. pneumoencephalography

17. The detection of this could indicate the presence of an old brain lesion.

e. computerized transaxial tomography

18. The insertion of a catheter into the femoral artery which allows for investigation of blood flow via any of three major arteries.

f. hypo-density

19. Also called air encephalogram.

g. hyperdensity

20. Won the Nobel Prize in 1901.

h. angiography

21. The Wada technique, used to anesthetize a hemisphere of the brain.

i. femorocerebral angiography

22. The detection of this could indicate an abnormality such as a tumor or bleed in the brain.

j. digital subtraction angiography

23. Electromagnetic vibrations of short wavelength which can penetrate biological tissue.

k. Carotid Sodium Amobarbital Injection

Electrophysiological Procedures

<u>Key Terms and Concepts</u>

electroencephalography
beta
theta
electrocorticogram
brain stem auditory evoked responses
somatosensory evoked responses
electromyography

gamma
alpha
delta
evoked potential
visual evoked responses
electrical stimulation

<u>Sentence Completion</u>

24.   During deep sleep, _____ waves are prominent.

25.   _____ is used to differentiate between peripheral nerve and central sensory pathway deficits.

26.   The _____ can diagnose a malfunction of the auditory nerve at the inferior colliculus.

27.   _____ activity is a low-amplitude and fast activity wave.

28.   At its inception, it was hoped that _____ would aid in mapping the cortex of the brain.

29.   _____ is a recording of the electrical activity of the brain.

30.   _____ is used to detect lesions along the visual nerve pathways.

31.   A type of EEG in which electrodes are placed directly on the surface of the brain is called _____.

32.   _____ waves are most likely to be associated with quiet, passive but wakeful states of arousal.

33.   In a deeply relaxed state, _____ waves are prominent.

34.   _____ assesses the electrical activity of a specific sensory process.

35.   _____ is used to diagnose neuromuscular disorders.

36.   _____ waves are associated with peak performance and high levels of arousal.

Imaging of Brain Metabolism

Key Terms and Concepts

regional cerebral blood flow   single-photon emission computerized tomography
positron emission tomography

True/False

37._____   Blood flow in the brain is not indicative of level of neural activity.

38._____   Earliest techniques to measure cerebral blood flow involved the use of nitrous oxide.

39._____   Current methods to measure regional cerebral blood flow involve the use of radioactive isotopes.

40._____   Single-photon emission computerized tomography (SPECT) provides a three-dimensional image.

41._____   SPECT can only be used if the patient remains perfectly still.

42._____   SPECT is far more expensive than positron emission tomography (PET).

43._____   PET uses a radioactive tracer to detect glucose and oxygen metabolism, as well as cerebral blood flow.

44._____   In PET the radioactive isotopes have a very long half-life of approximately two days.

45._____   Radionuclei used in PET have an excess negative charge.

46._____   Research using PET has shown that metabolic activity in individuals with head trauma and stroke is suppressed, even though CT and MRI are within normal limits.

47._____   Research using PET suggests that there are no differences between male and female brains.

Magnetic Imaging Procedures

Key Terms and Concepts

magnetic resonance imaging   functional MRI   magnetoencephalogram

True/False

48._____   Magnetic resonance imaging (MRI) provides better neuroanatomical pictures than does CT, especially when diagnosing underlying pathology.

49._____   MRI use requires injection of radioactive isotopes.

50._____   MRI uses a strong magnetic field to magnetize and align hydrogen protons.

51. _____ The "picture" which is created of the brain by use of MRI is actually a visualization of the density of hydrogen in the brain.

52. _____ Protons with short T1 values emit higher signal intensities and appear dark on MRI.

53. _____ With the exception of invasive methods, MRI was the first method available to visualize brain structures.

54. _____ Using MRI, images of the brain can be acquired for any plane, angle or orientation.

55. _____ Functional MRI can be used to measure the active brain.

56. _____ Neuronal activity generates electrical and magnetic fields.

57. _____ The recording of changes in the magnetic field is called magnetoencephalogram (MEG).

58. _____ MEG is recorded using the superconducting quantum interference device (SQUID).

59. _____ MEG is a relatively inexpensive way to measure brain activity.

60. _____ MEG is routinely used in clinical settings.

61. _____ MEG may be better than EEG in diagnosing epilepsy.

Cerebrospinal Fluid Studies

Key Terms and Concepts

lumbar puncture   cerebrospinal fluid

True/False

62. _____ The lumbar puncture differs from the spinal tap.

63. _____ The lumbar puncture is done in order to collect a sample of cerebrospinal fluid.

64. _____ The lumbar puncture is considered a non-invasive medical procedure.

65. _____ Lumbar puncture can be useful in the diagnosis of bacterial meningitis, multiple sclerosis, and viral infections.

Behavioral Examinations

Key Terms and Concepts

neurological exam   neuropsychological evaluation

True/False

66. _____ A neurologist is a physician who has specialized in the evaluation and treatment of neurological disorders.

67._____   During the neurological examination by the neurologist, it is common for an MRI and lumbar puncture to be performed.

68._____   The neurological examination takes about as long as the neuropsychological evaluation.

69._____   Neuropsychological evaluations are used to assist with diagnosis, patient management, intervention, rehabilitation, and discharge planning.

70._____   Neuropsychological findings are more sensitive to the progression of degenerative diseases than MRI.

71._____   MRI and CT are good indicators of an individual's level of functioning and good predictors of whether or not that individual will be able to function at work.

New Advances in Imaging Techniques: Mapping the Brain

Key Terms and Concepts

subtraction procedures   image analysis and quantification

True/False

72._____   Subtraction procedures are used to compare control and experimental conditions.

73._____   Approximately 3% of the healthy adult brain is cerebrospinal fluid.

74._____   Image analysis and quantification can create a three dimensional picture of the head, entire brain, or individual brain structures.

75._____   Structure and function of the brain can be examined simultaneously by superimposing the results of MRI over those of PET.

76._____   Complete understanding of the human brain will come when it has been completely, visually mapped.

77._____   Of great future interest is the imaging of individuals with healthy functioning brains in an effort to increase knowledge about brain function.

Post-Test
Multiple Choice

1. Which of the following was the earliest method of examining neural tissue?

   a. Electromyography.
   b. Computed transaxial tomography.
   c. Staining.
   d. Magnetic resonance imaging.

2. What color does silver chromate stain neurons?

   a. Black.
   b. Green.
   c. Blue.
   d. Red.

3. What is the Golgi method used for today?

   a. To diagnose epilepsy.
   b. To characterize specific cell types.
   c. To visualize internal cell structures.
   d. To provide an accurate account of the number of neurons in a given brain region.

4. Which of the following statements is true regarding the Nissl stain?

   a. The Nissl stain does not assist in providing an accurate count of neurons in a specific brain region.
   b. The Nissl stain is not a good method to use in order to view internal structures of neurons.
   c. The Nissl method stains the axon of the neuron.
   d. The Nissl method assists in the study of neurons in both normal and pathological states.

5. Which of the following is a staining technique in use today?

   a. Golgi method.
   b. Myelin staining.
   c. Horseradish peroxidase.
   d. All of the above.

6. Which of the following is a staining technique which can be used to chart axonal transport in the brain?

    a.   Golgi method.
    b.   Myeline staining.
    c.   Horseradish peroxidase.
    d.   Nissl method.

7. Who invented the X-Ray?

    a.   Wilhelm Conrad von Roentgen.
    b.   Erin D. Bigler.
    c.   Bloch and Purcell.
    d.   Benjamin Franklin.

8. X-Rays:

    a.   can penetrate biological tissue.
    b.   are electromagnetic vibrations of short wavelength.
    c.   can be detected on a photographic plate.
    d.   All of the above.

9. Which of the following is true about X-Rays?

    a.   X-Rays pass more easily through high-density tissue (i.e., bone).
    b.   X-Rays are absorbed by low-density tissue (i.e., water).
    c.   X-Rays are useful in diagnosing skull fractures.
    d.   X-Rays are three dimensional.

10. During a pneumoencephalographic procedure:

    a.   ventricles are filled with saline.
    b.   cerebrospinal fluid is removed.
    c.   ventricles are intentionally collapsed.
    d.   None of the above.

11. Which of the following is a disadvantage of the air encephalogram?

    a.   The patient often developed terrible headaches.
    b.   The patient often had to be inverted to undergo the procedure.
    c.   The patient had to be subjected to a lumbar puncture.
    d.   All of the above.

12. Where was the CT scan invented?

    a.   United States.
    b.   Great Britain.
    c.   Germany.
    d.   Brazil.

13. The CT uses:

    a.   X-Rays.
    b.   a magnetic field.
    c.   radioactive isotopes.
    d.   a lumbar puncture.

14. CT results consist of:

    a.   representations of "slices" of the brain.
    b.   three-dimensional likenesses of the brain.
    c.   color pictures of individual brain structures.
    d.   All of the above.

15. An angiography is:

    a.   an X-Ray of the brain stem.
    b.   an X-Ray of the subcortical structures.
    c.   an X-Ray of the blood vessels in the brain.
    d.   an X-Ray of the cerebral cortex.

16. Femorocerebral angiography was introduced because:

    a.   results were much more accurate than the alternative.
    b.   the procedure was safer than the alternative.
    c.   the procedure cost much less than the alternative.
    d.   All of the above.

17. Digital subtraction angiography is used:

    a.   to more easily differentiate the vascular system from brain tissue.
    b.   as an alternative to femorocerebral angiography so that no injection has to be made.
    c.   as an alternative to intravenous angiography so that no injection has to be made.
    d.   in order to more easily access the brachiocephalic artery.

18. What is a potential hazard associated with angiography?

    a.   Induced tumor.
    b.   Induced embolism.
    c.   Induced seizure.
    d.   Induced Parkinson's disease.

19. Angiography is particularly useful in the diagnosis of:

    a.   epilepsy.
    b.   schizophrenia.
    c.   Alzheimer's disease.
    d.   cerebrovascular disorders.

20. During the Wada technique:

    a.   a CT and lumbar puncture are used.
    b.   half of the body is anesthetized.
    c.   one hemisphere of the brain is anesthetized.
    d.   the entire brain is anesthetized.

21. The EEG records:

    a.   radiowaves.
    b.   magnetic fields.
    c.   electrical activity.
    d.   the newest rock and roll hits.

22. Who first discovered that patterns of neural electrical activity could be recorded?

    a.   Wilhelm Conrad von Roentgen.
    b.   Hans Berger.
    c.   Erin D. Bigler.
    d.   Bloch and Purcell.

23. What was Berger investigating when he experimented with early EEG?

    a.   Insomnia.
    b.   Narcolepsy.
    c.   Epilepsy.
    d.   Telepathy.

24. Which of the following is true regarding EEG?

    a.   It is an invasive procedure.
    b.   It involves a small amount of electrical shock to the patient.
    c.   It requires electrodes to be attached to the head.
    d.   All of the above.

25. A "spike" on the EEG record may indicate:

    a.   deep Stage 4 sleep.
    b.   seizure activity.
    c.   wakefulness.
    d.   brain death.

26. Which of the following is associated with drowsiness or a deeply relaxed state?

    a.   Gamma activity.
    b.   Alpha activity.
    c.   Theta activity.
    d.   Delta activity.

27. Which of the following is associated with peak performance states or hyper-arousal?

    a.   Gamma activity.
    b.   Beta activity.
    c.   Alpha activity.
    d.   Delta activity.

28. Which of the following is associated with deep Stage 4 sleep?

    a.   Beta activity.
    b.   Alpha activity.
    c.   Theta activity.
    d.   Delta activity.

29. Which of the following is associated with a quiet, resting but wakeful state?

    a.   Gamma activity.
    b.   Beta activity.
    c.   Alpha activity.
    d.   Theta activity.

30. Which of the following is associated with a narrow focus, anxiety, or over-arousal?

    a.   Gamma activity.
    b.   Beta activity.
    c.   Alpha activity.
    d.   Theta activity.

31. Seizures are a form of:

    a.   synchronous brain activity.
    b.   unsynchronous brain activity.
    c.   scattered brain activity.
    d.   psychosis.

32. What is the likelihood that you have had/will have a seizure at some point in your life?

    a.   <1%
    b.   1%
    c.   3%
    d.   10%

33. Which class of drugs can suppress seizures?

   a.   Selective serotonin reuptake inhibitors.
   b.   Benzodiazepines.
   c.   Amphetamines.
   d.   Monoamine oxidase inhibitors.

34. An electrocortigram involves:

   a.   placing extra electrodes on the scalp for a more accurate recording.
   b.   placing stronger/larger electrodes on the scalp for a more accurate recording.
   c.   placing electrodes directly on the cortex of the brain for a more accurate recording.
   d.   electroconvulsive therapy.

35. Which of the following diagnoses involves the use of EEG?

   a.   Sleep disorder.
   b.   Coma.
   c.   Epilepsy.
   d.   All of the above.

36. Brain electrical activity mapping (BEAM):

   a.   maps the brain's electrical activity as it occurs.
   b.   creates a map of the brain's electrical activity based on an average of activity recorded over several hours.
   c.   Creates a map of brain structures based on complicated subtraction formulas.
   d.   None of the above.

37. Which of the following is used to assess the integrity of the visual, auditory, and somatosensory pathways of the brain?

   a.   Electromyography.
   b.   Evoked potential.
   c.   Electroencephalogram.
   d.   Brain electrical activity mapping.

38. In which of the following can brain stem auditory evoked responses (BAER) diagnose a malfunction?

   a.   The auditory nerve at the superior olive.
   b.   The auditory nerve at the lateral lemniscus.
   c.   The auditory nerve at the cochlear nucleus.
   d.   All of the above.

39. For visual evoked responses (VER), over which brain regions are the electrodes placed?

     a.   Frontal and temporal.
     b.   Temporal and occipital.
     c.   Parietal and frontal.
     d.   Parietal and occipital.

40. Which of the following is used to diagnose neuromuscular disorders?

     a.   Electromyography.
     b.   Evoked potential.
     c.   Electroencephalogram.
     d.   Brain electrical activity mapping.

41. Regional cerebral blood flow (rCBF) requires:

     a.   removal of a portion of the skull for close inspection of the blood vessels.
     b.   an electrocorticogram.
     c.   injection of a radioactive isotope.
     d.   inhalation of nitrous oxide.

42. Which of the following is true of rCBF?

     a.   Regional cerebral blood flow measures information in the deepest regions of the brain.
     b.   Studies using rCBF have validated many brain-behavior relationships.
     c.   Regional cerebral blood flow is not sensitive to changes in neuronal metabolism.
     d.   None of the above.

43. Which of the following is true of single-photon emission computerized tomography (SPECT)?

     a.   SPECT is more expensive than positron emission tomography (PET).
     b.   SPECT provides a two-dimensional representation.
     c.   The SPECT tracer clears from the brain in approximately 15 minutes.
     d.   SPECT can be used to study subjects while they are performing neuropsychological tasks.

44. Which of the following is examined by PET?

     a.   Glucose metabolism.
     b.   Oxygen metabolism.
     c.   Blood flow.
     d.   All of the above.

45. Which of the following is true of PET?

    a.   PET requires a cyclotron.
    b.   The radionuclei injected into a patient during PET has an excess negative charge.
    c.   PET measures only glucose metabolism and blood flow.
    d.   PET is cost-effective and widely used clinically.

46. Using PET, which of the following differences has been found between the brains of males and females?

    a.   During a spatially-based problem solving task, male brains demonstrated maximum activity in the right frontal area.
    b.   During a spatially-based problem solving task, male brains demonstrated maximum activity in the right parietal-temporal lobe.
    c.   During a spatially-based problem solving task, female brains demonstrated maximum activity in the right frontal area.
    d.   During a spatially-based problem solving task, female brain demonstrated maximum activity throughout the entire brain.

47. Which of the following is true of magnetic resonance imaging (MRI)?

    a.   MRI utilizes radio frequencies.
    b.   MRI is based on the fact that the hydrogen nucleus generates a magnetic field.
    c.   MRI does not require the injection of a radioactive isotope.
    d.   All of the above.

48. MRI is used for:

    a.   the evaluation of cognitive deficits in relation to a specific neurological disorder.
    b.   diagnosing neurological conditions.
    c.   treating neurological conditions.
    d.   rehabilitation following traumatic brain injury.

49. The combined use of MRI and functional MRI (fMRI) can be used to:

    a.   superimpose information regarding brain activity over corresponding brain structures.
    b.   treat brain tumors by applying more accurate radioactive treatment.
    c.   provide a three-dimensional picture of the magnetic field of the brain.
    d.   measure electrical activity of the brain.

50. What is the procedure called which records the magnetic fields that accompany electrical activity of neurons?

    a.   Electroencephalogram.
    b.   Magnetic resonance imaging.
    c.   Functional magnetic resonance imaging.
    d.   Magnetoencephalogram.

51. The lumbar puncture takes a sample of:

    a.   neural tissue from the cortex.
    b.   cerebrospinal fluid.
    c.   myelinated axons.
    d.   the spinal cord.

52. What is cerebrospinal fluid examined for following a spinal tap?

    a.   Cell count.
    b.   Protein content.
    c.   Glucose levels.
    d.   All of the above.

53. Which of the following is tested by a neurologist during a neurological examination?

    a.   Cranial nerve functioning.
    b.   Rudimentary language functions.
    c.   Muscle tone.
    d.   All of the above.

54. A budding neuropsychologist needs to understand:

    a.   current neuroimaging technology.
    b.   neurological disorders and their associated cognitive deficits.
    c.   the social impact any given neurological condition may have on a patient.
    d.   All of the above.

55. What method allows for the visualization of a lesion from any angle or perspective?

    a.   Angiography.
    b.   CT.
    c.   Brain stem auditory evoked response.
    d.   Image analysis and quantification.

56. What is the normal ventricle-to-brain ratio (VBR) in healthy adults?

    a.   1.5%
    b.   2.5%
    c.   5%
    d.   10%

57. What is a common VBR in individuals with traumatic brain injury?

    a.   2%
    b.   4%
    c.   10%
    d.   20%

58. Which of the following is used to generate a three dimensional image of the brain?

    a.   CT.
    b.   Angiography.
    c.   PET.
    d.   Electrocorticogram.

Essay Questions

1.   Compare and contrast Golgi and Nissl stains.

2.   Discuss the advantages and disadvantages of CT, Angiography, EEG, and MRI.

3.   Outline the PET and MRI techniques.

Answer Key

Chapter Exercises

1. True (p.194)
2. False (p.194)
3. True (p.194)
4. False (p.195)
5. True (p.195)
6. True (p.195)
7. True (p.195)
8. False (p.195)
9. False (p.195)
10. True (p.195)
11. True (p.195)
12. True (p.195)
13. c (p.197)
14. j (p.200)
15. e (p.198)
16. h (p.200)
17. f (p.199)
18. i (p.200)
19. d (p.197)
20. a (p.196)
21. k (p.201)
22. g (p.199)
23. b (p.196)
24. delta (p.204)
25. Somatosensory evoked response (p.208)
26. brain stem auditory evoked response (p.207)
27. Beta (p.204)
28. electrical stimulation (p.208)
29. Electroencephalography (p.202)
30. Visual evoked response (p.208)
31. electrocorticogram (p.205)
32. Alpha (p.204)
33. theta (p.204)
34. Evoked potential (p.207)
35. Electromyography (p.210)
36. Gamma (p.204)
37. False (p.210)
38. True (pp.210,211)
39. True (p.211)
40. True (p.211)
41. False (p.212)
42. False (p.212)
43. True (p.212)
44. False (p.212)
45. False (p.212)
46. True (p.213)
47. False (pp.213,214)
48. True (p.215)
49. False (p.215)
50. True (pp.215,216)
51. True (p.216)
52. False (p.216)
53. False (p.218)
54. True (p.218)
55. True (p.217)
56. True (p.217)
57. True (p.217)
58. True (p.217)
59. False (p.217)
60. False (p.217)
61. True (p.217)
62. False (p.217)
63. True (p.218)
64. False (p.218)
65. True (p.218)
66. True (p.218)
67. False (p.219)
68. False (p.219)
69. True (p.220)
70. True (p.220)
71. False (p.220)
72. True (p.220)
73. False (p.221)
74. True (p.221)
75. True (p.221)
76. False (p.221)
77. True (p.221)

Post-Test

Multiple Choice

1. C (p.194)
2. A (p.194)
3. B (p.195)
4. D (p.195)
5. D (p.195)
6. C (p.195)
7. A (p.196)
8. D (p.196)
9. C (p.197)
10. B (p.197)
11. D (p.197)
12. B (p.197)
13. A (p.198)
14. A (pp.198,199)
15. C (p.200)
16. B (p.200)
17. A (p.200)
18. B (p.201)
19. D (p.201)
20. C (p.201)
21. C (p.202)
22. B (p.202)
23. D (p.202)
24. C (pp.202,203)
25. B (p.203)
26. C (p.204)
27. A (p.204)
28. D (p.204)
29. C (p.204)
30. B (p.204)
31. A (p.204)
32. D (p.204)
33. B (p.205)
34. C (p.205)
35. D (p.206)
36. A (p.207)
37. B (p.207)
38. D (p.207)
39. D (p.208)
40. A (p.210)
41. C (p.211)
42. B (p.211)
43. D (p.212)
44. D (p.212)
45. A (p.213)
46. A (p.214)
47. D (pp.215,216)
48. B (p.216)
49. A (p.217)
50. D (p.217)
51. B (p.218)
52. D (p.218)
53. D (p.219)
54. D (p.220)
55. D (p.218)
56. A (p.221)
57. B (p.221)
58. C (p.221)

Chapter 7

The Developing Brain
Developmental Disorders of Childhood

Chapter Outline

Post-Test

Answer Key

Overview

This chapter focuses on the neuropsychology of developmental disorders. An overview of the prenatal and postnatal development of the human brain and related emergence of cognitive functions is presented. The brain develops in accordance with genetically predetermined templates, or "blueprints," that guide the unfolding of structure and function. Unfortunately, the developing brain can be adversely impacted by genetic and chromosomal anomalies, trauma, disease, and toxins. A number of representative developmental disorders are presented to highlight the consequences of anomalies in brain development. The contribution of neuropsychology to the study of childhood developmental disorders is also provided.

Learning Objectives

- To develop an appreciation of the relationship of prenatal and postnatal anatomic development to cognitive and related neuropsychological functions.
- To understand the vulnerability of the developing brain to anomalies of structure and function, and the limitations in the emergence of functions following such trauma.
- To develop an understanding of the brain-behavior relationships of hydrocephalus, Turner's syndrome, and fetal alcohol syndrome.

Anatomic and Functional Development of the Brain

Key Terms and Concepts

neurogenesis	neural tube	progenitor cells	neurulation
spina bifida	anencephaly	corticogenesis	agyria
spines	synaptogenesis	myelin	pruning
polymicrogyria	prosodic	executive functions	working memory
inhibitory control	object permanence	phenylketonuria	teratogens
agenesis	dysgenesis	Kennard Principle	

True/False

1. _____ Neurogenesis refers to the process by which the human nervous system has evolved over the years.
2. _____ The central and peripheral nervous system develop approximately 18 days after conception.
3. _____ The progenitor cells of the neural tube eventually form the cerebellum.
4. _____ In healthy individuals, the neural tube remains open throughout fetal development.
5. _____ The posterior end of the neural tube eventually becomes the spinal cord.
6. _____ Neurulation refers to the process by which the neural tube is formed and closed during fetal development.
7. _____ A problem in the differentiation of neural cells during neurulation may result in spina bifida.
8. _____ Spina bifida occurs as the result of the demyelination of cells.

9._____ Failure of the posterior end of the neural tube to close may result in anencephaly.

10._____ Corticogenesis begins in the 6th month of fetal development.

11._____ During corticogenesis cells migrate inward to form the six cortical layers from the outside-in.

12._____ Disruptions in cell migration during corticogenesis may result in lissencephaly.

13._____ Lissencephaly, or agyria, is usually associated with cognitive difficulties in the later adult years.

14._____ The sprouting of dendrites is termed arborization.

15._____ Dendritic spines create synapses.

16._____ Most of arborization and spine growth occurs during the 2nd trimester.

17._____ The formation of synapses is termed synaptogenesis.

18._____ Synaptic development in the occipital lobe is nearly completed between the ages of 2 and 4 years.

19._____ Synaptic development in the prefrontal cortex is completed between the ages of 5 and 7 years.

20._____ Myelination begins in the cortical regions.

21._____ Myelination of the frontal lobes is completed by birth.

22._____ Pruning refers to the organized elimination of neurons.

23._____ Most pruning occurs prenatally.

24._____ The anterior end of the neural tube eventually forms three vesicles, which form the prosencephalon, mescephalon, and rhomcephalon.

25._____ At approximately 14 weeks the longitudinal and Sylvian fissures are visible.

26._____ Once the gyri are formed, intracortical connections have been established.

27._____ Polymicrogyria is associated with epilepsy.

28._____ The first and second ventricles of the forebrain become the lateral ventricles.

29._____ Diminished cerebrospinal fluid prenatally may result in hydrocephalus.

30._____ The motor cortex is fully developed by the 3rd trimester.

31._____ During the first 3 months of life, Broca's area develops much faster than its corresponding region in the right hemisphere.

32._____ From 3-12 months of age, nonverbal language development exceeds that of verbal language.

33._____   Prosodic aspects of speech include fluency and tempo of speech.

34._____   Lateralization of speech is typically completed by age 2 years.

35._____   During Piaget's sensorimotor stage, accelerated brain activity is noted in the parietal-occipital areas only.

36._____   In the dialectic period, accelerated brain activity is evident in the frontal regions.

37._____   Executive functions reflect supervisory, integrating and regulatory operations.

38._____   Working memory, inhibitory control and cognitive flexibility are considered executive functions.

39._____   Children completely lack executive functions.

40._____   Executive functions cease developing once the frontal lobes reach maximum synaptic density.

41._____   Object permanence is the ability to store a mental representation of an object in order to guide future behavior.

42._____   Object permanence reflects the development of working memory.

43._____   The ability to inhibit a response develops between the ages of 10-12 years.

44._____   Children with Attention-Deficit/Hyperactivity Disorder are more efficient on a task requiring executive planning (Tower of London-Drexel) than children without the disorder.

45._____   Damage to the frontal regions can result in disorders of emotional regulation.

46._____   Phenylketonuria is a disorder caused by environmental factors during pregnancy.

47._____   Teratogens are drugs which, if presented during fetal development, enhance central nervous system formation.

48._____   Agenesis refers to the failure of a given organ to develop.

49._____   Dysgenesis refers to the abnormal development of a given organ.

50._____   Examples of teratogens are influenza, alcohol, and lead.

51._____   Teratogens are the only dangers to the prenatal developing brain.

52._____   Plasticity refers to the notion that axons are more flexible and exhibit an ability to stretch during infancy.

53._____   The Kennard Principle states that recovery from brain trauma is greater if the injury is incurred later in the developmental period.

54._____   By the age of 5 years, the human brain is fully matured.

55._____   Focal injuries to a developing brain tend to be associated with relatively specific functional deficits.

56._____   Radiation treatment may adversely impact the rate of information processing in the brain.

57._____   A thorough neuropsychological evaluation is dependent on the neuropsychologist's knowledge of psychological, behavioral, neurological, social and medical issues.

Specific Developmental Disorders

Key Terms and Concepts

hydrocephalus	intraventricular hemorrhage	obstructive HC
nonobstructive HC	cocktail party syndrome	shunt
ultrasonography	cubitus valgus	Turner's syndrome
karotype	vestigal ovarian streaks	isochromosome
mosaic karotypes	gonadotropins	fetal alcohol syndrome
fetal alcohol effects	alcohol-related neurodevelopmental disabilities	
enuresis		

58._____   The life expectancy of children with anatomic brain abnormalities is approximately the same as for children with healthy brains.

59._____   Mental retardation and epilepsy are rare in children with anatomic brain malformations.

60._____   An excessive accumulation of cerebrospinal fluid within the brain's ventricles is called hydrocephalus.

61._____   The increased cerebrospinal fluid causes a decrease in intracranial pressure.

62._____   Hydrocephalus can be fatal.

63._____   Hydrocephalus is more common in girls than boys.

64._____   Congenital disorders which result in hydrocephalus include spina bifida and intraventricular hemorrhage.

65._____   Hydrocephalus is usually caused by an oversecretion of cerebrospinal fluid.

66._____   Noncommunicating hydrocephalus may be the result of a tumor or scarring.

67._____   The aqueduct of Sylvius is the most frequently obstructed pathway in noncommunicating hydrocephalus.

68._____   Communicating hydrocephalus refers to a problem reabsorbing cerebrospinal fluid into the blood stream.

69._____   If not properly treated, hydrocephalus can cause significant deficits of higher-order cognitive functions.

70._____   In children hydrocephalus can result in enlargement of the skull.

71._____   Neurological treatment of hydrocephalus involves the placement of a shunt.

72._____   Shunts have not been associated with seizure activity.

73._____   Some children with hydrocephalus and shunts exhibit normal intelligence.

74._____ The cocktail party syndrome refers to the observation that hydrocephalic children often appear to be intoxicated and exhibit significant motor impairment.

75._____ Ultrasonography is a technique used to assess a child prenatally for hydrocephalus.

76._____ Turner's syndrome is an inherited disorder.

77._____ Cubitus valgus refers to a failure to develop secondary sex characteristics.

78._____ A karotype refers to the visual representation of the configuration of a chromosome.

79._____ Individuals with Turner's syndrome tend to be significantly taller than individuals without the disorder.

80._____ The life expectancy of an individual with Turner's syndrome is significantly shorter than for individuals without the disorder.

81._____ In Turner's syndrome, the second X chromosome may be missing.

82._____ The presence of normal chromosomes in some cells and abnormal chromosomes in other cells is referred to as isochromosome.

83._____ Individuals with Turner's syndrome are likely to exhibit verbal deficits, while having preserved visual-spatial abilities.

84._____ Positron emission tomography (PET) has shown that individuals with Turner's syndrome have decreased activity in the parietal and occipital lobes.

85._____ No evidence exists suggesting that individuals with Turner's syndrome exhibit frontal system dysfunction.

86._____ Gonadotropins stimulate the functions of the ovaries.

87._____ Individuals with Turner's syndrome experience significant social difficulties as they grow older.

88._____ Turner's syndrome is considered an acquired disorder.

89._____ Fetal alcohol syndrome is considered an acquired disorder.

90._____ Individuals with fetal alcohol syndrome may experience microcephaly, seizures, below average intelligence, and learning disabilities.

91._____ All children affected with fetal alcohol syndrome are mentally retarded.

92._____ Examples of alcohol-related neurodevelopmental disabilities are impulsivity and sensory-motor impairments.

93._____ Amount of alcohol consumed is not a factor in determining severity of fetal alcohol syndrome.

94._____ Dizygotic twins born to an alcoholic mother generally exhibit the same pattern of deficits.

95._____ Cognitive deficits associated with fetal alcohol syndrome generally resolve as the child matures.

96._____ Enuresis refers to the pattern of cognitive deficits observed in individuals with fetal alcohol syndrome.

Post-Test
Multiple Choice

1.   The earliest stage of brain development is called:

      e.   neurogenesis.
      f.   neuromigration.
      g.   neuroevolution.
      h.   neurulation.

2.   The peripheral and central nervous systems begin to develop at:

      a.   at the time of conception.
      b.   8 days post-conception.
      c.   18 days post-conception.
      d.   28 days post-conception.

3.   The cavity of the neural tube eventually becomes:

      a.   the glia of the brain.
      b.   the neurons of the brain.
      c.   the spinal cord.
      d.   the ventricular system.

4.   The cells lining the wall of the neural tube are called:

      a.   preneurons.
      b.   progenitor cells.
      c.   oligodendrocytes.
      d.   astrocytes.

5.   The neural tube closes at what point?

      a.   5 days post-conception.
      b.   15 days post-conception.
      c.   25 days post-conception.
      d.   35 days post-conception.

6.   The formation and closing of the neural tube is called:

      a.   neurogenesis.
      b.   neurulation.
      c.   necrosis.
      d.   corticogenesis.

7. When cells in the posterior end of the neural tube fail to differentiate properly, the result can be:

    a.   anencephaly.
    b.   agyria.
    c.   lissencephaly.
    d.   spina bifida.

8. A condition which can result from failure of the anterior end of the neural tube to close is called:

    a.   anencephaly.
    b.   agyria.
    c.   lissencephaly.
    d.   spina bifida.

9. Corticogenesis begins in which embryonic week?

    a. 1st
    b. 2nd
    c. 4th
    d. 6th

10. During corticogenesis, the neuronal sheets, or laminae, will become:

    a.   the five layers of the cerebral cortex.
    b.   the six layers of the cerebral cortex.
    c.   the seven layers of the cerebral cortex.
    d.   the neural tube.

11. At what time have most cortical neurons reached their locations?

    a. 4th week
    b. 8th week
    c. 12th week
    d. 18th week

12. Problems with cell migration during the 11th to 13th weeks of gestation may result in _____, which is characterized by an underdevelopment of the cortical gyri.

    a.   lissencephaly
    b.   spina bifida
    c.   anencephaly
    d.   hydrocephalus

13. Children with agyria usually do not live beyond the age of _____.

    a.   2 weeks
    b.   2 months
    c.   2 years
    d.   5 years

14. The process by which dendrites begin to sprout is termed:

    a.   synaptogenesis.
    b.   arborization.
    c.   corticogenesis.
    d.   neurogenesis.

15. Most dendritic growth occurs between birth and _____ months.

    a.   6
    b.   12
    c.   18
    d.   24

16. The process by which synapses are formed is termed:

    a.   synaptogenesis.
    b.   arborization.
    c.   corticogenesis.
    d.   neurogenesis.

17. The human occipital lobe achieves synaptic density comparable to that of an adult at the age of:

    a.   6-12 months.
    b.   2-4 years.
    c.   5-10 years.
    d.   18-21 years.

18. The prefrontal cortex achieves synaptic density comparable to that of an adult at the age of:

    a.   6-12 months.
    b.   2-4 years.
    c.   5-10 years.
    d.   18-21 years.

19. Increases in synaptic density in the brain are associated with:

    a.   neurological disorders originating in the dendrites and axons.
    b.   the emergence of brain functions.
    c.   associated neuronal regeneration.
    d.   increased cerebral spinal fluid.

20. The white insulating sheath, which serves to increase efficacy of neuronal transmission, is called:

    a.   white matter.
    b.   myelin.
    c.   agyria.
    d.   a spine.

21. The complete myelination of the brain occurs by:

    a.   infancy.
    b.   childhood.
    c.   adolescence.
    d.   adulthood.

22. In the early months of neurodevelopment, how many neurons are produced?

    a.   Not enough. Neurons have to regenerate throughout the lifetime.
    b.   Just enough. Humans are born with all of the neurons they will ever have and they must utilize them wisely.
    c.   Too many. Humans are born with an excess of neurons which have to be eliminated.
    d.   One.

23. Pruning is:

    a.   random.
    b.   organized.
    c.   orchestrated by the cerebellum.
    d.   what you do to your rose bushes every year.

24. What percentage of neurons are pruned during childhood?

    a.   10%
    b.   20%
    c.   40%
    d.   50%

25. Polymicrogyria is associated with which of the following?

    a.   Mental retardation.
    b.   Epilepsy.
    c.   Learning Disabilities.
    d.   All of the above.

26. From the age of 3 to 12 months, which of the following is true?

    a. The speech and orofacial areas of the left hemisphere exceed that of the right hemisphere.
    b. The speech and orofacial areas of the right hemisphere exceed that of the left hemisphere.
    c. The speech and orofacial areas of the left and right hemisphere develop at an equal rate.
    d. There is no development in the speech and orofacial areas of the right and left hemispheres during this time.

27. Which of the following is a prosodic aspect of speech?

    a. Rhythm of speech.
    b. Vocabulary.
    c. Specific language spoken.
    d. Spelling ability.

28. Speech lateralizes by what age?

    a. 2 years.
    b. 4 years.
    c. 6 years.
    d. 8 years.

29. Quantified electroencephalogram (QEEG) studies have shown _____ stages of brain development.

    a. 3
    b. 4
    c. 5
    d. 6

30. These stages correlate to whose stages of cognitive maturation?

    a. Freud.
    b. Piaget.
    c. Adler.
    d. Maslow.

31. What is the correct order of Piaget's Stages of Cognitive Development?

    a.   Sensorimotor, Concrete Operations, Preoperational, Formal Operations, Dialectic Operations.

    b.   Sensorimotor, Preoperational, Formal Operations, Concrete Operations, Dialectic Operations.

    c.   Sensorimotor, Dialectic Operations, Preoperational, Concrete Operations, Formal Operations.

    d.   Sensorimotor, Preoperational, Concrete Operations, Formal Operations, Dialectic Operations.

32. During the Preoperational stage, which brain regions exhibit heightened activity on QEEG?

    a.   Centro-central, parieto-occipital, temporo-temporal and fronto-temporal.

    b.   Centro-central, parieto-occipital and temporo-temporal.

    c.   All cortical regions.

    d.   Fronto-temporal.

33. During the Dialectic Operations stage, which brain regions exhibit heightened activity on QEEG?

    a.   Centro-central, parieto-occipital, temporo-temporal and fronto-temporal.

    b.   Centro-central, parieto-occipital and temporo-temporal.

    c.   All cortical regions.

    d.   Fronto-temporal.

34. Executive functions are:

    a.   advanced cognitive processes such as memory and speech.

    b.   present only in truly brilliant individuals such as Einstein and Freud.

    c.   considered to be supervisory or control functions.

    d.   not present until adulthood.

35. Which of the following is considered to be an executive function?

    a.   Long-term memory.

    b.   Inhibitory control.

    c.   Expressive language.

    d.   Motor speed.

36. Which of the following statements is true regarding the development of executive functions?

    a.   Executive functions emerge in adolescence once maximum synaptic density of the frontal lobes has been reached.

    b.   Executive functions are fully developed by adolescence.

    c.   Executive functions continue to develop even after maximum synaptic density of the frontal lobes is achieved.

    d.   Executive functions begin to decline in adolescence once neurons begin to undergo pruning.

37. Object permanence refers to:

    a.   the theory that humans tend to want to keep important objects permanently.
    b.   the concept that only humans can store in their memory a mental representation of an object and utilize that information at a later time.
    c.   the concept of storing in memory a mental representation of an object for the purpose of guiding behavior.
    d.   the tendency for very young children to be unable to recognize that an object continues to exist even when it is out of sight.

38. In humans, there is evidence that the abilities to inhibit reflexive reactions and coordinate multiple actions (i.e., rudimentary executive functioning) develop as early as:

    a.   1 month.
    b.   5 months.
    c.   12 months.
    d.   2 years.

39. Infants are unable to make a two-directional reach to retrieve an object placed behind a wall prior to the age of:

    a.   1 month.
    b.   4-6 months.
    c.   8-12 months.
    d.   2 years.

40. On the Tower of London – DX, what pattern of performance was observed with younger children?

    a.   Younger children spent less time planning their moves prior to trying to solve the puzzles.
    b.   Younger children utilized more moves in an effort to solve the puzzles.
    c.   Younger children broke rules more often than older children.
    d.   All of the above.

41. Which of the following is a genetic disorder?

    a.   Turner's syndrome.
    b.   Dysgenesis.
    c.   Phenylketonuria.
    d.   Traumatic brain injury.

42. Which of the following is a potential teratogen?

    a.   Prenatal vitamins.
    b.   Vaccines.
    c.   Orange juice.
    d.   Chicken noodle soup.

43. The failure of an organ to develop is termed:

    a.   agenesis.
    b.   dysgenesis.
    c.   anencephaly
    d.   aphasia.

44. The abnormal development of an organ is termed:

    a.   agenesis.
    b.   dysgenesis.
    c.   anencephaly.
    d.   aphasia.

45. The prenatal brain is most vulnerable to structural damage during which weeks of development?

    a.   1-2.
    b.   1-9.
    c.   3-4.
    d.   3-8.

46. Recovery of function following neurological insult is referred to as:

    a.   neuronal regeneration.
    b.   brain plasticity.
    c.   compensation syndrome.
    d.   axonal shearing.

47. The Kennard Principle holds that:

    a.   recovery from brain damage is greater if the injury is sustained later in development.
    b.   recovery from brain damage is greater if the injury is sustained earlier in development.
    c.   recovery from brain damage is the same regardless of when in development it is sustained.
    d.   there is no recovery from brain damage.

48. The Kennard Principle has been:

    a.   shown to be absolutely true.
    b.   shown to be mostly true.
    c.   shown to be absolutely false.
    d.   shown to be mostly false.

49. Young children who suffer an injury to the language areas of the left hemisphere are likely to:

    a.   develop a life-long aphasic disorder.
    b.   maintain language function in the left hemisphere, with a restructuring of other left-hemisphere-related abilities.
    c.   shift language functions to the right hemisphere.
    d.   lose the ability to speak entirely.

50. In adequately assessing a child via a neuropsychological evaluation, which of the following must be taken into consideration?

    a.   The context of the chief complaint.
    b.   Knowledge of any existing medical problems.
    c.   The normal neuropsychological development of children.
    d.   All of the above.

51. An excessive accumulation of cerebrospinal fluid is called:

    a.   hydrocephalus.
    b.   hydranencephaly.
    c.   Turner's syndrome.
    d.   fetal alcohol syndrome.

52. An excess of cerebrospinal fluid results in:

    a.   decreased intracranial pressure.
    b.   increased intracranial pressure.
    c.   unstable intracranial pressure.
    d.   no changes in intracranial pressure.

53. Which of the following is a consequence secondary to the expansion of cerebral ventricles?

    a.   Damaged neurons.
    b.   Increased dendritic sprouting.
    c.   Agyria.
    d.   Agenesis.

54. A tumor of the choroid plexus may cause:

    a.   an oversecretion of cerebrospinal fluid.
    b.   an obstruction of cerebrospinal passages.
    c.   impaired absorption of cerebrospinal fluid.
    d.   None of the above.

55. Noncommunicating hydrocephalus results from:

    a.   an oversecretion of cerebrospinal fluid.
    b.   an obstruction of cerebrospinal passages.
    c.   impaired absorption of cerebrospinal fluid.
    d.   None of the above.

56. Communicating hydrocephalus results from:

    a.   an oversecretion of cerebrospinal fluid.
    b.   an obstruction of cerebrospinal passages.
    c.   impaired reabsorption of cerebrospinal fluid.
    d.   None of the above.

57. Which of the following is used to treat hydrocephalus?

    a.   Removal of one of the cerebral vesicles.
    b.   Shunt.
    c.   Hemispherectomy.
    d.   Electroconvulsive Therapy.

58. A shunt is typically placed through the _____ lobe of the right hemisphere.

    a.   occipital.
    b.   frontal.
    c.   temporal.
    d.   parietal.

59. Without the use of the shunt, how many individuals with hydrocephalus would survive until adulthood?

    a.   10%
    b.   25%
    c.   50%
    d.   75%

60. Hydrocephalic children with shunts tend to exhibit which of the following neuropsychological deficits when compared to healthy children?

    a.   Memory.
    b.   Hyperverbal communication.
    c.   Reading comprehension
    d.   All of the above.

61. Identification of hydrocephalus in utero is possible through:

    a.   biopsy.
    b.   amniocentesis.
    c.   ultrasonography.
    d.   magnetic Resonance Imaging.

62. Which of the following disorders is genetic?

    a.   Tuberous Sclerosis Complex.
    b.   Prader-Willi Syndrome.
    c.   Klinefelter Syndrome.
    d.   Lesch-Nyhan Disease.

63. Which of the following disorders is chromosomal?

    a.   Williams Syndrome.
    b.   Mild Brain Trauma.
    c.   Fragile X Syndrome.
    d.   Friedreich's Ataxia.

64. Turner's syndrome is characterized by:

    a.   tall stature.
    b.   cubitus valgus.
    c.   overdeveloped secondary sexual characteristics.
    d.   All of the above.

65. Turner's syndrome affects:

    a.   females only.
    b.   males only.
    c.   both males and females equally.
    d.   both males and females, but most often females.

66. Mosaic karotypes constitute _____ of Turner's syndrome cases.

    a.   10-20%
    b.   20-25%
    c.   25-30%
    d.   30-35%

67. Intellectual functioning of children with Turner's syndrome is generally:

    a.   below-average to low-average.
    b.   low-average to average.
    c.   average to above-average.
    d.   above-average.

68. Which neuropsychological deficit is associated with Turner's syndrome?

    a.   Mathematics.
    b.   Mental rotation.
    c.   Visual-spatial abilities.
    d.   All of the above.

69. In young children with Turner's syndrome, which of the following statements is true:

    a.   They exhibit an awareness of their differences, which negatively impacts peer relations.
    b.   They exhibit anxiety and depression.
    c.   They exhibit poor self-esteem.
    d.   They exhibit few difficulties and are generally accepted by peers.

70. Which of the following accounts for the majority of brain damage experienced by children and adolescents?

    a.   Turner's syndrome.
    b.   Traumatic head injuries.
    c.   Environmental toxins.
    d.   Malnutrition.

71. Which of the following is a determinant of functional outcome following brain trauma?

    a.   Age of onset.
    b.   Premorbid intelligence.
    c.   Medical intervention.
    d.   All of the above.

72. An acquired disorder, which is 100% preventable is:

    a.   traumatic brain injury.
    b.   fetal alcohol syndrome.
    c.   concussions.
    d.   None of the above.

73. Fetal alcohol effects are:

    a.   the characteristic facial features associated with fetal alcohol syndrome.
    b.   the neurological symptoms associated with fetal alcohol syndrome, such as seizures and tremors.
    c.   the cardiac problems associated with fetal alcohol syndrome, such as the ventricular septal defect.
    d.   the cognitive and functional impairments present in children who have been exposed to alcohol in utero, but who do not exhibit the physical characteristics of fetal alcohol syndrome.

74. In alcoholic mothers the rate of fetal alcohol syndrome and fetal alcohol effects is:

    a.   2 per 1000 live births.
    b.   10 per 1000 live births.
    c.   25 per 1000 live births.
    d.   200 per 1000 live births.

75. Which of the following neuroanatomic changes is associated with fetal alcohol syndrome?

    a.   Agenesis of the hippocampus.
    b.   Decreased ventricle size.
    c.   Dysgenesis of the corpus callosum.
    d.   All of the above.

76. Which of the following statements is true regarding adolescents with fetal alcohol syndrome?

    a.   By late adolescence most of the cognitive deficits have resolved.
    b.   Adolescents with fetal alcohol syndrome are at high risk of abusing alcohol and drugs.
    c.   Communication disorders become progressively worse during adolescence.
    d.   By late adolescence brain function will have deteriorated significantly and the individual will likely require residential placement for medical problems.

Essay Questions

1.   Compare Piaget's developmental stages to current knowledge regarding neurological maturation.

2.   Compare and contrast the three underlying causes of hydrocephalus and describe the neuropsychological deficits of the disorder.

3.   Discuss the physical, cognitive and emotional difficulties associated with Turner syndrome.

Answer Key

Chapter Exercises

1. False (p.228)
2. True (p.229)
3. False (p.229)
4. False (p.229)
5. True (p.229)
6. True (p.229)
7. True (p.229)
8. False (p.229)
9. False (p.229)
10. False (p.229)
11. False (p.229)
12. True (p.230)
13. False (p.230)
14. True (p.230)
15. True (p.230)
16. False (p.230)
17. True (p.230)
18. True (p.230)
19. False (p.230)
20. False (p.230)
21. False (p.230)
22. True (p.231)
23. False (p.231)
24. True (p.231)
25. True (p.231)
26. True (p.232)
27. True (p.232)
28. True (p.232)
29. False (p.233)
30. False (p.233)
31. False (p.233)
32. True (p.233)
33. True (pp.233,234)
34. False (p.234)
35. False (pp.234,235)
36. True (p.235)
37. True (p.235)
38. True (p.238)
39. False (p.238)
40. False (p.238)
41. True (p.238)
42. True (p.238)
43. False (p.238)
44. False (p.239)
45. True (p.240)
46. False (p.240)
47. False (p.241)
48. True (p.241)
49. True (p.241)
50. True (p.241)
51. False (p.241)
52. False (p.241)
53. False (p.241)
54. False (p.243)
55. False (p.243)
56. True (p.245)
57. True (p.245)
58. False (pp.245,246)
59. False (p.246)
60. True (p.246)
61. False(p.246)
62. True (p.247)
63. False (p.247)
64. True (p.247)
65. False (p.248)
66. True (p.248)
67. True (p.248)
68. True (p.248)
69. True (p.249)
70. True (p.249)
71. True (p.249)
72. False (p.249)
73. True (p.250)
74. False (p.250)
75. True (p.250)
76. False (p.251)
77. False (p.251)
78. True (p.251)
79. False (p.251)
80. False (p.251)
81. True (p.251)
82. False (p.251)
83. False (p.252)
84. True (p.252)
85. False (p.253)
86. True (p.253)
87. True (p.253)
88. False (p.254)
89. True (p.254)
90. True (p.255)
91. False (p.255)
92. True (p.255)
93. False (p.255)
94. False (p.256)
95. False (p.257)
96. False (p.257)

Post-Test

Multiple Choice

1. A (p.228)
2. C (p.229)
3. D (p.229)
4. B (p.229)
5. C (p.229)
6. B (p.229)
7. D (p.229)
8. A (p.229)
9. D (p.229)
10. B (p.229)
11. D (p.230)
12. A (p.230)
13. C (p.230)
14. B (p.230)
15. C (p.230)
16. A (p.230)
17. B (p.230)
18. D (p.230)
19. B (p.230)
20. B (p.230)
21. D (p.230)
22. C (p.231)
23. B (p.231)
24. C (p.231)
25. D (p.232)
26. B (p.233)
27. A (pp.233,234)
28. C (p.234)
29. C (p.234)
30. B (pp.234,235)
31. D (pp.234,235)
32. B (p.235)
33. D (p.235)
34. C (p.235)
35. B (p.238)
36. C (p.238)
37. C (p.238)
38. B (p.238)
39. C (pp.236,237)
40. D (p.239)
41. C (p.240)
42. B (p.241)
43. A (p.241)
44. B (p.241)
45. D (p.241)

46. B (p.241)
47. B (p.241)
48. D (p.241)
49. C (p.243)
50. D (pp.244,245)
51. A (p.246)
52. B (p.246)
53. A (p.249)
54. A (p.248)
55. B (p.248)
56. C (p.248)
57. B (p.249)
58. D (p.249)
59. B (p.249)
60. D (p.249)
61. C (p.250)
62. D (p.251)
63. C (p.251)
64. B (p.251)
65. A (p.251)
66. D (p.251)
67. B (p.252)
68. D (p.253)
69. D (p.253)
70. B (p.254)
71. D (p.254)
72. B (p.254)
73. D (p.255)
74. C (p.255)
75. C (p.256)
76. B (p.257)

Chapter 8

The Developing Brain
Learning and Neuropsychiatric Disorders of Childhood

Chapter Outline

Post-Test

Answer Key

Overview

Chapter 8 presents a discussion of learning disorders, pervasive developmental disorders, and disruptive behavioral disorders of childhood that can significantly hinder development and adaptation. Historically, these disorders have not been clearly linked to anomalies of the brain prompting an emphasis on environmental factors as causative. However, advances in neuroscience are revealing that brain abnormalities may, in fact, play a prominent role in the etiology of learning and neuropsychiatric disorders. Three representative disorders are examined in detail: nonverbal learning disability syndrome, autism/Asperger's syndrome, and attention-deficit/hyperactivity disorder. These disorders exemplify the contributions of neuropsychology to the understanding of brain-behavior relationships that characterize each of these disorders.

Learning Objectives

- To develop an appreciation of the contributions of neuropsychology to the conceptualization, identification, and treatment of learning, pervasive developmental, and disruptive behavioral disorders of childhood.
- To be cognizant of the clinical features, pathogenesis, neuropsychological models, neuropsychological assessment procedures, developmental course and treatment interventions pertinent to nonverbal learning disability syndrome, autism/Asperger's syndrome, and attention-deficit/hyperactivity disorder.
- To understand the advances in the identification of etiological factors, preventative strategies, and treatment alternatives to reverse or significantly modify pervasive developmental disorders such as autism/Asperger's syndrome.

Learning Disabilities

Key Terms and Concepts

dyslexia
dysgraphia
flicker fusion rates
parvocellular visual system
phonological processing
ectopia
working memory
nonverbal learning disability syndrome
pragmatics of language

dyscalculia
social emotional learning disability
magnocellular visual system
saccadic eye movements
planum temporale
cytoarchitectonic dysplasia
lexicon stores
metacognition

Sentence Completion

1. The magnocellular visual system is activated during _____.

2. The _____ is the speed at which two distinct visual images become a single image when presented quickly.

3. A child experiencing cognitive deficits which produce socioemotional disturbances may have a _____.

4. The _____ is responsive to stationary objects and fine spatial details.

5. _____, or focal pathologic changes of the cortical structure of the left plenum temporale, is evident in individuals with dyslexia.

6. The _____ is characterized by visual-perceptual, tactile-perceptual, psychomotor and novel problem solving deficits.

7. _____ is a learning disability exhibited by impairment in reading.

8. The _____ is implicated in phonological processing.

9. The ability to understand your own cognitive processes is called _____.

10. The ability to store information for a short period so that it can be processed is termed _____.

11. The _____ is responsive to visual movement and rapid stimulus change.

12. An _____ is a small group of abnormally situated neurons.

13. The emotional and social content of a message is also called the _____.

14. _____ is a learning disability exhibited by impairment in arithmetic.

15. A conceptual location of our internal dictionaries is called _____.

16. The application of rules for translating letters and letter sequences into corresponding speech-sound equivalents is called _____.

17. _____ is a learning disability exhibited by impairment in written expression.

Pervasive Developmental Disorders

Key Terms and Concepts

autism	Asperger's syndrome	autistic aloneness
joint attention	echolalia	neologisms
hyperplexia	savant skills	emotional perception
theory of mind	stuck-in-set perseveration	fragile X
executive planning	response inhibition	canalesthesia
asociality	extended selective attention	response cost
overcorrection		

True/False

18. _____ Pervasive developmental disorders are associated with mild neuropsychological deficits.

19. _____ Verbal and nonverbal language may be impaired in an individual with a pervasive developmental disorder.

20. _____ Mental retardation is often observed in individuals with a pervasive developmental disorder.

21. _____ Asperger's disorder and Rett's disorder are examples of pervasive developmental disorders.

22. _____ An individual with an autistic disorder is not likely to exhibit stereotyped behavior.

23. _____ Asperger's syndrome or disorder is a form of autism.

24. _____ Autistic aloneness refers to the phenomenon that occurs when children exhibit difficulty relating to individuals with autism and tend to shy away from them.

25. _____ An individual with autism is not likely to exhibit difficulties sharing activities with others.

26. _____ Joint attention refers to the difficulty of individuals with autism to reciprocate attention between themselves and others.

27. _____ Echolalia refers to the repetition of the words of others.

28. _____ Individuals with autism may invent their own words.

29. _____ Imaginative play is overdeveloped in children with autism.

30. _____ The prevalence of autism is 1 in 100.

31. _____ Females have a higher rate of autism.

32. _____ At least half of children with autism also exhibit mental retardation.

33. _____ Some individuals with autism exhibit average intelligence.

34. _____ Hyperlexia is a reading learning disability.

35._____	Individuals with autism are more likely to experience seizures than the general population.
36._____	Asperger's syndrome is a very severe form of autism.
37._____	Individuals with Asperger's syndrome exhibit a significant impairment in verbal and nonverbal communication skills.
38._____	Individuals with Asperger's syndrome are less likely to exhibit echolalia than individuals with autism.
39._____	It is theorized that autism arises out of a genetic predisposition in conjunction with an early neurological insult.
40._____	Autism is localized to one dysfunctional area in the brain.
41._____	Serotonin is implicated in autism.
42._____	Hyperserotonemia refers to a deficit in serotonin.
43._____	The diagnosis of autism can be made with the exclusive use of standardized neuropsychological tests.
44._____	Emotional perception refers to the ability to accurately perceive emotions.
45._____	The theory of mind refers to the understanding that other people have mental states which influence their behavior.
46._____	Executive dysfunction is present in both autism and Asperger's syndrome.
47._____	Stuck-in-set perseveration occurs when an autistic individual gets a song "stuck" in his/her head and hums it over and over.
48._____	Executive planning requires complex, means-end problem solving.
49._____	Response inhibition occurs when an individual engages in an impulsive behavior.
50._____	Canalesthesia refers to the lack of sensation individuals with autism have in various parts of their bodies.
51._____	Individuals with autism experience impaired affective assignment.
52._____	Asociality refers to the lack of social interest and motivation to form emotional attachments to others.
53._____	Extended selective attention refers to the extraordinary ability of individuals with autism to focus, which subsequently leads to increased learning.
54._____	Autism is usually detected in infancy.
55._____	Autism is a chronic, life-long disorder.
56._____	Most children with autism are placed in a regular educational program.
57._____	Most children with autism have no difficulty making friends.
58._____	About 80% of autistic individuals are unable to maintain competitive employment.
59._____	About ½ of autistic individuals will require life-long residential placement.

60._____   Autism generally resolves in early adulthood.

61._____   Behavior modification is typically used in the treatment of autism.

62._____   Response-cost refers to a behavior management technique in which appropriate
             responses result in the rewarding of a targeted behavior.

Disruptive Behavioral Disorders

Key Terms and Concepts

attention-deficit/hyperactivity disorder (ADHD)
Tourette syndrome
shifting attention
encode attention
posterior attentional system
vigilance attentional system
interference control

phenylketonuria
focus-execute attention
sustain attention
stable attention
anterior attentional network
prepotent response

Matching

63.	Change attentional focus flexibly.	a.	ADHD
64.	Visual orienting system.	b.	phenylketonuria
65.	One of three interrelated processes linked to behavioral inhibition.	c.	Tourette syndrome
66.	Characterized by vocal and motor tics.	d.	focus-execute attention
67.	Consistency of attentional effort.	e.	shifting attention
68.	Requires selective attention and rapid perceptual-motor output.	f.	sustain attention
69.	Controls and coordinates other brain regions in executing voluntary attention.	g.	encode attention
70.	System which sustains alertness.	h.	stable attention
71.	Disorder characterized by inattention, impulsivity, and hyperactivity.	i.	posterior attentional system
72.	Protection of an ongoing mental operation from disruption.	j.	anterior attentional network
73.	Vigilant attention.	k.	vigilance attentional system
74.	Maintain information while performing another task.	l.	prepotent response
75.	A genetic metabolic disorder.	m.	interference control

1. Which disorder comprises 50% of the population of child psychiatric clinics?

    i.   Nonverbal learning disability.
    j.   Schizophrenia.
    k.   Autism.
    l.   Attention deficit/hyperactivity disorder.

2. A learning disability which involves impairment in reading is called:

    a.   dyscalculia.
    b.   dyslexia.
    c.   autism.
    d.   dysgraphia.

3. A learning disability which involves impairment in written expression is called:

    a.   dyscalculia.
    b.   dyslexia.
    c.   autism.
    d.   dysgraphia.

4. A learning disability which involves impairment in arithmetic is called:

    a.   dyscalculia.
    b.   dyslexia.
    c.   autism.
    d.   dysgraphia.

5. What percentage of school age children are affected by dyslexia?

    a.   1-2%
    b.   2-4%
    c.   4-9%
    d.   10-15%

6. The ratio of dyslexia cases in boys versus girls is:

    a.   1:2
    b.   2:1
    c.   2:3
    d.   3:2

7. How much more likely is a child of a dyslexic parent to exhibit dyslexia, than a child of a non-dyslexic parent?

    a.   2 times.
    b.   3 times.
    c.   5 times.
    d.   8 times.

8. What is the most common learning disability?

    a.   Dyscalculia.
    b.   Dyslexia.
    c.   Autism.
    d.   Dysgraphia.

9. Which chromosomes are implicated in dyslexia?

    a.   2 and 13.
    b.   5 and 16.
    c.   6 and 15.
    d.   125 and 1683.

10. What percentage of the variance in dyslexia is genetic?

    a.   25%
    b.   50%
    c.   75%
    d.   100%

11. Dyslexia may be attributable to:

    a.   visual perceptual anomalies.
    b.   auditory language dysfunction.
    c.   mental retardation.
    d.   Both a and b.

12. The flicker fusion rates of individuals with dyslexia are _____ when presented with stimuli of low spatial density and contrast.

    a.   faster
    b.   slower
    c.   more inconsistent
    d.   absent

13. The magnocellular visual system is sensitive to:

    a.   color.
    b.   fine spatial details.
    c.   spatial location.
    d.   high contrast.

14. The parvocellular visual system is sensitive to:

    a.   rapid stimulus change.
    b.   stationary objects.
    c.   low contrast.
    d.   spatial location.

15. Which of the following represents the disruption of the magnocellular and parvocellular visual systems in dyslexia?

    a.   The magnocellular visual system is completely impaired and fails to operate.
    b.   The parvocellular visual system is completely impaired and fails to operate.
    c.   The parvocellular visual system fails to inhibit the magnocellular visual system.
    d.   The magnocellular visual system fails to inhibit the parvocellular visual system.

16. The application of rules for translating letters and letter sequences into corresponding speech-sound equivalents is called:

    a.   phonological processing.
    b.   cytoarchitectonic dysplasia.
    c.   lexicon storage.
    d.   the phonological model of dyslexia.

17. Difficulty translating letter strings into word sounds refers to the concept of:

    a.   phonological processing.
    b.   lexicon storage.
    c.   word decoding.
    d.   cytoarchitectonic dysplasia.

18. In individuals with dyslexia, word recognition difficulties are most evident when presented with:

    a.   any familiar words.
    b.   familiar and abnormally lengthy words.
    c.   unfamiliar words.
    d.   All of the above.

19. In adulthood, dyslexia:

   a. completely disappears.
   b. continues but is largely compensated for.
   c. continues with significant deficits which preclude many types of employment
       due to severe reading/spelling difficulties.
   d. None of the above.

20. Which of the following neuroanatomical structures is implicated in phonological processing?

   a. Occipital cortex.
   b. Raphe nucleus.
   c. Corpus callosum.
   d. Planum temporale.

21. In non-reading disordered individuals, the planum temporale is:

   a. smaller in the left hemisphere.
   b. larger in the left hemisphere.
   c. symmetrical.
   d. absent in the right hemisphere.

22. The presence of ectopias and cytoarchitectonic dysplasia in individuals with dyslexia, suggest
    that abnormal neural development occurs between the:

   a. 2nd and 3rd month of fetal development.
   b. 3rd and 5th month of fetal development.
   c. 5th and 7th month of fetal development.
   d. 7th and 9th month of fetal development.

23. Which of the following neuroanatomical structures is implicated in dyslexia?

   a. Planum temporale.
   b. Frontal cortex.
   c. Corpus callosum.
   d. All of the above.

24. A reading and spelling (i.e., R-S) learning disability is characterized by:

   a. preserved psycholinguistic skills.
   b. poor visual-perceptual skills.
   c. preserved nonverbal problem solving skills.
   d. impaired psychomotor abilities.

25. A non-verbal learning disability (NVLD) is characterized by:

    a.   impaired psycholinguistic skills.
    b.   preserved tactile-perceptual skills.
    c.   preserved psychomotor abilities.
    d.   impaired tactile-perceptual abilities.

26. Which of the following is hypothesized to be true about the right cerebral hemisphere?

    a.   The right hemisphere is more diffusely organized than the left.
    b.   The right hemisphere shows more specialization for interregional integration of information than the left.
    c.   The right hemisphere possesses more association regions than the left.
    d.   All of the above.

27. Which of the following is believed to emanate from the right hemisphere?

    a.   Auditory perception.
    b.   Socioemotional skills.
    c.   Psycholinguistic skills.
    d.   All of the above.

28. The nonverbal learning disability syndrome can by caused by:

    a.   damage to white fibers which access the right cerebral hemisphere.
    b.   damage to white fibers which connect cortical regions within the right hemisphere.
    c.   damage to white fibers which link cortical to subcortical regions within the right hemisphere.
    d.   All of the above.

29. The ability to comprehend one's own cognitive processes is called:

    a.   insight.
    b.   judgment.
    c.   executive processing.
    d.   metacognition.

30. Which of the following is a frequent deficit observed in the nonverbal learning disability syndrome?

    a.   Reading.
    b.   Mathematics.
    c.   Spelling.
    d.   Expressive language.

31. Which of the following is a common error made by individuals with nonverbal learning disability syndrome?

    a.   Misreading mathematical symbols.
    b.   Failure to remember mathematical rules.
    c.   Poorly formed numbers.
    d.   All of the above.

32. The pragmatics of language refers to:

    a.   the practicality of word choice when speaking.
    b.   the ability to retrieve accurately from lexicon stores.
    c.   the emotional and social content of a message.
    d.   quality of speech.

33. An individual with nonverbal learning disability syndrome is likely to:

    a.   exhibit poor social judgment.
    b.   be especially skilled in social interactions.
    c.   have a speech impediment.
    d.   exhibit dyslexia.

34. Adolescents with nonverbal learning disability syndrome are likely to:

    a.   form peer relationships as well as anyone else.
    b.   act out and engage in impulsive behavior.
    c.   exhibit poor verbal skills.
    d.   become isolated and withdrawn.

35. An individual with nonverbal learning disability syndrome may be at a higher risk for:

    a.   developing post-traumatic stress disorder.
    b.   committing suicide.
    c.   developing mental retardation.
    d.   None of the above.

36. An individual with a pervasive development disorder:

    a.   will likely outgrow the disorder by adulthood.
    b.   has a high probability of not achieving normal adaptive functioning.
    c.   is not likely to exhibit mental retardation.
    d.   Both a and c.

37. Which of the following is an example of a pervasive developmental disorder?

    a.   Attention deficit/hyperactivity disorder.
    b.   Fetal alcohol syndrome.
    c.   Turner syndrome.
    d.   Autistic disorder.

38. Autism is characterized by:

    a. preserved social relatedness.
    b. the presence of repetitive behaviors.
    c. intense emotional attachments to other people.
    d. preserved language functioning.

39. Which of the following is generally considered a subtype of autism?

    a. Asperger's Disorder.
    b. Rett's Disorder.
    c. Childhood Disintegrative Disorder.
    d. Attention-Deficit/Hyperactivity Disorder.

40. In autism, a state of separation and disconnection from other people is known as:

    a. joint attention.
    b. autistic aloneness.
    c. separation anxiety.
    d. None of the above.

41. The ability to reciprocate attention to another individual is called:

    a. joint attention.
    b. autistic aloneness.
    c. neologism.
    d. echolalia.

42. An invented word is a:

    a. word salad.
    b. poverty of speech.
    c. echolalia.
    d. neologism.

43. Disruption of an autistic individual's routine is likely to result in:

    a. no change in the child.
    b. increased flexibility and adaptation to the environment.
    c. the exhibition of significant anxiety.
    d. neologisms.

44. The ratio of males:females with autism is:

    a. 1:1
    b. 1-2:2
    c. 2-4:2
    d. 2-6:1

45. What percentage of children with autism exhibit mental retardation?

    a.   10-20%
    b.   30-50%
    c.   50-80%
    d.   95%

46. The acquisition of reading skills at an early age, though without reading comprehension is known as:

    a.   dyslexia.
    b.   dysgraphia.
    c.   hyperlexia.
    d.   aphasia.

47. Skills which are overdeveloped in individuals with limited cognitive capacity are known as:

    a.   executive functions.
    b.   savant skills.
    c.   Rainman syndrome.
    d.   hyperintelligent skills.

48. Individuals with Asperger's syndrome are likely to display:

    a.   significant impairment in verbal and nonverbal communication abilities.
    b.   cognitive deficits.
    c.   a lack of imaginative play.
    d.   inattention and impulsivity.

49. The percentage of autism in siblings of individuals with autism is:

    a.   3-6%
    b.   6-10%
    c.   10-15%
    d.   50%

50. In identical twins, the co-occurrence rate of autism is:

    a.   5-10%
    b.   10-36%
    c.   36-96%
    d.   100%

51. Which neurotransmitter is implicated in autism?

    a.   Dopamine.
    b.   Serotonin.
    c.   Epinephrine.
    d.   Norepinephrine.

52. Which of the following should be included in the neuropsychological evaluation of an individual with suspected autism?

    a.   Observations of the child with family members.
    b.   Review of medical records.
    c.   Speech and language evaluation.
    d.   All of the above.

53. The problem-solving profile of individuals with Asperger's syndrome is consistent with which of the following disorders?

    a.   Mental retardation.
    b.   Dyslexia.
    c.   Dysgraphia.
    d.   Nonverbal learning disability syndrome.

54. The ability to identify and comprehend feeling states is known as:

    a.   emotional perception.
    b.   theory of mind.
    c.   stuck-in-set perseveration.
    d.   autistic aloneness.

55. The understanding that other people have mental states which influence their behavior is called:

    a.   emotional perception.
    b.   theory of mind.
    c.   stuck-in-set perseveration.
    d.   autistic aloneness.

56. Which of the following is an example of an executive function?

    a.   Working memory.
    b.   Executive planning.
    c.   Response inhibition.
    d.   All of the above.

57. The fragmentation in the processing of incoming information from the various sensory modalities is known as:

    a.   canalesthesia.
    b.   impaired affective assignment.
    c.   asociality.
    d.   extended selective attention.

58. Which of the following is implicated in canalesthesia?

    a.   Serotonin.
    b.   Parietal association area.
    c.   Corpus callosum.
    d.   Hippocampus.

59. Which of the following is implicated in asociality?

    a.   Serotonin.
    b.   Parietal association area.
    c.   Corpus callosum.
    d.   Hippocampus.

60. Which of the following is implicated in extended selective attention?

    a.   Serotonin.
    b.   Parietal association area.
    c.   Corpus callosum.
    d.   Hippocampus.

61. How many higher functioning individuals with autism achieve independent living?

    a.   One quarter.
    b.   One third.
    c.   One half.
    d.   Two-thirds.

62. Behavior modification can be used to:

    a.   strengthen appropriate actions.
    b.   reduce inappropriate behaviors.
    c.   generate behaviors.
    d.   All of the above.

63. Which of the following is a typical behavior modification technique used in the treatment of autism?

    a.   Physical punishment.
    b.   Overcorrection.
    c.   Psychotherapy.
    d.   All of the above.

64. Which of the following is a core symptom pattern of attention-deficit/hyperactivity disorder (ADHD)?

    a.   Impulsivity.
    b.   Memory problems.
    c.   Speech and language deficits.
    d.   All of the above.

65. Prevalence of ADHD in childhood populations is:

    a.   1-2%
    b.   2-3%
    c.   3-7%
    d.   7-10%

66. What is the ratio of ADHD in boys and girls?

    a.   1:1.
    b.   1:2.
    c.   2:1.
    d.   At least 3:1.

67. Which of the following is most likely to occur in conjunction with ADHD?

    a.   Hydrocephalus.
    b.   Autism.
    c.   Agyria.
    d.   Oppositional defiant disorder.

68. What percentage of children with ADHD also exhibit learning disabilities?

    a.   1-2%
    b.   5-10%
    c.   10-15%
    d.   15-20%

69. Which of the following has been implicated in ADHD?

    a.   Frontal lobes.
    b.   Basal ganglia.
    c.   Corpus callosum.
    d.   All of the above.

70. The diagnosis of ADHD is best made by:

    a.   brain scanning, usually MRI.
    b.   evaluation with ADHD-specific neuropsychological tests.
    c.   neurological evaluation.
    d.   ruling out everything else.

71. According to Mirsky, what are the four elements of attention?

    a.   Focus, sustain, vigilant and encode.
    b.   Focus-execute, sustain, shift and encode.
    c.   Focus, divide, shift and encode.
    d.   Focus-execute, divide, sustain and encode.

72. Which type of attention involves changing attentional focus in a flexible manner?

    a.   Focus-execute.
    b.   Shifting.
    c.   Sustained.
    d.   Encoding.

73. Which type of attention provides the capacity to maintain information while performing other tasks?

    a.   Focus-execute.
    b.   Shifting.
    c.   Sustained.
    d.   Encoding.

74. Which type of attention pertains to vigilance?

    a.   Focus-execute.
    b.   Stable.
    c.   Sustained.
    d.   Encoding.

75. Which type of attention involves selective attending and rapid perceptual-motor output?

    a.   Focus-execute.
    b.   Shifting.
    c.   Sustained.
    d.   Encoding.

76. Which type of attention correlates to the consistency of attentional effort?

    a.   Shifting.
    b.   Stable.
    c.   Sustained.
    d.   Encoding.

77. In Posner's model of attentional functioning, the visual orienting system is called the:

    a.   Anterior attentional network.
    b.   Posterior attentional system.
    c.   Vigilance attentional system.
    d.   None of the above.

78. Which system prepares and sustains alertness for high priority information?

    a.   anterior attentional network.
    b.   posterior attentional system.
    c.   viglinance attentional system.
    d.   disengagement.

79. What are the three tiers of Barkley's executive model of ADHD?

    a.   Attentional control, behavioral inhibition, behavioral self-restraint.
    b.   Behavioral inhibition, behavioral self-restraint, executive functions.
    c.   Behavioral inhibition, executive functions, attentional control.
    d.   Behavioral inhibition, executive functions, behavioral output.

80. What percentage of children with ADHD, continue to manifest symptoms in adulthood?

    a.   10-15%
    b.   15-30%
    c.   30-50%
    d.   50-65%

81. Ritalin, which is used to treat ADHD, is a(n):

    a.   depressant medication.
    b.   anti-depressant medication.
    c.   stimulant medication.
    d.   anti-anxiety medication.

82. Which of the following is a drawback to using ADHD medications?

    a.   Side-effects.
    b.   Difficulties with medication compliance in children.
    c.   Medications do not improve concurrent learning disabilities.
    d.   All of the above.

Essay Questions

1. What are the main neuroanatomical correlates of dyslexia?

2. Compare and contrast autism and Asperger's syndrome.

3. Discuss the neurological substrates of attention-deficit/hyperactivity disorder (ADHD).

Answer Key

Chapter Exercises

1. saccadic eye movements (p.264)
2. flicker fusion rate (p.263)
3. social emotional learning disability (p.262)
4. parvocellular visual system (p.264)
5. Cytoarchitectonic dysplasia (p.265)
6. nonverbal learning disability syndrome (p.267)
7. Dyslexia (p.262)
8. planum temporale (p.265)
9. metacognition (p.269)
10. working memory (p.266)
11. magnocellular visual system (p.264)
12. ectopia (p.265)
13. pragmatics of language (p.270)
14. Dyscalculia (p.262)
15. lexicon store (p.266)
16. phonological processing (p.264)
17. Dysgraphia (p.262)
18. False (p.272)
19. True (p.272)
20. True (p.272)
21. True (p.273)
22. False (p.273)
23. True (p.273)
24. False (p.273)
25. False (p.273)
26. True (p.273)
27. True (p.27)
28. True (p.273)
29. False (p.274)
30. False (p.274)
31. False (p.274)
32. True (p.274)
33. True (p.274)
34. True (p.274)
35. True (pp.274,275)
36. False (p.275)
37. False (p.275)
38. True (p.275)
39. True (pp.275,278)
40. False (p.278)
41. True (p.278)
42. False (p.278)
43. False (p.279)
44. True (p.279)
45. True (p.279)
46. True (p.279)
47. False (p.280)
48. True (p.280)
49. False (p.280)
50. False (p.280)
51. True (p.280)
52. True (p.280)
53. False (p.280)
54. False (p.281)
55. True (p.281)
56. False (p.281)
57. False (p.281)
58. True (p.282)
59. True (p.282)
60. False (p.282)
61. True (p.282)
62. False (p.282)
63. e (p.287)
64. i (p.289)
65. l (p.290)
66. c (p.287)
67. h (p.288)
68. d (p.287)
69. j (p.289)
70. k (p.289)
71. a (p.283)
72. m (p.290)
73. f (p.287)
74. g (p.288)
75. b (p.287)

Post-Test

Multiple Choice

1. D (p.261)
2. B (p.262)
3. D (p.262)
4. A (p.262)
5. C (p.263)
6. D (p.263)
7. D (p.263)
8. B (p.263)
9. C (p.263)
10. B (p.263)
11. D (p.263)
12. B (p.263)
13. C (p.264)
14. B (p.264)
15. D (p.264)
16. A (p.264)
17. C (p.265)
18. C (p.265)
19. B (p.265)
20. D (p.265)
21. B (p.265)
22. C (pp.265,266)
23. D (p.266)
24. C (p.267)
25. D (p.267)
26. D (p.267)
27. B (p.268)
28. D (p.268)
29. D (p.269)
30. B (p.270)
31. D (p.270)
32. C (p.270)
33. A (pp.270,271)
34. D (p.271)
35. B (p.272)
36. B (p.272)
37. D (p.273)
38. B (p.273)
39. A (p.273)
40. B (p.273)
41. A (p.273)
42. D (p.273)
43. C (p.274)
44. D (p.274)
45. C (p.274)
46. C (p.274)
47. B (p.274)
48. D (p.275)
49. A (p.278)
50. C (p.278)
51. B (p.278)
52. D (p.279)
53. D (p.279)
54. A (p.279)
55. B (p.279)
56. D (p.280)
57. A (p.280)
58. D (p.280)
59. A (p.281)
60. B (p.281)
61. B (p.282)
62. D (p.282)
63. B (p.282)
64. A (p.283)
65. C (p.283)
66. D (p.283)
67. D (p.283)
68. D (p.284)
69. D (p.284)
70. D (p.285)
71. B (p.287)
72. B (p.287)
73. D (p.287)
74. C (p.287)
75. A (p.287)
76. B (p.288)
77. B (p.289)
78. C (p.289)
79. D (p.290)
80. D (p.291)
81. C (p.292)
82. D (p.293)

Chapter 9

Cerebrovascular Disorders

Neuropsychological Deficits Associated with Stroke

Neuropsychological Risk Factors
        Necrosis
        Disinhibition
        Disconnection Syndrome
Attention Deficits
Motor and Sensory Impairment
Memory Problems
Deficits in Abstract Reasoning
Cognitive Deficits Associated with Right Brain Stroke
        Visual-Spatial Deficits
Cognitive Deficits Associated with Left Brain Stroke
Anterior vs. Posterior Strokes
Emotional and Behavioral Changes Following a Stroke
        Depression
        Apathy
        Euphoria
        Impulsive Behavior
        Lack of Initiation
        Poor Judgment

Post-Test

Answer Key

Overview

The normal functioning central nervous system can be affected by a number of neurological disorders and diseases. In this chapter we focus on the most common neurological problems and neuropsychological sequelae that are associated with cerebrovascular accidents. The brain is dependent on a constant supply of oxygen and disruption of its blood supply can be related to, among other causes, the blockage of a cerebral artery or a bleed within the blood system of the brain. For each type of cerebrovascular dysfunction, we outline the neuropathology, the neuropsychological sequelae, appropriate treatments, and case examples of patients. While these disorders may produce a host and at times multiple cognitive disabilities, often such dysfunction is relatively localized in terms of the anatomical area involved and the corresponding neuropsychological sequelae. An understanding of the neuropsychological correlates associated with an impairment of the blood supply to the brain is important for the neuropsychology student, because these disorders can produce cognitive disabilities which are often localized in terms of the anatomical area involved. In addition, the different types of cerebrovascular accidents are often encountered in neuropsychological practice and many neuropsychologists work in the assessment and rehabilitation of such disorders. As a result, cerebrovascular disorders provide an excellent neuropsychological perspective of brain pathology and its relevance to known brain anatomy, biological processes of the brain, and their behavioral product.

Learning Objectives

- To learn about the cardiovascular system of the brain.
- To be able to differentiate the types of cerebrovascular disorders.
- To understand the neuropsychological manifestations associated with cerebrovascular disorders.

The Pathological Process of Brain Damage

Key Terms and Concepts

lesions	necrosis	anoxia
hypoxia	sleep apnea	hydrocephalus
communicating hydrocephalus	obstructive hydrocephalus	

Sentence Completion

1. _____ is a condition marked by reduced oxygen supply to the brain during sleep.

2. Increased cerebrospinal fluid in the brain due to circulation blockage is referred to as _____.

3. _____ is a condition marked by a complete absence of oxygen to the brain.

4. A brain _____ results in holes or cavities within the brain.

5.	An increase in intracranial pressure and increased presence of cerebrospinal fluid is known as _____.

6.	Increased cerebrospinal fluid in the brain due to impaired reabsorption is known as _____.

7.	_____ is a condition marked by diminished oxygen supply to the brain.

8.	_____ occurs when neurons die.

Overview of Cerebrovascular Disorders

Key Terms and Concepts

stroke   cerebrovascular accident   intracranial pressure

True/False

9._____	In developed countries, cerebrovascular disorders are the leading cause of death.

10._____	The average age of a stroke victim is 80 years.

11._____	Stroke typically results in neuron death.

12._____	Right and left hemisphere strokes result in similar functional deficits.

13._____	The three main risks to an individual suffering a stroke are decreased oxygen to the brain, increased intracranial pressure, and exposure to toxins.

Types of Cerebrovascular Disorders

ischemia	infarction	hemorrhage
Transient Ischemic Attack	migraine	aura
thrombosis	atherosclerosis	platelets
endothelium	embolism	hematoma
intracerebral	subarachnoid hemorrhage	aneurysm
arteriovenous malformation		

Matching

14. Loss of blood to the brain due to the blockage of an artery.

    a. ischemia

15. Fat deposits which reduce artery size.

    b. infarction

16. Often experienced prior to a migraine.

    c. hemorrhage

17. Within the brain.

    d. Transient Ischemic Attack

18. A temporary lack of blood supply to the brain.

    e. migraine

19. A blood clot which has moved.

    f. aura

20. Abnormal collection of blood vessels in the brain.

    g. thrombosis

21. A vascular disorder characterized by a severe headache.

    h. atherosclerosis

22. Accumulation of blood in the subarachnoid space.

    i. platelets

23. Disk-shaped cells found in blood.

    j. endothelium

24. A blood clot formed within a blood vessel.

    k. embolism

25. Bleeding in the brain which results in displacement of brain tissue.

    l. hematoma

26. The accumulation of blood within tissue.

    m. intracerebral

27. Weak areas in the walls of arteries.

    n. subarachnoid hemorrhage

28. The layer of cells lining blood vessels.

    o. aneurysm

29. An acute focal neurologic deficit which is evidenced by a transient loss of function.

    p. arteriovenous malformation

Diagnosing Cerebrovascular Disease

Key Terms and Concepts

computed tomography   angiography   stenosis
noninvasive tests

True/False

30._____   The CT is a relatively safe procedure.

31._____   Unfortunately, hemorrhage is not easily detected by CT.

32._____   Transient ischemic attacks are easily detected by CT.

33._____   The most accurate diagnostic procedure for vascular disorders is angiography.

34._____   Angiography is a risk-free procedure.

35._____   Angiography is most often used for diagnosis via the venous system.

36._____   Stenosis refers to the narrowing of an artery.

37._____   Aneurysms and arteriovenous malformations are diagnosable using angiography.

38._____   Noninvasive tests are more accurate in diagnosing cerebrovascular disorders than invasive tests.

Treatment and Prognosis of Vascular Disorders

Key Terms and Concepts

collateral blood vessel   anastomosis   aneurysm clip
heparin   embolization   risk factors for stroke

True/False

39._____   Strokes of large arteries may result in coma and death.

40._____   Collateral blood vessels provide a redundancy in blood supply which is advantageous following a stroke.

41._____   The communication between collateral blood vessels is referred to as anastomosis.

42._____   Prior strokes increase an individual's likelihood of having a permanent disability.

43._____   Following a stroke, surgery is sometimes necessary.

194

44._____   Lowering a patient's blood pressure may be indicated as treatment for stroke.

45._____   Anti-coagulant agents are indicated for patients with a hemorrhage.

46._____   An arteriovenous malformation may be treated by intentionally embolizing it.

47._____   Women have a higher risk of stroke than men.

48._____   Hypertension is a risk factor for stroke.

49._____   Diabetes and high cholesterol have not been identified as risk factors for stroke.

50._____   Smokers are at increased risk of stroke.

51._____   Consuming large quantities of alcohol has shown to be associated with reduced risk of stroke.

52._____   Obesity is a risk factor for stroke.

Neuropsychological Deficits Associated with Stroke

<u>Key Terms and Concepts</u>

disinhibition	disconnection	attention deficits
motor and sensory impairment	memory problems	abstract reasoning deficits
right brain stroke	visual-spatial deficits	left brain stroke
anterior stroke	posterior stroke	depression
apathy	euphoria	impulsive behavior
lack of initiation	poor judgment	

<u>Sentence Completion</u>

53.   _____ occurs when pathways of neurons are disrupted.

54.   One who appears "too happy" and energetic is said to be in a state of _____.

55.   _____ is reflected by an individual's inability to start even simple tasks.

56.   _____ may be reflected by a lack of insight and/or the use of poor judgment.

57.   A deficiency in the ability to monitor one's own behavior is referred to as _____.

58.   Unintentionally knocking things over might reflect _____ following a right hemisphere stroke.

59.   Behaviors such as impulsiveness and hypersexuality reflect _____.

60.   A seeming indifference following a stroke is referred to as _____.

61.   _____ may come without any warning.

62.   Inability to sustain attention or select information are examples of the _____ seen in individuals who have suffered a stroke.

63.   An _____ is more likely to result in disinhibition while a _____ is more likely to be associated with a visual field deficit.

64.   Even though stroke is associated with _____, immediate and long-term memory are usually preserved.

65.   Language comprehension may be impaired after a _____, while visual-spatial abilities are more likely to follow a _____.

66.   _____ may present as motor slowing or be as severe as paralysis.

67.   Poor sleep, decreased appetite, crying spells, and feelings of failure are symptoms of _____.

Post-Test
Multiple Choice

1.   What is the generic term for any pathological effect on brain tissue?

      a.   Tumor.
      b.   Hypoxia.
      c.   Necrosis.
      d.   Lesion.

2.   The brain requires _____ of the body's oxygen.

      a.   5%
      b.   10%
      c.   20%
      d.   50%

3.   What is another term for neuronal cell death?

      a.   Tumor.
      b.   Hypoxia.
      c.   Necrosis.
      d.   Lesion.

4.   What is the term for a complete loss of oxygen to the brain?

      a.   Lesion.
      b.   Necrosis.
      c.   Hypoxia.
      d.   Anoxia.

5.   What is the term for a reduced level of oxygen to the brain?

      a.   Lesion.
      b.   Necrosis.
      c.   Hypoxia.
      d.   Anoxia.

6.   What is the general rule of thumb for necrosis in cases of anoxia?

      a.   An anoxic episode lasting 1-2 minutes will result in necrosis.
      b.   An anoxic episode lasting 4-6 minutes will result in necrosis.
      c.   An anoxic episode lasting 8-10 minutes will result in necrosis.
      d.   An anoxic episode lasting 20 minutes will result in necrosis.

7.   Which of the following is most likely to result in hypoxia (as opposed to anoxia)?

    a.   Cardiac arrest in a deep sea diver.
    b.   Mountain climbing in the Himalayas.
    c.   Gun-shot wound to the head.
    d.   Near-drowning accident.

8.   Hypoxic episodes associated with sleep apnea are most likely to occur:

    a.   in REM sleep.
    b.   in Stage Four sleep.
    c.   in conjunction with Delta waves.
    d.   in Stage Three sleep.

9.   Interference with the reabsorption of cerebrospinal fluid may result in:

    a.   sleep apnea.
    b.   anoxia.
    c.   communicating hydrocephalus.
    d.   obstructive hydrocephalus.

10.   What is the most common cause of neurologic disability in the Western world?

    a.   Hydrocephalus.
    b.   Sleep apnea.
    c.   Cardiovascular disease.
    d.   Cerebrovascular disease.

11.   What is the average age of a stroke victim?

    a.   49 years.
    b.   59 years.
    c.   69 years.
    d.   79 years.

12.   A stroke:

    a.   is the disruption of any vital fluid needed in the brain.
    b.   is the eruption of a blood vessel anywhere in the body.
    c.   results from a blockage of the blood supply or a bleed in the brain.
    d.   usually results in death.

13.   A stroke:

    a.   may result in hypoxia or anoxia.
    b.   may result in a decrease in intracranial pressure.
    c.   does not compromise the blood-brain barrier defenses.
    d.   All of the above.

14. What is the term for a "temporary" stroke?

    a.   Ischemia.
    b.   Hemorrhage.
    c.   Infarction.
    d.   Hypoxia.

15. What is the term for a loss of blood caused by the blockage of an artery?

    a.   Ischemia.
    b.   Hemorrhage.
    c.   Infarction.
    d.   Hypoxia.

16. What is the term for the rupture of a blood vessel which results in the accumulation of blood within brain tissue?

    a.   Ischemia.
    b.   Hemorrhage.
    c.   Infarction.
    d.   Hypoxia.

17. Which of the following is true regarding Transient Ischemic Attacks (TIAs)?

    a.   Recovery takes place over 1-2 weeks.
    b.   The patient typically returns to a level of normal functioning.
    c.   Anoxia is usually a consequence of a TIA.
    d.   The complete loss of consciousness associated with a TIA typically last only about 4-6 minutes.

18. A TIA impacting posterior circulation is likely to result in:

    a.   aphasia.
    b.   limb weakness.
    c.   dysarthria.
    d.   double vision.

19. Which of the following has been reported as an aura preceding a migraine headache?

    a.   flashes of light.
    b.   blurred vision.
    c.   skin numbness.
    d.   All of the above.

20.   Which of the following cranial nerves is implicated in migraine headaches?

    a.   Occulomotor.
    b.   Olfactory.
    c.   Vagus.
    d.   Trigeminal.

21.   Which of the following neurotransmitters is implicated in migraine?

    a.   Norepinephrine.
    b.   Serotonin.
    c.   Dopamine.
    d.   Acetylcholine.

22.   The formation of a blood clot in a blood vessel is known as:

    a.   ischemia.
    b.   thrombosis.
    c.   embolism.
    d.   hematoma.

23.   The build up of fat deposits in arteries is known as:

    a.   thrombosis.
    b.   hemorrhage.
    c.   atherosclerosis.
    d.   hematoma.

24.   Which of the following is an anti-thrombotic agent?

    a.   Aspirin.
    b.   Tylenol.
    c.   No-doze.
    d.   Motrin.

25.   Which of the following refers to a blood clot which has traveled from one part of the body to another?

    a.   thrombosis.
    b.   hemorrhage.
    c.   hematoma.
    d.   embolism.

26.   _____ is a weak spot in a blood vessel.

    a.   thrombosis.
    b.   embolism.
    c.   aneurysm.
    d.   hematoma.

27. Which of the following has the worst prognosis?

   a. TIA.
   b. Hemorrhage.
   c. Migraine headache.
   d. Thrombosis.

28. A collection of abnormal blood vessels in the brain is known as:

   a. Subarachnoid hemorrhage.
   b. Intracerebral hemorrhage.
   c. Arteriovenous malformation.
   d. Aneurysm.

29. Which of the following information does a CT provide following a stroke?

   a. Size of hemorrhage.
   b. Edema.
   c. Displacement of brain structures.
   d. All of the above.

30. Which of the following is the most accurate diagnostic procedure for vascular disorders?

   a. CT scan.
   b. Angiography.
   c. Neurological examination.
   d. Neuropsychological examination.

31. Why is the use of angiography limited?

   a. It is cost-prohibitive.
   b. There are risks associated with the procedure.
   c. Angiography is not very accurate in the diagnosis of vascular disorders.
   d. All of the above.

32. Which of the following would be considered a good prognostic indicator?

   a. A stroke in a large blood vessel.
   b. The presence of a collateral blood vessel.
   c. A history of one other stroke.
   d. A lesion in the brain stem.

33. Which of the following may be indicated following hemorrhage?

   a. Surgical intervention.
   b. Anticoagulant.
   c. Artificial embolization.
   d. All of the above.

34. Which of the following is a predisposing factor for stroke?

   a. Gender.
   b. Age.
   c. Ethnicity.
   d. All of the above.

35. Which of the following is a risk factor for stroke?

   a. Heart disease.
   b. Hypertension.
   c. Obesity.
   d. All of the above.

36. An increase in behavior, accompanied by behavioral and personality changes following a stroke is known as:

   a. Disconnection syndrome.
   b. Disinhibition.
   c. Dysarthria.
   d. Dementia.

37. The severing of pathways resulting in cognitive deficits not consistent with the location of the stroke is called:

   a. Disconnection syndrome.
   b. Disinhibition.
   c. Dysarthria.
   d. Dementia.

38. Motor deficits may be evidenced by:

   a. Decline in motor speed.
   b. Reduction in motor strength.
   c. Reduction in fine motor coordination.
   d. All of the above.

39. Which of the following is most likely to be impacted by stroke?

   a. Long-term memory.
   b. Immediate memory.
   c. Short-term memory.
   d. All of the above.

40.   Which of the following is most likely to be observed following stroke?

        a.   Impaired judgment.
        b.   Lack of insight.
        c.   Abstract reasoning deficits.
        d.   All of the above.

For questions 41 – 51 please answer either   a. Right hemisphere stroke.
                                               b. Left hemisphere stroke.

41.   Impaired language comprehension.

42.   Impaired visual-spatial abilities.

43.   Deficits are not as striking and obvious.

44.   Patient may be aphasic.

45.   Patient may be euphoric.

46.   Patient often depressed.

47.   Shorter hospitalization.

48.   Diagnosed more quickly.

49.   May have problems estimating the distance between objects.

50.   Motor problems on the right side of the body.

51.   Patient may experience an inability to communicate through written language.

52.   Which of the following statements is true regarding depression following a stroke?

        a.   Depression is uncommon following a stroke.
        b.   Onset of depression is usually 6-12 months following the stroke.
        c.   Depression is most likely to occur following a TIA.
        d.   All of the above.

53.   Which of the following may be present following a stroke?

        a.   Emotional lability.
        b.   Euphoria.
        c.   Apathy.
        d.   All of the above.

54.   The inability to start a behavior is referred to as:

        a.   akinesia.
        b.   Perseveration.
        c.   motor impersistence.
        d.   stenosis.

Essay Questions

1.   Compare and contract ischemic attacks, infarctions, and hemorrhage.

2.   What are the various ways to diagnose cerebrovascular disease and what are the advantages, and disadvantages of each?

3.   Discuss the various cognitive differences between individuals with right and left hemisphere strokes.

Answer Key

Chapter Exercises

1. Sleep apnea (p.300)
2. obstructive hydrocephalus (p.301)
3. Anoxia (pp.299,300)
4. lesion (p.299)
5. hydrocephalus (p.300,301)
6. communicating hydrocephalus (p.301)
7. Hypoxia (p.300)
8. Necrosis (p.299)
9. False (p.301)
10. False (p.301)
11. True (p.301)
12. False (p.302)
13. True (p.302)
14. b (p.302)
15. h (p.304)
16. f (p.306)
17. m (p.305)
18. a (p.302)
19. k (p.304)
20. p (p.306)
21. e (p.306)
22. n (p.305)
23. i (p.304)
24. g (p.303)
25. c (p.302)
26. l (p.305)
27. o (p.305)
28. j (p.304)
29. d (p.302)
30. True (p.308)
31. False (p.308)
32. False (p.308)
33. True (p.308)
34. False (p.308)
35. False (p.308)
36. True (p.308)
37. True (p.308)
38. False (p.308)
39. True (p.309)
40. True (p.309)
41. True (p.309)
42. True (p.309)
43. True (p.309)
44. True (p.309)
45. False (p.310)
46. True (p.310)
47. False (p.310)
48. True (p.310)
49. False (p.310)
50. True (p.310)
51. False (p.310)
52. True (pp.310,311)
53. Disconnection (p.312)
54. euphoria (p.318)
55. Lack of initiation (p.319)
56. Abstract reasoning deficits (p.313)
57. poor judgment (p.319)
58. visual-spatial deficits (p.314)
59. disinhibition (p.312)
60. apathy (p.318)
61. Impulsive behavior (p.318)
62. attention deficits (p.312)
63. anterior stroke, posterior stroke (p.315)
64. memory problems (p.313)
65. left brain stroke, right brain stroke (p.313)
66. Motor and sensory impairment (p.312)
67. depression (p.318)

Post-Test

Multiple Choice

1. D (p.299)
2. C (p.299)
3. C (p.299)
4. D (pp.299,300)
5. C (p.300)
6. B (p.300)
7. B (p.300)
8. A (p.300)
9. C (p.301)
10. D (p.301)
11. C (p.301)
12. C (p.301)
13. A (p.302)
14. A (p.302)
15. C (p.302)
16. B (p.302)
17. B (p.303)
18. D (p.303)
19. D (p.306)
20. D (p.306)
21. B (p.307)
22. B (p.303)
23. C (p.304)
24. A (p.304)
25. D (p.304)

26. C (p.305)
27. B (p.305
28. C (p.306)
29. D (p.308)
30. B (p.308)
31. B (p.308)
32. B (p.309)
33. A (pp.309,310)
34. D (p.310)
35. D (p.310)
36. B (p.312)
37. A (p.312)
38. D (p.312)
39. C (p.313)
40. D (p.313)
41. B (pp.313,315)
42. A (pp.313,314)
43. A (pp.313,314)
44. B (p.315)
45. A (p.318)
46. B (p.318)
47. B (p.314)
48. B (p.314)
49. A (p.314)
50. B (p.314)
51. B (p.314)
52. B (p.318)
53. D (p.318)
54. A (p.319)

Chapter 10

Tumors and Traumatic Head Injury

Overview
Learning Objectives
Tumors of the Brain
Types of Intracranial Tumors
    Infiltrating Tumors
    Non-Infiltrating Tumors
        Meningiomas
        Metastatic Tumor
        Acoustic Neuroma
        Pituitary Tumors
    Childhood Tumors
    Diagnosis of Brain Tumors
    Treatment of Brain Tumors
Brain Tumors and Neuropsychology
Traumatic Head Injury
Epidemiology of Traumatic Head Injury
Mechanism of Impact: Neuronal Shearing, Stretching, and Tearing
    Penetrating Head Injury
    Closed Head Injury
    Assessing the Severity of Brain Injury
Complications of Moderate and Severe Brain Injury
    Edema
    Brain Herniation
    Intracranial Bleeding
    Hematomas (Extradural and Subdural)
    Skull Fractures
Mild Head Injury: "Concussion"
    Post Concussional Syndrome
Treatment of Head Injuries
Neuropsychological Manifestations
    Anterograde and Retrograde Amnesia
    Neuropsychological Evaluation
Other Neurologic Disorders
    Brain Abscess
    Infections
    Neurotoxins

Post-Test

Answer Key

Overview

This chapter focuses on two common neurological disorders, brain tumors and traumatic brain injury (TBI). The two pathologies are outlined and contrasted in terms of their overall effect on the integrity of cortical processes. In general, tumors are considered to be focal disorders of the brain, because most often they are associated with more-or-less circumscribed damage to the brain. In contrast, traumatic brain injuries most often involve dysfunction of the entire brain. Other less frequently encountered neurological disorders including brain abscess, infections, and neurotoxins are also discussed in this chapter. Brain tumors and brain injuries affect a significant proportion of the population and may lead to many debilitating conditions. Neuropsychologists play an important role in evaluating the cognitive profile of those patients and in participating actively in the rehabilitation of these conditions. Furthermore, neuropsychologists are at the forefront in research of tumor treatment and TBI rehabilitation. Neuropsychologists are most interested in how such conditions result in specific neuropsychological deficits and disabilities in adaptive behaviors. Particularly the area of mild brain injury has received recent attention and practicing neuropsychologists have played an important role in its diagnosis and treatment.

Learning Objectives

- To be able to list the major types of brain tumors, their symptoms, and their treatment.
- To understand the mechanism of both penetrating and closed traumatic head injury.
- To know the different neuropsychological manifestations of traumatic head injuries.

Tumors of the Brain

Key Terms and Concepts

tumor	neoplasm	infiltrative tumor
non-infiltrative tumor	malignant	benign
metastasis	neuromas	grade

1. Tumor classification which indicates that the tumor cells are invading other tissue and are likely to spread.

   a. tumor

2. An encapsulated tumor.

   b. neoplasm

3. The spreading of malignant cells through the blood stream.

   c. infiltrative tumor

4. A tumor made up of nerve cells and nerve fibers.

   d. non-infiltrative tumor

5. A growth of tissue in which the multiplication of cells is uncontrolled and progressive.

   e. malignant

6. Tumor classification which indicates that the cell growth is non-infiltrative and will not spread.

   f. benign

7. A tumor which takes over an area of the brain and destroys neural tissue.

   g. metastasis

8. A means of evaluating and rating tumors.

   h. neuromas

9. Another term for a tumor within the brain.

   i. grade

Types of Intracranial Tumors

Key Terms and Concepts

glioma	glioblastoma multiforme	astrocytoma
oligodendroglioma	meningioma	metastatic tumor
acoustic neuroma	pituitary tumor	functioning adenoma
nonfunctioning adenoma	acidophillic adenoma	chromophobic adenoma
basophillic adenoma	Cushing's syndrome	medulloblastoma
pinealoma		

Sentence Completion

10. An _____ is a benign tumor within the auditory canal arising from Schwann cells.

11. _____ is a tumor found in the anterior lobe of the pituitary gland and can result in Cushing's syndrome.

12. The most common type of non-infiltrating tumor is the _____.

13.   _____ is a tumor found in the anterior aspects of the pituitary gland and is
       associated with hyper- or hypopituitarism.

14.   _____ play a direct role on the functioning of the pituitary gland.

15.   The most common form of infiltrative tumor is the _____.

16.   A _____ is encapsulated and malignant and has its primary site in another part
       of the body.

17.   An _____ is an infiltrative tumor of astrocytes.

18.   A _____ produces symptoms caused by pressure on the pituitary gland and
       adjacent structures.

19.   The _____ is a tumor of the pineal body.

20.   _____ is a systemic illness which results in changes in bone structure,
       hypertension, and diabetes.

21.   A very destructive and fatal glioma is the _____.

22.   _____ is a tumor found in the anterior lobe of the pituitary gland and is
       associated with giantism.

23.   The _____ is divided into two categories, functioning and nonfunctioning
       adenomas.

24.   The _____ accounts for two-thirds of all tumors in children.

25.   An _____ is an infiltrative tumor which effects young adults.

True/False

26._____   Meningiomas are more common in men.

27._____   Pituitary adenomas accounts for 45% of brain tumors.

28._____   Sudden onset headache, nausea, and seizures may indicate a tumor.

29._____   CT and MRI have made the diagnosis of tumor more accurate.

30._____   CT and MRI are able to diagnose the type of tumor.

31._____   Surgical resection of the tumor is the preferred treatment.

32._____   The blood brain barrier interferes with the ability of anti-cancer agents to enter
              brain tissue.

33._____ Family functioning has an impact on the outcome of children treated for cancer.

34._____ The diagnosis and treatment of cancer in children has an impact on family functioning.

Brain Tumors and Neuropsychology

True/False

35._____ It is possible for a tumor to reach a large size before resulting in clinical symptoms.

36._____ A glioblastoma multiforme can destroy the entire affected cerebral hemisphere.

37._____ Tumors of the frontal lobes are most likely to be meningiomas or gliomas.

38._____ Occipital lobe tumors are most frequently associated with expressive and receptive aphasias.

39._____ Parietal lobe tumors are likely to result in inattention and changes in motivation.

40._____ A tumor of the basal ganglia may result in tremors.

41._____ In an individual with seizures due to a tumor, an aura may provide information regarding the location of a tumor.

42._____ Acoustic neuromas are likely to be accompanied by significant cognitive loss as well as hearing impairment.

43._____ Neuropsychological evaluations are useful in establishing a baseline of cognitive performance prior to surgical resection of a tumor.

44._____ Neuropsychological evaluations are useful in establishing cognitive changes following surgical resection of a tumor.

45._____ Verbal-semantic memory may be impacted following radiotherapy.

Traumatic Head Injury

Key Terms and Concepts

Tensile strength	retrograde degeneration	anterograde degeneration
penetrating head injury	closed head injury	acceleration
deceleration	impact injury	countercoup injury
Glasgow Coma Scale	coma	edema
intracranial pressure	brain herniation	transtentorial herniation
subdural hematoma	extradural hematoma	epidural hematoma
intracranial bleeding	skull fractures	post-traumatic epilepsy
concussion	post concussional syndrome	sexuality
post-traumatic amnesia	retrograde amnesia	anterograde amnesia

True/False

46._____ Sports account for 10% of all head injuries.

47._____   Motor vehicle accidents are the leading cause of head injuries.

48._____   Males are more likely to sustain a head injury than females.

49._____   Tensile strength refers to the amount of physical strength an axon can endure.

50._____   The deterioration of the axon, leading to cell death, is known as retrograde degeneration.

51._____   The rupture of the cell body, leading to deterioration of the axon is known as anterograde degeneration.

52._____   A head injury caused by a bullet from a gun is referred to as a closed head injury.

53._____   Individuals who have suffered a gunshot wound to the brain stem have a fairly good prognosis.

54._____   In the case of a penetrating head injury, the neuropsychologist serves a role in identifying current level of functioning as well as making recommendations for rehabilitation.

55._____   A motor vehicle accident provides an example of a deceleration injury.

56._____   Professional ice hockey players are evaluated neuropsychologically pre-season due to their risk of closed head injury.

57._____   A countercoup injury occurs when the brain rebounds after impact.

58._____   On the Glasgow Coma Scale, a score of 10 or less indicates a severe head injury.

59._____   Coma is synonymous with sleep.

60._____   Individuals in a coma exhibit sleep-wake cycles when monitored with EEG.

61._____   An injury to the reticular activating system rarely results in coma.

62._____   An injury to the brain stem rarely results in coma.

63._____   When an individual emerges from a coma, there appears to be a sudden awakening with the patient regaining normal levels of awareness quickly.

64._____   Edema of the brain refers to swelling.

65._____   The most significant complication of edema of the brain is the resulting increase in intracranial pressure.

66._____   The displacement or deformation of the brain is referred to as brain herniation.

67._____   An upward displacement of the parahippocampal gyrus and uncus through the tentorial hiatus is known as transtentorial herniation.

68._____   Herniation of the brain can lead to a deterioration in consciousness, coma and eventually death.

69._____   Decreasing a patient's blood pressure can result in a decrease in intracranial pressure.

70._____   A partial or full lobectomy (surgical removal of a part of the brain) may be necessary to decrease intracranial pressure following a closed head injury.

71._____ Subdural hematomas are caused by an excess of cerebrospinal fluid which accumulates between the dura and the arachnoid space.

72._____ Subdural hematomas generally present within the first hour after the closed head injury.

73._____ Subdural hematoma is diagnosed using CT.

74._____ An extradural hematoma is a bleed between the skull and the dura.

75._____ Extradural hematomas are more common than are subdural hematomas.

76._____ Epidural hematomas account for 1-3% of bleeds in closed head injuries.

77._____ Coagulated blood must be removed surgically.

78._____ Intracranial and epidural hematomas are associated with skull fractures.

79._____ Skull fractures increase chances of infection, cerebrospinal fluid leaks, and bleeding.

80._____ Seizures are extremely rare following traumatic brain injury.

81._____ If an individual is going to experience a seizure as a result of a brain injury, it will typically be experienced within days of the injury.

82._____ Concussion is associated with neurological changes.

83._____ Individuals who have experienced a mild traumatic brain injury will have a Glasgow Coma Scale score of 13 or above.

84._____ Over a million people experience a mild traumatic brain injury each year.

85._____ All individuals who experience a mild traumatic brain injury regain full recovery in three to six months.

86._____ Mild traumatic brain injuries are easily detected by CT and MRI.

87._____ Neuropsychologists are in a unique position of assessing individuals with mild traumatic brain injury.

88._____ Headache, dizziness, and memory problems are symptoms of post concussional disorder.

89._____ Professional soccer players are at risk of developing electroencephalographic (EEG) abnormalities and neuropsychological dysfunction.

90._____ Following a severe closed head injury, most of the recovery occurs within the first six months.

91._____ Rehabilitation should begin once the natural healing process has finished.

92._____ The inability to problem solve and make informed decisions can significantly impact a head injured individual's quality of life.

93._____ The length of post-traumatic amnesia is a prognostic indicator in head injury.

Other Neurologic Disorders

<u>Key Terms and Concepts</u>

brain abscess   meningitis   herpes encephalitis
immunodeficiency virus   neurotoxins

<u>True/False</u>

94._____   A brain abscess arises from an infection in the brain.

95._____   Meningitis is a bacterial or viral infection of the meninges.

96._____   Herpes encephalitis attacks the brain stem and medulla oblongata.

97._____   The HIV/AIDS virus does not attack specific brain structures, rather is opens the
             brain up to infections and other diseases.

98._____   Neurotoxins are defined as any substance which is poisonous to the brain.

99._____   Pesticides, alcohol, and lead are examples of neurotoxins.

Post-Test
Multiple Choice

1. An enlargement or new growth of tissue in which the multiplication of cells is uncontrolled and progressive is known as:

    e.   tumor.
    f.   malignant.
    g.   benign.
    h.   metastasis.

2. A tumor of the brain is also referred to as:

    a.   an infiltrative tumor.
    b.   a non-infiltrative tumor.
    c.   a neoplasm.
    d.   malignant.

3. Brain tumors make up _____ of all cancers.

    a.   1%
    b.   5%
    c.   10%
    d.   50%

4. Brain tumors are most common in:

    a.   infancy.
    b.   childhood.
    c.   early and middle adulthood.
    d.   the elderly.

5. A tumor which takes over neighboring areas of the brain and destroys neural tissue is known as:

    a.   a neoplasm.
    b.   an infiltrative tumor.
    c.   a non-infiltrative tumor.
    d.   benign.

6. A tumor which is encapsulated and easily distinguished from neural tissue is known as:

    a.   a neoplasm.
    b.   an infiltrative tumor.
    c.   a non-infiltrative tumor.
    d.   malignant.

7. Which of the following is a tumor classification indicating that the tumor cells are likely to re-grow and spread?

    a.   Malignant.
    b.   Benign.
    c.   Meningioma.
    d.   None of the above.

8. Which of the following is a tumor classification indicating that the cell growth is surrounded by a fibrous capsule and will not spread?

    a.   Malignant.
    b.   Benign.
    c.   Metastatic.
    d.   None of the above.

9. The spreading of malignant tumor cells to other parts of the body is known as:

    a.   grading.
    b.   metastasis.
    c.   infiltration.
    d.   progression.

10. Which of the following indicates a fast growing tumor with a poor prognosis?

    a.   Grade 1.
    b.   Grade 2.
    c.   Grade 3.
    d.   Grade 4.

11. What is the most common form of infiltrative tumor?

    a.   Glioma.
    b.   Meningioma.
    c.   Acoustic neuroma.
    d.   Pituitary tumor.

12. Which of the following tumors has the worst prognosis?

    a.   Oligodendroglioma.
    b.   Pituitary tumor.
    c.   Astrocytoma.
    d.   Glioblastoma multiforme.

13. Meningiomas represent _____ of all brain tumors.

    a.   5%
    b.   15%
    c.   25%
    d.   45%

14. Which of the following statements is true regarding meningiomas?

    a.   Meningiomas are more prominent in men.
    b.   Meningiomas grow quickly.
    c.   Neuropsychological deficits are often profound.
    d.   Meningiomas may not be diagnosed until autopsy.

15. Which of the following may result in metastatic tumors?

    a.   Skin cancer.
    b.   Breast cancer.
    c.   Lung cancer.
    d.   All of the above.

16. Which of the following may be the cause of tinnitus, unilateral loss of taste, and partial deafness?

    a.   Astrocytoma.
    b.   Oligodendroglioma.
    c.   Acoustic neuroma.
    d.   Meningioma.

17. A pituitary tumor which causes symptoms due to pressure on the pituitary is called a:

    a.   meningioma.
    b.   functioning adenoma.
    c.   nonfunctioning adenoma.
    d.   infiltrative tumor.

18. Which of the following might result in giantism?

    a.   Basophillic adenoma.
    b.   Acidophillic adenoma.
    c.   Chromophobic adenoma.
    d.   Cushing's syndrome.

19. Which of the following may indicate the presence of a tumor?

    a.   Seizure.
    b.   Nausea.
    c.   Loss of cognitive function.
    d.   All of the above.

20. Which is the most efficient diagnostic tool for tumors?

    a.   Neurological examination.
    b.   Neuropsychological examination.
    c.   Brain scanning.
    d.   Spinal tap.

21. Neuropsychological deficits associated with tumor are dependent on:

    a.   size of tumor.
    b.   location of tumor.
    c.   grade of tumor.
    d.   All of the above.

22. Which of the following tumors is most likely to result in stereognosis and apraxia?

    a.   Frontal lobe tumor.
    b.   Parietal lobe tumor.
    c.   Temporal lobe tumor.
    d.   Occipital lobe tumor.

23. Which of the following domains is most likely to be impacted by radiation therapy?

    a.   Memory.
    b.   Motor control.
    c.   Attention.
    d.   Language.

24. Sports account for _____ of all head injuries.

    a.   7%
    b.   17%
    c.   27%
    d.   37%

25. Which of the following sports is the most dangerous?

    a.   Skiing.
    b.   Diving.
    c.   Equestrian events.
    d.   Triathlon.

26. Which of the following is the leading cause of head injuries?

    a.   Sports injuries.
    b.   Car accidents.
    c.   Industrial accidents.
    d.   Violence.

27. Which of the following statements is true regarding head injury?

    a.   Females are more likely to suffer a head injury than males.
    b.   Individuals between the ages of 15 and 24 years are most likely to incur a head injury.
    c.   Infants are at a high risk of sustaining a head injury.
    d.   Alcohol is not a risk factor for head injury.

28. The destruction of the axon, subsequently leading to cell death is known as:

    a.   anterograde degeneration.
    b.   retrograde degeneration.
    c.   axonal shearing.
    d.   plasticity.

29. Which of the following is an example of a closed head injury?

    a.   Gun shot wound.
    b.   Concussion.
    c.   Surgical resection of a tumor.
    d.   Stabbing.

30. Which of the following is the primary technique used by males in completed suicides?

    a.   Slitting wrists.
    b.   Overdose.
    c.   Hanging.
    d.   Firearm.

31. Which of the following is an example of an acceleration injury?

    a.   Hitting a tree head-first.
    b.   Being struck by a baseball bat.
    c.   Falling and hitting your head on the ground.
    d.   None of the above.

32. Which of the following is a risk of closed head injury?

    a.   Ruptured blood vessels.
    b.   Shearing of nerves.
    c.   The tearing of the brain away from the skull.
    d.   All of the above.

33. If you received a head injury and were administered the Glasgow Coma Scale, which of the following scores would you most like to receive?

    a.   5.
    b.   8.
    c.   10.
    d.   14.

34. Within the verbal response dimension of the Glasgow Coma Scale, how many points would an individual receive if they were able to make verbal responses without recognizable words?

    a.   4.
    b.   3.
    c.   2.
    d.   1.

35. Which of the following statements is true regarding coma?

    a.   Being in a coma is similar to being in a deep sleep.
    b.   When a person arises from a coma, all cognitive functions are restored shortly afterwards.
    c.   Coma is related to damage of the reticulating activating system.
    d.   On the Glasgow Coma Scale, a coma is defined as a score of 13 or less.

36. Which of the following refers to the swelling of the brain?

    a.   Herniation.
    b.   Transtentorial herniation.
    c.   Hematoma.
    d.   Edema.

37. Which of the following might result in herniation of the brain?

    a.   Tumor.
    b.   Decreased intracranial pressure.
    c.   Coma.
    d.   Hyperventilation.

38. Which of the following is the "last resort" way to decrease intracranial pressure?

    a.   Electroconvulsive therapy.
    b.   Surgical removal of an intact portion of the brain.
    c.   Lobotomy.
    d.   Induce pharmacologic coma.

39. Which of the following is a danger associated with subdural hematoma?

    a.   Brain herniation.
    b.   Risk of death.
    c.   Coma.
    d.   All of the above.

40. Which of the following is the preferred treatment for subdural hematoma?

    a.   Surgical removal of neural tissue.
    b.   Surgical removal of coagulated blood.
    c.   Draining of the bleed.
    d.   Psychoanalysis.

41. Which of the following is the most difficult to treat?

    a.   Intracerebral hematomas.
    b.   Epidural hematomas.
    c.   Subdural hematomas.
    d.   None of the above.

42. Which of the following is more likely to occur in conjunction with a skull fracture than a head injury with no skull fracture?

    a.   Memory problems.
    b.   Identifiable neurological deficits.
    c.   Infection.
    d.   Attentional deficits.

43. Which of the following is a risk factor for developing seizures following a head injury?

    a.   Gender.
    b.   Memory functioning prior to the injury.
    c.   Post-traumatic amnesia.
    d.   Age.

44. A concussion:

    a.   has no neurological impact on the brain.
    b.   is a humorous and harmless neurological phenomenon.
    c.   is a form of mild head injury which is not associated with neurological effects.
    d.   causes the death of neurons.

45. Which of the following is true regarding a mild head injury?

    a.   The loss of consciousness should not exceed two hours.
    b.   The Glasgow Coma Scale should be 13 or above.
    c.   Post-traumatic amnesia should be no greater the 72 hours.
    d.   Mild head injuries are rare.

46. A neuropsychological evaluation is especially important in mild traumatic brain injury because:

    a. all individuals with concussions have lasting neuropsychological deficits.
    b. memory deficits in individuals with mild traumatic brain injury should be expected to last at least 24 months.
    c. mild traumatic brain injury is often not detected using brain scanning techniques.
    d. None of the above.

47. Which of the following statements is true regarding head injuries?

    a. Mild head injuries are easily diagnosed and treated medically.
    b. The sequelae of mild head injuries are well-known to the medical community.
    c. Mild head injuries do not result in neuronal death.
    d. Head injuries are cumulative in effect.

48. Which of the following is a typical symptom of post concussional syndrome?

    a. Unilateral motor deficits.
    b. Concentration problems.
    c. Seizures.
    d. All of the above.

49. In which of the following sports is the goal to produce neurological deficits in your opponents?

    a. Football.
    b. Boxing.
    c. Ice Hockey.
    d. Badminton.

50. Which of the following is the most critical thing that must be done for a head injury victim at the scene in order to minimize cognitive deficits?

    a. Order baseline neuropsychological testing.
    b. Implement rehabilitation strategies.
    c. Neurological assessment.
    d. Establish an open airway.

51. Most recovery following a head injury occurs:

    a. in the first week following the injury.
    b. in the first two months following the injury.
    c. in the first six months following the injury.
    d. Recovery progresses systematically and lasts the lifetime of the patient.

52. Which of the following problems may adversely impact the sexuality of a head injury survivor?

     a.   Physical limitations.
     b.   Sexual dysfunction.
     c.   Problem solving deficits.
     d.   All of the above.

53. Brain abscesses are the result of:

     a.   tumors.
     b.   infections.
     c.   bleeds.
     d.   head injuries.

54. Which of the following is the result of a bacterial infection of the meninges?

     a.   HIV.
     b.   Herpes encephalitis.
     c.   Meningitis.
     d.   Tumor.

Essay Questions

1.   Compare and contrast infiltrative and non-infiltrative tumors.

2.   Review the complications of severe head injury.

3.   Discuss the possible outcomes of a mild traumatic brain injury.

Answer Key

Chapter Exercises

1. e (p.323)
2. d (p.323)
3. g (p.323)
4. h (p.323)
5. a (p.323)
6. f (p.323)
7. c (p.323)
8. i (p.323,324)
9. b (p.323)
10. acoustic neuroma (p.326)
11. Basophilic adenoma (p.326)
12. meningioma (p.325)
13. Chromophobic adenoma (p.326)
14. Functioning adenomas (p.326)
15. glioma (p.324)
16. metastatic tumor (p.325)
17. astrocytoma (p.324)
18. nonfunctioning adenoma (p.326)
19. pinealoma (p.327)
20. Cushing's syndrome (p.326)
21. Glioblastoma multiforme (p.324)
22. Acidophillic adenoma (p.326)
23. pituitary tumor (p.326)
24. medulloblastoma (p.326)
25. oligodendroglioma (p.325)
26. False (p.325)
27. False (p.327)
28. True (p.327)
29. True (p.327)
30. False (p.327)
31. True (p.328)
32. True (p.328)
33. True (pp.330,331)
34. True (pp.330,331)
35. True (p.328)
36. True (p.328)
37. True (p.329)
38. False (p.329)
39. False (p.329)
40. True (p.329)
41. True (p.329)
42. False (p.329)
43. True (p.329)
44. True (p.329)
45. True (pp.332,333)
46. False (p.329)
47. True (p.333)
48. True (p.333)
49. True (p.334)
50. True (p.334)
51. True (p.334)
52. False (p.335)
53. False (p.335)
54. True (pp.336,337)
55. True (p.336)
56. True (p.338)
57. True (p.338)
58. False (p.338)
59. False (p.338)
60. True (p.338)
61. False (p.338)
62. False (p.338)
63. False (p.339)
64. True (p.340)
65. True (p.340)
66. True (p.340)
67. False (p.340)
68. True (p.340)
69. True (p.340)
70. True (p.340)
71. False (p.341)
72. False (p.341)
73. True (p.341)
74. True (p.341)
75. False (p.341)
76. True (p.341)
77. True (p.341)
78. True (p.341)
79. True (p.342)
80. False (p.342)
81. False (p.342)
82. True (p.343)
83. True (p.344)
84. True (p.344)
85. False (p.344)
86. False (p.345)
87. True (p.345)
88. True (p.346)
89. True (p.346)
90. True (p.347)
91. False (p.347)
92. True (pp.350,351)
93. True (p.347)
94. True (p.351)
95. True (p.352)
96. False (p.352)
97. True (p.353)
98. True (p.353)
99. True (p.353)

Post-Test

Multiple Choice

1. A (p.323)
2. C (p.323)
3. B (p.323)
4. C (p.323)
5. B (p.323)
6. C (p.323)
7. A (p.323)
8. B (p.323)
9. B (p.323)
10. D (p.324)
11. A (p.324)
12. D (p.324)
13. B (p.325)
14. D (p.325)
15. D (p.325)
16. C (p.326)
17. C (p.326)
18. B (p.326)
19. D (p.327)
20. C (p.327)
21. D (p.328)
22. B (p.329)
23. A (pp.332,333)
24. B (p.329)
25. C (p.329)
26. B (p.332)
27. B (pp.333,334)
28. B (p.334)
29. B (p.335)
30. D (p.335)
31. B (p.336)
32. D (p.338)
33. D (p.338)
34. C (p.339)
35. C (pp.338,339)
36. D (p.340)
37. A (p.340)
38. B (p.340)
39. D (p.341)
40. C (p.341)
41. A (p.341)
42. C (p.342)
43. C (p.342)
44. C (pp.342,343)
45. B (p.344)
46. C (p.345)
47. D (p.349)
48. B (p.346)
49. B (p.346)
50. D (p.346)
51. C (p.347)
52. D (p.350,351)
53. B (p.351)
54. C (p.352)

Chapter 11

Disorders of the Brain
Normal Aging and Dementia:
Alzheimer's Disease

Chapter Outline

Overview

The elderly are the fastest growing segment of the U.S. population. Due to this change in demographics, increasing research interest has been aimed at understanding the neuropsychological conditions that target the elderly. Among these conditions are a group of disorders, collectively known as the dementias, which result in global declines in cognitive and behavioral functioning. There is no one cause for dementia and, in fact, the precise etiologies for the dementias are still a mystery. Also, for many dementias there is no known cure. Dementia is often progressive, eventually affecting numerous higher mental facilities. In short, dementia may be thought of as the "thief of the mind," first robbing memory, communication ability, or visuospatial skills, but then returning to steal other aspects of mental functioning. Psychological studies of the elderly have established that aging is itself not necessarily associated with dementia. Aging instead is associated with predictable changes in patterns of abilities in crystallized and fluid intelligence. Healthy and active individuals in their 60s, 70s, and 80s do not differ substantially in the level of their cognitive skills or abilities in relation to their past level of functioning. Relatively stable skills include well-learned verbal abilities such as reading, writing, and speaking, simple arithmetic ability, and immediate and long-term memory. In contrast, short term memory, abstract and novel problem solving, and behavioral slowing are examples of types of functioning that may be compromised by the normal aging processes. The current chapter is important for the neuropsychology student because it examines the important differences between normal aging and dementia. Questions regarding the aging brain and neuropsychological functioning are also addressed. This chapter presents an in-depth look at the most common dementia syndrome namely, Alzheimer's disease. This cortical dementia is examined from a neuropathological, neuropsychological, and behavioral perspective. Neuropsychologists play an important role in the comprehensive assessment of relevant medical, functional, psychosocial, and neuropsychological factors in the assessment of dementia. Specifically, neuropsychological assessment of mental status and cognitive abilities yields valuable information about the prognosis of the disease, is important in monitoring the patient's health, and assists the patient in making future life plans.

Learning Objectives

- To know the differences in cognitive decline associated with normal aging compared to the neuropsychological deficits seen in Alzheimer's disease.
- To be able to differentiate the subtypes of dementia, including cortical versus subcortical, static versus progressive, and reversible versus irreversible.
- To understand the major neurological, neuropsychological, and behavior symptoms associated with Alzheimer's disease.

Normal Aging

Key Terms and Concepts

dementia	crystallized intelligence	fluid intelligence
neurofibrillary tangles	senile plaques	striate cortex
neostriatum	atrophy	

1. The degeneration of neurons is referred to as _____.

2. _____ and _____ have been implicated in Alzheimer's disease but are also present in normal aging.

3. Novel reasoning is a form of _____.

4. The _____ loses 15-20% of neurons between young adulthood and old age.

5. _____ results in an abnormal cognitive decline.

6. The _____ does not lose a significant number of neurons over the life span.

7. Habitual ways of solving problems is a form of _____.

Defining Dementia

cortical dementia	subcortical dementia	static dementia
progressive dementia	reversible dementia	irreversible dementia
delirium		

8. A dementia which affects the gray matter primarily.   a.   cortical dementia

9. A transient cognitive problem associated with confusion.   b.   subcortical dementia

10. A dementia which cannot currently be arrested.   c.   static dementia

11. A dementia which is the result of a disease process and gets worse over time.   d.   progressive dementia

12. Often confused with delirium.   e.   reversible dementia

13. A dementia which affects the white matter primarily.   f.   irreversible dementia

14. A steady state cognitive disorder.   g.   delirium

Alzheimer's Disease

Alzheimer's disease   beta-amyloid   acetylcholine
multi-infarct dementia   declarative memory   language functioning
visual-spatial functioning   intellectual functioning   executive functioning
metacognitive   orientation/attention   motor/sensory
depression

True/False

15._____   Alzheimer's disease is a subcortical dementia.

16._____   Alzheimer's disease is an irreversible dementia.

17._____   Alzheimer's disease represents 25% of all diagnostic dementia cases.

18._____   There is a single identifiable cause of Alzheimer's disease.

19._____   Individuals with doctoral degrees cannot get Alzheimer's disease.

20._____   A strong genetic component has been identified in Alzheimer's disease.

21._____   A brain biopsy is the only way to diagnose Alzheimer's disease medically.

22._____   Diagnosis of Alzheimer's disease includes ruling out all other dementias.

23._____   In Alzheimer's disease, the cerebral cortex, hippocampus, and amygdala are
              negatively impacted.

24._____   Gyri are thinned, sulci widened, and ventricles enlarged in Alzheimer's disease.

25._____   Primary motor areas are usually targeted in Alzheimer's disease.

26._____   Neurofibrillary tangles and senile plaques are observed in Alzheimer's disease.

27._____   Senile plaques are composed of tau proteins.

28._____   Senile plaques are mostly likely to be found in the frontal and temporal regions
              as well as the hippocampal formation.

29._____   Tangles and plaques are only found in individuals with Alzheimer's disease.

30._____   Senile plaques contain beta-amyloid.

31._____   Beta-amyloid is coded on chromosome 14.

32._____ The ApoE3 variant of apolipoprotein substantially increases the risk of developing Alzheimer's disease.

33._____ The neurotransmitter associated with memory functioning in Alzheimer's disease is serotonin.

34._____ CT and MRI scans of the brain are regularly used to rule out Alzheimer's disease.

35._____ Multi-infarct dementia is caused by multiple small strokes.

36._____ Memory is rarely affected in Alzheimer's disease.

37._____ Decline in memory in individuals over aged 65 is normal.

38._____ Memory impairments in Alzheimer's disease are specific to encoding.

39._____ Intrusions and perseverations are likely to be noted in an individual with Alzheimer's disease.

40._____ Retrieval cues greatly enhance memory in individuals with Alzheimer's disease.

41._____ Individuals with Alzheimer's disease profit from repetition and practice when attempting to remember or learn.

42._____ Individuals with Alzheimer's typically have little difficulty organizing information semantically.

43._____ Short-term memory span is generally much more impaired in Alzheimer's disease than declarative long-term memory.

44._____ Individuals with Alzheimer's disease are able to perform relatively well on motor learning tasks.

45._____ Individuals with Alzheimer's disease are able to perform well on priming tasks.

46._____ The striatum is relatively preserved in Alzheimer's disease.

47._____ Language difficulties exhibited by individuals with Alzheimer's disease early in the disease process are usually word-finding and naming problems.

48._____ Visual-spatial problems are usually evident very early in the disease process.

49._____ Abstract reasoning and conceptualization are preserved in Alzheimer's disease.

50._____ Bradyphrenia refers to very slow information processing.

51._____ Metacognitive difficulties are apparent in Alzheimer's disease.

52._____ Individuals with Alzheimer's disease have little difficulty with planning, problem solving, and organization.

53._____ Orientation for person, place and time can be impaired in the moderate to severe stages of Alzheimer's disease.

54._____ Sense of smell is impaired in Alzheimer's disease.

55._____ Auditory problems are common in individuals with Alzheimer's disease.

56._____ Paranoia sometimes accompanies significant memory deficits.

57._____   10% of individuals with Alzheimer's disease also experience depression.

58._____   Depression can mimic dementia.

Treatment

<u>Key Terms and Concepts</u>

acetylcholine   Physostigmine   Tacrine
nerve growth factor   neurotrophins   estrogen replacement therapy

<u>True/False</u>

59._____   There is a cure for Alzheimer's disease.

60._____   Eating chocolate, and thus increasing choline intake, may improve memory
                 (don't we wish).

61._____   Pharmacologic interventions targeting acetylcholine have met with mixed
                 results and are accompanied by serious side effects.

62._____   Physostigmine is a cholinergic augmenting drug.

63._____   Tacrine use is associated with liver toxicity.

64._____   Nerve growth factor, a neurotrophin, may eventually result in the promotion of
                 the growth of existing cholinergic neurons.

65._____   Estrogen replacement has shown little promise in the prevention of Alzheimer's
                 disease.

66._____   Hallucinations may be experienced by individuals with Alzheimer's disease.

67._____   Reinforcement based strategies are effective in increasing learning in individuals
                 with Alzheimer's disease.

68._____   Environmental manipulation is an effective manner in which to manage an
                 individual in the later stage of Alzheimer's disease.

Post-Test
Multiple Choice

1. What percentage of the United States population is over age 65?

    i.   1%
    j.   11%
    k.   21%
    l.   31%

2. In the year 2030, approximately what percentage of the population of the United States will be over age 65?

    a.   1%
    b.   10%
    c.   20%
    d.   30%

3. Approximately how many people over 65 live in nursing homes?

    a.   1 million.
    b.   3 million.
    c.   5 million.
    d.   10 million.

4. What percentage of individuals who are 85-years-old suffer from a dementia?

    a.   1%
    b.   5%
    c.   8%
    d.   18%

5. What cognitive capacity is basically resistant to the effects of normal aging?

    a.   Fund of learned information.
    b.   New learning.
    c.   Abstract problem solving.
    d.   All of the above.

6. In the Nun Study, poor linguistic ability in early life was found to be related to:

    a.   the development of a dementia later in life.
    b.   brain changes characteristic of Alzheimer's disease later in life.
    c.   lower cognitive functioning later in life.
    d.   All of the above.

7. Which of the following neuroanatomic changes takes place during normal aging?

    a.   Cerebral blood vessels burst.
    b.   The cortical surface is flattened.
    c.   Neurons regenerate.
    d.   Increase in brain size.

8. Which of the following does not lose a significant number of neurons throughout the life span?

    a.   Neostriatum.
    b.   Frontal cortex.
    c.   Striate cortex.
    d.   None of the above.

9. Dementia is:

    a.   senility.
    b.   old-timer's disease.
    c.   a behavioral syndrome.
    d.   hardening of the arteries.

10. An example of a cortical dementia is:

    a.   Alzheimer's disease.
    b.   Parkinson's disease.
    c.   Alcoholic dementia.
    d.   Tumor.

11. An example of a subcortical dementia is:

    a.   Alzheimer's disease.
    b.   Fragile X syndrome.
    c.   Parkinson's disease.
    d.   Herpes Encephalitis.

12. Which of the following is a criterion for dementia?

    a.   Loss of intellectual function.
    b.   Deficits in multiple areas of cognitive function.
    c.   Memory impairment.
    d.   All of the above.

13. Which of the following is a progressive dementia?

    a.   Alcoholic dementia.
    b.   Huntington's disease.
    c.   Herpes Encephalitis.
    d.   Lead poisoning.

14. Delirium is:

    a.   a serious debilitating dementia.
    b.   a transient cognitive problem.
    c.   a permanent condition.
    d.   never mistaken for a dementia.

15. A symptom of a delirium is:

    a.   an altered state of consciousness.
    b.   memory impairment.
    c.   disorientation.
    d.   All of the above.

16. What percentage of dementias does Alzheimer's disease represent?

    a.   10%
    b.   25%
    c.   50%
    d.   75%

17. Which of the following is related to an increased chance of developing Alzheimer's disease?

    a.   High levels of education.
    b.   Down's syndrome.
    c.   Nicotine use.
    d.   Unhealthy lifestyle.

18. Which chromosomes appear to be related to Alzheimer's disease?

    a.   2, 13, 21
    b.   1, 13, 21
    c.   1, 14, 21
    d.   1, 14, 19

19. Alzheimer's disease can be definitively diagnosed through:

    a.   brain scanning techniques.
    b.   neuropsychological evaluation.
    c.   neurological evaluation.
    d.   brain biopsy.

20. Which of the following is affected in Alzheimer's disease?

    a.   Cerebral cortex.
    b.   Hippocampus.
    c.   Amygdala.
    d.   All of the above.

21. Which sensory modality is negatively impacted early in Alzheimer's disease?

    a.   Tactile.
    b.   Olfactory.
    c.   Auditory.
    d.   Visual.

22. Neurofibrillary tangles are composed of:

    a.   tau proteins.
    b.   twisted dendrites.
    c.   beta-amyloid.
    d.   apolipoprotein E4.

23. Neuritic or senile plaques contain:

    a.   an increase in neurotransmitters.
    b.   twisted dendrites.
    c.   beta-amyloid.
    d.   apolipoprotein E4.

24. What developmental disability shows hope in helping to understand Alzheimer's disease?

    a.   Dyslexia.
    b.   Fragile X syndrome.
    c.   Fetal alcohol syndrome.
    d.   Down's syndrome.

25. If the apolipoprotein E4 is inherited from both parents, the risk for developing Alzheimer's disease is:

    a.   10%
    b.   30%
    c.   50%
    d.   90%

26. Which neurotransmitter is linked to the memory deficits observed in Alzheimer's disease?

    a.   Serotonin.
    b.   Acetylcholine.
    c.   Dopamine.
    d.   Norepinephrine.

27. The EEG's of Alzheimer patients are likely to show:

    a.   a general increase in brain activity.
    b.   a general decrease in brain activity.
    c.   increase Stage 4 sleep.
    d.   increased REM sleep.

28. Which of the following is most reliably associated with increasing cognitive impairment in Alzheimer's disease?

    a.   Degree of cerebral atrophy.
    b.   Slowing observed via EEG.
    c.   Degree of ventricular enlargement.
    d.   All of the above.

29. What are deficits associated with early and mid-stages of Alzheimer's disease?

    a.   Decreased strength.
    b.   Decreased motor speed.
    c.   Confluent aphasia.
    d.   Impaired memory.

30. Which of the following might reflect an early symptom of Alzheimer's disease?

    a.   Forgetting the name and face of a spouse.
    b.   Forgetting how to get around the house in which you have lived for 30 years.
    c.   Disorientation.
    d.   Being unable to remember what to buy at the grocery store.

31. Which of the following is true about individual's with Alzheimer's disease?

    a.   They are able to benefit from retrieval cues to assist memory.
    b.   They are able to profit from practice.
    c.   They exhibit flat learning curves.
    d.   They exhibit problems with retrieval, but not with encoding or consolidation of memories.

32. On which of the following would an individual with Alzheimer's disease be expected to perform reasonably well?

    a.   A verbal priming task.
    b.   A motor learning task.
    c.   A declarative memory task.
    d.   A task requiring semantic organization.

33. Which of the following language difficulties would be typical of an individual in the early stages of Alzheimer's disease?

    a.   Stuttering.
    b.   Global aphasia.
    c.   Comprehension difficulties.
    d.   Word finding problems.

34. Which of the following deficits would be expected on visual-spatial measures?

    a.   Problems with spatial construction.
    b.   Problems with visual integration.
    c.   Problems with copying and drawing.
    d.   All of the above.

35. Which of the following is evident in Alzheimer's disease?

    a.   Bradyphrenia.
    b.   Anomic aphasia.
    c.   Neurotoxin exposure.
    d.   Increased metacognitive awareness.

36. Which of the following psychiatric difficulties is relatively common in individuals with Alzheimer's disease?

    a.   Paranoia.
    b.   Schizophrenia.
    c.   Anorexia Nervosa.
    d.   Paraphilia.

37. In the case of dementias, it is most often necessary to make a differential diagnosis between which conditions?

    a.   Dementia and Psychosis.
    b.   Dementia and Bipolar Disorder.
    c.   Dementia and Depression.
    d.   Dementia and Pica.

38. Which of the following methods has been attempted to improve the cognitive functions of individuals with Alzheimer's disease?

    a.   Neurosurgery.
    b.   Cholinergic augmenting drugs.
    c.   Decreasing dietary intake of choline.
    d.   Brain transplant.

39. Which of the following research areas shows promise in developing a means to reverse the effects of Alzheimer's disease?

    a.   Consumption of dietary choline.
    b.   Nerve growth factor.
    c.   Cholinergic inhibiting drugs.
    d.   Brain transplant.

40. Post-menopausal women on hormone (Estrogen) replacement therapy are:

    a.   more likely to develop Alzheimer's disease.
    b.   less likely to develop Alzheimer's disease.
    c.   just as likely as individuals who are not on hormone replacement therapy to develop Alzheimer's disease.
    d.   None of the above.

41. Which of the following techniques might be used to assist an individual with significant cognitive deficits due to Alzheimer's disease?

    a.   Restructure the environment to increase safety.
    b.   Redirection of inappropriate behavior.
    c.   Provision of stimulating activities.
    d.   All of the above.

Essay Questions

1.   What are the differences between a dementia and delirium?

2.   Discuss the memory deficits associated with Alzheimer's disease.

3.   Discuss treatment options for individuals with Alzheimer's disease.

Answer Key

Chapter Exercises

1. atrophy (p.360)
2. Senile plaques, neurofibrillary tangles (pp.359,360)
3. fluid intelligence (p.358)
4. neostriatum (p.359)
5. Dementia (p.357)
6. striate cortex (p.359)
7. crystallized intelligence (p.358)
8. a (p.363)
9. g (p.363)
10. f (pp.363,364)
11. d (p.363)
12. e (p.363)
13. b (p.363)
14. c (p.363)
15. False (p.364)
16. True (p.364)
17. False (p.364)
18. False (p.364)
19. False (p.365)
20. False (p.365)
21. True (p.366)
22. True (p.366)
23. True (p.366)
24. True (p.366)
25. False (p.367)
26. True (p.367)
27. False (p.367)
28. True (p.367)
29. False (p.367)
30. True (p.367)
31. False (p.368)
32. False (p.368)
33. False (p.368)
34. True (p.368)
35. True (p.369)
36. False (p.369)
37. True (p.370)
38. False (p.370)
39. True (p.370)
40. False (p.370)
41. False (pp.370,371)
42. False (pp.371,372)
43. False (p.372)
44. True (p.372)
45. False (p.372)
46. True (p.373)
47. True (p.373)
48. False (p.373)
49. False (p.374)
50. True (p.374)
51. True (pp.374,375)
52. False (p.375)
53. True (p.375)
54. True (p.375)
55. False (p.375)
56. True (p.375)
57. False (p.376)
58. True (p.376)
59. False (p.377)
60. False (p.377)
61. True (p.377)
62. True (p.377)
63. True (p.377)
64. True (p.378)
65. False (p.378)
66. True (pp.378,379)
67. False (p.379)
68. True (p.379)

Post-Test

Multiple Choice

1. B (p.357)
2. C (p.357)
3. A (p.357)
4. D (p.357)
5. A (p.358)
6. D (p.359)
7. B (p.359)
8. C (p.359)
9. C (p.361)
10. A (p.361)
11. C (p.361)
12. D (p.362)
13. B (p.363)
14. B (p.363)
15. D (p.363)
16. C (p.364)
17. B (p.365)
18. C (p.365)
19. D (p.366)
20. D (p.366)
21. B (p.367)
22. A (p.367)
23. C (p.367)
24. D (p.368)
25. D (p.368)
26. B (p.368)
27. B (p.368)
28. C (p.368)
29. D (p.369)
30. D (pp.369,370)
31. C (pp.369,370)
32. B (p.372)
33. D (p.373)
34. D (pp.373,374)
35. B (p.373)
36. A (p.375)
37. C (p.376)
38. B (p.377)
39. B (pp.377,378)
40. B (p.378)
41. D (p.379)

Chapter 12

Disorders of the Brain
Subcortical and Mixed Dementias

Chapter Outline

Overview

This chapter reviews the differential diagnosis between dementia subtypes including Parkinson's, Huntington's, and Creutzfeld-Jacob disease. Although the differences in presentation of these subtypes can be quite complex, the practicing neuropsychologist may see many different exemplars of dementia. Subcortical dementias are so named because, although these conditions often affect cortical areas and functioning, the structures that are prominently damaged are subcortical. For example, Parkinson's disease and Huntington's disease attack the basal ganglia; Parkinson's disease is known to target the substantia nigra, and Huntington's disease originates in the caudate nucleus. Creutzfeld-Jacob disease affects yet another non-cortical structure, the cerebellum. The common behavioral feature characterizing these, and most subcortical dementias, is slowed cognitive and motor dysfunction. What is interesting is the manner in which each disease affects the motor system in a different way. The complexities of the motor system can be truly appreciated through the examination of these diseases. These dementias, however, do not represent only motor system dysfunction. Although motor problems present great physical limitations and hardship, the dementias presented in this chapter are progressive and involve multiple functional systems. The study and recognition of dementias requires much experience with a number of dementia subtypes, and careful assessment and observation of behavioral differences. In this endeavor, neuropsychologists work in close conjunction with neurologists specializing in geriatrics.

Learning Objectives

- To learn the major neuropsychological symptoms associated with subcortical dementias.
- To be able to differentiate the clinical presentation of Parkinson's, Huntington's, and Creutzfeld-Jacob disease.
- To understand the neuropsychological profile of Parkinson's disease, including motor, visual-spatial, executive functioning, language, speech, memory, mood, emotion, personality, and insight.

Parkinson's Disease

Key Terms and Concepts

subcortical dementia	Parkinsonism	Lewy bodies
resting tremor	bradykinesia	micrographia
rigidity	hypokinesia	festinating gait
masked face	visual-spatial	executive functioning
dysphonia	tachiphemia	palilalia
memory	anticholinergics	pallidotomy
thalotomy		

Sentence Completion

1.   _____ refers to the tightening of muscles and joints seen in individuals with Parkinson's disease.

2.   _____ were the first treatment for Parkinson's disease.

3.   _____ deficits in individuals with Parkinson's disease are exhibited by organizational and retrieval difficulties.

4.   _____ refers to the slow and small handwriting of individuals with Parkinson's disease.

5.   A loss of voice amplitude and vocal emotional expression is called _____ .

6.   An individual suffering from difficulty retrieving learned information and/or abnormalities of mood and motivation may have a _____ .

7.   _____ is a surgery which lesions a part of the globus pallidus.

8.   A _____ is characterized by rhythmic shaking.

9.   _____ refers to the reduced facial expression of individuals with Parkinson's disease.

10.   _____ refers to segmented accelerated bursts of speech.

11.   A _____ is characterized by rapid small steps.

12.   _____ is marked by tremor, rigidity, and slowness of movement.

13.   _____ refers to the reduced motor initiation observed in individuals with Parkinson's disease.

14.   _____ is a surgery which lesions a part of the thalamus.

15.   Found within dying cells, _____ are small tightly packed granular structures with ring-like filaments.

16.   The Judgment of Line Orientation Test measures _____ skills.

17.   _____, a poverty of movement, is a motor symptom of Parkinson's disease.

18.   _____ is exhibited by compulsive word or phrase repetition.

19.   Tests of _____ have shown that individuals with Parkinson's disease have difficulties with changing mental sets, maintaining mental sets, and temporal structuring.

243

Huntington's Disease

20._____ Huntington's disease is a result of the deterioration of the caudate nucleus.

21._____ The gene for Huntington's disease remains unidentified.

22._____ Huntington's disease is a static subcortical dementia.

23._____ There is an effective treatment for Huntington's disease.

24._____ There is no cure for Huntington's disease.

25._____ The gene for Huntington's disease is located on the short arm of chromosome 4.

26._____ Most people at risk of developing Huntington's disease have opted not to receive testing to determine if they have it.

27._____ In Huntington's disease, in addition to deterioration of the caudate nucleus, the putamen and hippocampus may also be involved.

28._____ The frontal lobes are spared in Huntington's disease.

29._____ Huntington's patients exhibit significant difficulties encoding new information.

30._____ The suicide rate in Huntington's disease patient is lower than in other degenerative disorders.

31._____ The emotional symptoms in Huntington's disease often precede the debilitating motor symptoms.

32._____ Chorea refers to twisting and grimacing movements of the face and body.

Creutzfeld-Jacob Disease

Key Terms and Concepts

Creutzfeld-Jacob disease   Gerstmann-Straussler-Scheinker syndrome
Kuru

True/False

33._____ Creutzfeld-Jacob disease is the most quickly progressing dementia.

34._____ Creutzfeld-Jacob disease is also referred to as a spongiform encephalopathy because it results in extensive holes in the brains of victims.

35._____ Dr. Hans Gerhard Creutzfeldt was an assitant of Alois Alzheimer.

36._____ Creutzfeld-Jacob disease is twice as common as Huntington's disease.

37._____ Gerstmann-Straussler-Scheinker syndrome is a familial variant of Creutzfeld-Jacob disease.

38._____ Kuru is a spongiform encephalopathy caused by eating the brains of infected sheep.

39._____ Mad cow disease refers to bovine spongiform encephalopathy.

40._____ It is possible that Creutzfeld-Jacob disease incubates slowly in the spleen.

41._____ Scrapie-associated fibrils are synonymous with prions.

42._____ In Creutzfeld-Jacob disease, motor symptoms precede emotional symptoms.

Post-Test
Multiple Choice

1. Subcortical dementia is characterized by which of the following?

    m. Retrieval difficulty.
    n. Slow cognitive processing.
    o. Executive dysfunction.
    p. All of the above.

2. Which of the following is not considered a subcortical dementia?

    a. Alzheimer's disease.
    b. Huntington's disease.
    c. Parkinson's disease.
    d. Creutzfeldt-Jacob disease.

3. Parkinsonism can be caused by:

    a. Parkinson's disease.
    b. encephalitis.
    c. carbon monoxide poisoning.
    d. All of the above.

4. Parkinsonism is characterized by:

    a. aphasia.
    b. rigidity.
    c. psychosis.
    d. loss of vision.

5. Parkinson's disease peaks between the ages of:

    a. 40-50.
    b. 50-54.
    c. 56-60.
    d. 60-64.

6. Parkinson's disease is characterized by:

    a. loss of pigmentation in the substantia nigra.
    b. loss of dopaminergic cells in the substantia nigra.
    c. Lewy bodies in the substantia nigra.
    d. All of the above.

7. Which of the following may be one of the first symptoms noticed by an individual with Parkinson's disease?

    a.   Resting tremor.
    b.   Masked face.
    c.   Depression.
    d.   Cogwheel rigidity.

8. Which of the following is considered a positive symptom of Parkinson's disease?

    a.   Resting tremor.
    b.   Bradykinesia.
    c.   Gait disturbance.
    d.   Hypokinesia.

9. The poverty of movement observed in individuals with Parkinson's disease is also referred to as:

    a.   hypokinesia.
    b.   bradykinesia.
    c.   cogwheel rigidity.
    d.   masked face.

10. The rapid, small steps taken by individuals with Parkinson's disease are referred to as:

    a.   hypokinesia.
    b.   migrographia.
    c.   festinating.
    d.   bradykinesia.

11. Which of the following is a problem commonly experienced by individuals with Parkinson's disease?

    a.   Visual acuity.
    b.   Abstract reasoning.
    c.   Aphasia.
    d.   Changing mental set.

12. The low voice amplitude and lack of vocal emotional expression observed in individuals with Parkinson's disease is referred to as:

    a.   festinating.
    b.   dysphonia.
    c.   palilalia.
    d.   tachiphemia.

13. The segmented accelerated bursts of speech observed in individuals with Parkinson's disease are referred to as:

    a.   festinating.
    b.   dysphonia.
    c.   palilalia.
    d.   tachiphemia.

14. The compulsive word or phrase repetition observed in individuals with Parkinson's disease is referred to as:

    a.   festinating.
    b.   dysphonia.
    c.   palilalia.
    d.   tachiphemia.

15. Which of the following is the most common memory deficit observed in individuals with Parkinson's disease?

    a.   Free recall.
    b.   Recognition.
    c.   Digit repetition.
    d.   Verbal priming.

16. Which of the following was the first documented treatment for Parkinson's disease?

    a.   Pallidotomy.
    b.   Levodopa.
    c.   Anticholinergics.
    d.   Thalotomy.

17. Side effects of dopaminergic medications include:

    a.   hypomania.
    b.   sleep disturbance.
    c.   perceptual disturbances.
    d.   All of the above.

18. Which of the following is a risk involved with pallidotomy surgery?

    a.   Blindness.
    b.   Memory difficulty and confusion.
    c.   Speech dysfunction.
    d.   None of the above.

19. Which of the following statements is true regarding dopaminergic medications?

    a.   Dopaminergic medications are an effective cure for Parkinson's disease for most patients.

    b.   Dopaminergic medications are a time-limited treatment for the motor symptoms of Parkinson's disease.

    c.   Dopaminergic medications, while not a cure, effectively manage motor symptoms of the disease for the life of most Parkinson's patients.

    d.   Dopaminergic medications are no longer used because they are not the cure they were once believed to be.

20. Why was the pallidotomy discontinued in the 1960s?

    a.   The surgery resulted in an unacceptable number of premature deaths in Parkinson's patients.

    b.   The surgery did not have a significant impact on the motor symptoms of Parkinson's patients.

    c.   The surgery was ruled unethical by the American Medical Association.

    d.   Doctors thought that levodopa would eliminate the need for brain surgery.

21. Huntington's disease impacts the:

    a.   prefrontal cortex.
    b.   globus pallidus.
    c.   caudate nucleus.
    d.   substantia nigra.

22. Huntington's disease is:

    a.   hereditary.
    b.   caused by a virus.
    c.   caused by eating infected neural tissue.
    d.   None of the above.

23. Which of the following difficulties is observed in individuals with Huntington's disease?

    a.   Recognition memory deficits.
    b.   Perseveration.
    c.   Receptive aphasia.
    d.   Expressive aphasia.

24. Which of the following is higher in Huntington's disease than in other degenerative disorders?

    a.   Co-occurrence of Alzheimer's disease.
    b.   Risk of developing pica.
    c.   Risk of developing anorexia nervosa.
    d.   Suicide rate.

25. Which of the following is seen in both Huntington's and Parkinson's patients?

    a.   Motor slowness.
    b.   Wide gait.
    c.   Dysarthric speech quality.
    d.   None of the above.

26. Which of the following diseases is the rarest?

    a.   Alzheimer's disease.
    b.   Parkinson's disease.
    c.   Huntington's disease.
    d.   Creutzfeldt-Jacob disease.

27. Which of the following is the most quickly progressing dementia?

    a.   Alzheimer's disease.
    b.   Parkinson's disease.
    c.   Huntington's disease.
    d.   Creutzfeldt-Jacob disease.

28. Which of the following is a disease contracted by cannibalism?

    a.   Creutzfeldt-Jacob disease.
    b.   Kuru.
    c.   Gerstmann-Straussler-Scheinker syndrome.
    d.   Huntington's disease.

29. Mad cow disease is synonymous with:

    a.   bovine spongiform encephalopathy.
    b.   Kuru.
    c.   scrapie.
    d.   cow tipping.

30. Spongiform encephalopathy is so termed because:

    a.   of the holes in the brains of patients.
    b.   a sponge is constantly needed to keep patients clean.
    c.   the brains of patients swell when water is added.
    d.   None of the above.

31. What is the focus of current research with regards to spongiform encephalopathies?

    a.   Cannibilistic tribes of New Guinea.
    b.   Prions.
    c.   Amyloid plaques.
    d.   Really angry cows.

32. Which of the following is a motor symptom observed in individuals with Creutzfeldt-Jacob disease?

     a.   A "drunk" stagger.
     b.   Slurred speech.
     c.   Uncoordinated movements.
     d.   All of the above.

33. Once the dementing process has begun in individuals with Creutzfeldt-Jacob disease or Kuru, approximately how rapidly does it progress?

     a.   One month.
     b.   Three-four months.
     c.   Two years.
     d.   Three-four years.

Essay Questions

1.   Compare and contrast the etiology and neuropsychological symptoms of Parkinson's disease, Huntington's disease, and Creutzfeldt-Jacob disease.

2.   Discuss the treatments available for Parkinson's disease.

3.   If you were at risk of developing Huntington's disease, would you want to be tested to know if you would develop the disease and why?

Answer Key

Chapter Exercises

1. Rigidity (p.388)
2. Anti-cholinergics (p.391)
3. Memory (p.390)
4. Micrographia (p.387)
5. Dysphonia (p.390)
6. subcortical dementia (p.384)
7. Pallidotomy (p.392)
8. resting tremor (p.386)
9. Masked face (p.387)
10. Tachiphemia (p.390)
11. festinating gait (p.387)
12. Parkinsonism (p.384)
13. Hypokinesia (p.387)
14. Thalotomy (p.392)
15. Lewy bodies (p.385)
16. visuospatial (p.389)
17. Bradykinesia (p.387)
18. Palilalia (p.390)
19. executive function (p.389)
20. True (p.393)
21. False (p.393)
22. False (p.393)
23. False (p.393)
24. True (p.393)
25. True (p.396)
26. True (p.396)
27. True (pp.395,396)
28. False (p.396)
29. False (p.397)
30. False (p.397)
31. True (p.397)
32. True (p.397)
33. True (p.398)
34. True (p.398)
35. True (p.398)
36. False (p.398)
37. True (p.398)
38. False (p.399)
39. True (p.399)
40. True (p.399)
41. True (p.400)
42. False (p.401)

Post-Test

Multiple Choice

1. D (p.384)
2. A (p.383)
3. D (p.383)
4. B (p.383)
5. D (p.384)
6. D (pp.385,386)
7. C (p.386)
8. A (p.387)
9. B (p.387)
10. C (p.387)
11. D (p.389)
12. B (p.390)
13. D (p.390)
14. C (p.390)
15. A (p.390)
16. C (p.391)
17. D (p.392)
18. B (p.392)
19. B (p.392)
20. D (p.391)
21. C (p.393)
22. A (p.393)
23. B (p.397)
24. D (p.397)
25. A (p.398)
26. D (p.398)
27. D (p.398)
28. B (p.399)
29. A (p.399)
30. A (p.398)
31. B (pp.400,401)
32. D (p.401)
33. B (p.401)

Chapter 13

Disorders of the Brain
Alterations of Consciousness

Chapter Outline

Overview

In this chapter both normal and abnormal alterations of conscious alertness are examined, including sleep and seizure disorders. In sleep, circadian rhythms fluctuate throughout the day and night. These daily rhythms, as people move from waking to sleeping and dreaming, provide lessons for the study of the limits of normal brain alterations of consciousness. Disruptions in the flow of these rhythms can result in a variety of sleep disorders, which often result in some type of cognitive disruption. Seizures represent yet another set of disorders of consciousness. Seizures are the outward behavioral manifestation of excessive, excitatory, synchronous neuronal firing. The behavioral symptoms of seizures are related to the scope and the location of the brain focus. Seizure events of various types represent alterations of consciousness affecting daytime alertness. While seizures can occur as a result of a variety of causes, most people with repeat seizures are considered to have an epileptic syndrome, which is potentially more threatening to brain functioning than an isolated seizure event. The neuroanatomy and neurophysiology of epilepsy is discussed as well as the neuropsychological consequences and types of treatments available. Neuropsychologists are active in the assessment of cognitive dysfunction associated with sleep disorders, and the assessment and treatment planning of seizure patients for surgical evaluations. The inherent complexities in studying alterations of consciousness in the human brain present both the most complex and perhaps the most interesting aspects of neuropsychology.

Learning Objectives

- To understand and appreciate both normal and abnormal alterations of consciousness in the human brain.
- To learn the basic stages of sleep and associated disorders.
- To be able to classify the different types of seizure disorders and identify their neuropsychological manifestations.

Rhythms of Consciousness

Key Terms and Concepts

agnosia	neglect	synthesthesia	circadian
epileptic syndrome	ultradian	REM	

Sentence Completion

1. _____ rhythms are reflected in daily levels of consciousness.

2. The dreaming stage of sleep is synonymous with _____.

3. _____ reflects an unawareness of one side of the body.

4. Individuals with a seizure disorder are said to have an _____.

5. A visual _____ would be exhibited by an inability to recognize an object.

6. _____ represents an alteration in the integration of sensory-perceptual experiences.

7. _____ rhythms are reflected in short cycles of approximately 90 minutes.

The Brain and Mind in Sleep

<u>Key Terms and Concepts</u>

NREM	suprachiasmatic nucleus	reticular activating system
atonia	benzodiazepines	lucid dreaming
obstructive sleep apnea	central sleep apnea	uvulopalotopharyngoplasty
narcolepsy	cataplexy	hypnagogic hallucinations
sleep paralysis		

<u>True/False</u>

8._____   Delta waves occur during the deepest stage of sleep.

9._____   Individuals wake easily out of Stage 4 sleep.

10._____   NREM sleep is comprised of four stages.

11._____   Sleepwalking occurs during REM sleep.

12._____   50% of sleep in adults is spent in REM sleep.

13._____   Time spent in Stage 4 sleep decreases with age.

14._____   Both male and female sexual response is increased in REM sleep.

15._____   The suprachiasmatic nucleus of the hypothalamus regulates the sleep/wake cycle.

16._____   The ventrolateral preoptic area is less active during sleep than wakefulness.

17._____   REM sleep occurs approximately every 60 minutes.

18._____   The reticular activating system is thought to initiate REM sleep.

19._____   During dreams the occipital cortex is activated as if we were "watching" our dreams.

20._____   Paralysis during REM sleep is believed to protect individuals from acting out their dreams while asleep.

21._____   An increase in muscle tone is called atonia.

22._____   During REM sleep norepinephrine and serotonin levels in the brain are decreased.

23._____   REM sleep is thought to assist in memory consolidation.

24._____   The hippocampus produces theta waves during Stage 4 and REM sleep.

25._____   Deprivation of REM sleep results in increased learning of a task.

26._____   Benzodiazepines are prescribed primarily for anxiety and sleep disturbances.

27._____   Benzodiazepine use has not been associated with memory difficulty.

28._____   50% of dreams are disturbing, with the most reported themes being falling or being chased.

29._____   Most current dream theorists agree with Freud's original dream theories regarding sex and aggression.

30._____   The current view of dream analysis is that dreams must be interpreted by a psychoanalyst.

31._____   Dreams are felt to be a reflection of current life events and emotional states.

32._____   Lucid dreaming is synonymous to day dreaming.

33._____   Adults are more likely to experience lucid dreaming than children.

34._____   During lucid dreams, individuals have access to memories.

35._____   Sleep apnea is a rare disorder.

36._____   Sleep apnea is characterized by the disruption of breathing during sleep.

37._____   Sleep apnea is diagnosed when an individual is awakened secondary to apnea 10 times an hour during the night.

38._____   Obstructive sleep apnea may occur following a collapse of the upper airway.

39._____   In central sleep apnea, breathing disruptions are the direct result of neurological dysfunction.

40._____   Sleep apnea is not known to result in cognitive deficits.

41._____   Females are more likely than males to experience sleep apnea.

42._____   Sleep apnea can result in hypoxia.

43._____   The continuous positive airway pressure (CPAP) device is a cure for sleep apnea.

44._____   A uvulopalotopharyngoplasty involves the removal of the uvula.

45._____   Narcolepsy is characterized by daytime episodes of spontaneous sleep.

46._____   Aside from the "sleep attacks" during the day, individuals with narcolepsy do not experience other difficulties with the sleep-wake cycle.

47._____   Cataplexy may result in falls.

48._____   Cataplexy is associated with Stage 4 sleep.

49._____ Hypnagogic hallucinations are always of an anxiety-producing topic.

50._____ Sleep paralysis occurs when an individual is asleep and thus they have no conscious awareness of the experience.

51._____ Narcolepsy is a form of epilepsy.

The Runaway Brain: Seizure Disorders

Key Terms and Concepts

partial seizure	generalized seizure	tonic
clonic	aura	prodromal phase
postictal	automatisms	simple seizures
secondarily generalized seizure	Jacksonian seizures	complex partial seizures
temporal lobe epilepsy	eliptogenic	nucleus reticularis thalami
Wada test		

True/False

52._____ Partial seizures result when the entire brain is involved.

53._____ Generalized seizures result when the abnormal neuronal firing is confined to a specific brain region.

54._____ Tonic refers to the stiffening of the body.

55._____ Clonic refers to the "jerking" motions exhibited by individuals experiencing a seizure.

56._____ An aura may be represented by an unpleasant smell.

57._____ During the prodromal phase, or aura, some individuals are able to halt a seizure.

58._____ The phase following a seizure is referred to as postictal.

59._____ Abrupt limpness or loss of muscle tone is referred to as atonia.

60._____ Automatisms may be observed in absence seizures.

61._____ Absence seizures are more common in children than in adults.

62._____ Partial seizures may evolve into generalized seizures.

63._____ There are three main types of partial seizures, simple, secondarily generalized, and complex partial.

64._____ Simple seizures may be classified in some individuals as an aura.

65._____ A complex partial seizure begins as a simple seizure and spreads, eventually generalizing to the entire brain.

66._____ Temporal lobe epilepsy is typically exhibited through complex partial seizures.

67._____   Complex partial seizures usually emanate from the frontal lobes.

68._____   The most common emotional sensation experienced in conjunction with a complex partial seizure is fear.

69._____   During a complex partial seizure, it is possible for an individual to walk around.

70._____   The eliptogenic focus refers to the site of onset of seizure activity.

71._____   EEG is used to localize seizure focus.

72._____   All seizures can be localized.

73._____   Disruption in the thalamocortical circuitry has been attributed to absence seizures.

74._____   The nucleus reticularis thalami is able to influence both cerebral hemispheres.

75._____   The Wada test is used as a means to localize language and memory to one cerebral hemisphere and thus determine the effect removing specific brain tissue will have on functional outcome.

76._____   Emotional disturbances and memory deficits are common in individuals with complex partial seizures involving the temporal lobe.

77._____   Absence seizures are best treated by anticonvulsants which prolong the inhibitory action of GABA in the brain.

78._____   Neurosurgery for seizure disorders involves removing the eliptogenic focus.

79._____   Countering an aura consisting of an unpleasant smell with that of a pleasant smell usually causes increased seizure activity.

Post-Test
Multiple Choice

1. An agnosia may occur in which sensory modality?

    a. Visual.
    b. Auditory.
    c. Olfactory.
    d. All sensory modalities.

2. An example of neglect would be:

    a. the inability to recognize an object visually.
    b. the unawareness of specific smells.
    c. the unawareness of one side of the body.
    d. the inability to recognize any smells.

3. Alterations of consciousness during the day and night occur as the result of _____ rhythms.

    a. ultradian
    b. circadian
    c. psychological
    d. reggae

4. Individuals who experience repeated seizures have:

    a. an epileptic syndrome.
    b. a traumatic brain injury.
    c. mental retardation.
    d. hydrocephalus.

5. Ninety minute rhythms which occur in humans are referred to as:

    a. ultradian.
    b. circadian.
    c. synthesthetic.
    d. agnostic.

6. A means of studying brain activity through brain wave frequencies is called:

    a. Magnetic Resonance Imaging.
    b. Positron Emission Tomography.
    c. Computerized Axial Tomography.
    d. Electroencephalogram Monitoring.

7. During REM, individuals are:

    a.   awake.
    b.   in a coma.
    c.   dreaming.
    d.   meditating.

8. Which of the following characterizes the deepest stage of sleep?

    a.   Alpha waves.
    b.   Theta waves.
    c.   K complexes.
    d.   Delta waves.

9. REM stands for:

    a.   Rhythmic Eye Movement.
    b.   Rapid Eye Movement.
    c.   Rhythmic Electrical Measurement.
    d.   Real Extreme Mindmeld.

10. As a person falls to sleep, which of the following statements is true?

    a.   EEG pattern moves from low amplitude fast waves to high amplitude slow waves.
    b.   EEG pattern moves from high amplitude slow waves to low amplitude fast waves.
    c.   EEG pattern moves from low amplitude slow waves to high amplitude fast waves.
    d.   None of the above.

11. What percentage of time is spent in Stage 1 sleep?

    a.   5%.
    b.   10%.
    c.   25%.
    d.   45%.

12. What percentage of time is spent in REM sleep?

    a.   5%.
    b.   10%.
    c.   25%.
    d.   45%.

13. During REM sleep:

      a.   the body is active and may kick (nocturnal myoclonus).
      b.   theta waves are prominent.
      c.   the body is paralyzed.
      d.   delta waves are prominent.

14. In adults, the proportion of NREM sleep to REM sleep in any given night is approximately:

      a.   50:50.
      b.   25:75.
      c.   75:25.
      d.   10:90.

15. In infants, the proportion of NREM sleep to REM sleep in any given night is approximately:

      a.   50:50.
      b.   25:75.
      c.   75:25.
      d.   10:90.

16. In the elderly, which stages of sleep become sparse or non-existent?

      a.   Stages 1, 2 and REM.
      b.   Stages 1, 4 and REM.
      c.   Stages 3, 4 and REM.
      d.   Stage 4 and REM.

17. Which of the following occurs during Stage 4 sleep?

      a.   The immune system is active.
      b.   Delta waves are prominent.
      c.   Growth hormone is released.
      d.   All of the above.

18. The suprachiasmic nucleus of the hypothalamus is thought to:

      a.   function as a circadian clock.
      b.   function as an ultradian clock.
      c.   function as an initiator of Stage 1 sleep.
      d.   function as an initiator of REM sleep.

19. Without cues from the sun, how long would daily sleep-wake cycles be in humans?

     a.   12 hours.
     b.   24 hours.
     c.   25 hours.
     d.   30 hours.

20. In extreme cases, disruption of the sleep-wake cycle can result in:

     a.   improved cognition.
     b.   adjustment to the disruption, ultimately leading to the ability to function indefinitely with no sleep.
     c.   death.
     d.   None of the above.

21. Which of the following is thought to play a role in initiating sleep onset?

     a.   thalamocortical loop.
     b.   ventrolateral preoptic area.
     c.   Factor S.
     d.   All of the above.

22. During the night, REM sleep occurs every _____ minutes.

     a.   20
     b.   30
     c.   60
     d.   90

23. What is responsible for the activation and deactivation of REM sleep?

     a.   Factor S.
     b.   Reticular Activating System.
     c.   Ventrolateral Preoptic Area.
     d.   Thalamocortical Loop.

24. The reticular activating system is located in the:

     a.   thalamus.
     b.   hypothalamus.
     c.   temporal lobe.
     d.   brain stem.

25. Which of the following areas of the brain are activated during REM sleep?

      a.   occipital lobe.
      b.   hippocampus.
      c.   medulla.
      d.   All of the above.

26. During REM sleep:

      a.   serotonin is decreased.
      b.   norepinephrine is increased.
      c.   acetylcholine is decreased.
      d.   there are no changes associated with neurotransmitters.

27. Long-term potentiation in the hippocampus occurs during the production of _____ rhythms.

      a.   alpha.
      b.   theta.
      c.   delta.
      d.   All of the above.

28. During sleep, new information is:

      a.   not interfered with, thus facilitating memory consolidation.
      b.   reprocessed and strengthened, thus facilitating memory consolidation.
      c.   placed in temporary storage for use the next day, thus facilitating memory consolidation.
      d.   forgotten at a higher rate than when awake because it cannot be consciously integrated.

29. REM sleep:

      a.   facilitates new learning.
      b.   interferes with new learning.
      c.   has no impact on new learning.
      d.   None of the above.

30. Sleeping pills:

      a.   have no impact on memory.
      b.   enhance memory.
      c.   can cause anterograde amnesia.
      d.   can cause retrograde amnesia.

31. Which neurotransmitter is most affected by benzodiazepines?

    a.   Serotonin.
    b.   Acetylcholine.
    c.   Norepinephrine.
    d.   Gamma-aminobutyric acid.

32. What is it called when an individual is awakened by a terrifying dream?

    a.   Nightmare.
    b.   Panic Disorder.
    c.   Sleep Anxiety Attack.
    d.   Post-Traumatic Stress Disorder.

33. Psychological functions of dreams are currently believed to be:

    a.   the representation of unconscious aggressive and sexual urges.
    b.   the "cleansing" of the brain of unnecessary information.
    c.   the representation of conscious aggressive and sexual urges.
    d.   the representation of current life experiences and emotional states.

34. Conscious knowledge that one is dreaming is called:

    a.   conscious dreaming.
    b.   lucid dreaming.
    c.   day dreaming.
    d.   impossible.

35. During lucid dreams, the dreamer:

    a.   knows he/she is dreaming and can control the length of REM sleep as a result.
    b.   has control over the outcome of his/her dreams.
    c.   has access to available waking thoughts and memories.
    d.   is in Stage 4 sleep.

36. _____ is the most common disorder evaluated in Sleep Disorder Centers.

    a.   Narcolepsy
    b.   Sleep apnea
    c.   Cataplexy
    d.   Sleep paralysis

37. How many times during an hour must loss of breath and subsequent awakening occur for a diagnosis of sleep apnea?

    a.   1.
    b.   5.
    c.   10.
    d.   20.

38. The most serious complication related to sleep apnea is:

    a.   disruption in the normal stages of sleep.
    b.   headaches.
    c.   insomnia.
    d.   heart failure.

39. When the body weight of an individual impairs respiration during sleep, _____ occurs.

    a.   central sleep apnea.
    b.   peripheral sleep apnea.
    c.   obstructive sleep apnea.
    d.   hypertension.

40. When the brain fails to send necessary neurological messages to regulate breathing, _____ occurs.

    a.   central sleep apnea.
    b.   peripheral sleep apnea.
    c.   obstructive sleep apnea.
    d.   hypertension.

41. Neuropsychological problems associated with sleep apnea include:

    a.   visual disturbances.
    b.   memory problems.
    c.   decreased motor speed.
    d.   problems with expressive speech.

42. Which of the following are risk factors for sleep apnea?

    a.   Age.
    b.   Gender.
    c.   Weight.
    d.   All of the above.

43. The nasal continuous positive airway pressure (CPAP) device is:

    a.   surgically inserted in the upper airway to prevent obstructive sleep apnea.
    b.   worn at night to maintain upper airway flow during sleep.
    c.   utilized following uvulopalotopharyngoplasty.
    d.   considered a cure for sleep apnea.

44. Spontaneous sleep which occurs during periods of wakefulness is called:

    a.   cataplexy.
    b.   narcolepsy.
    c.   sleep apnea.
    d.   excessive daytime sleepiness.

45. Sudden episodes of loss of muscle tone are called:

    a.   cataplexy.
    b.   narcolepsy.
    c.   sleep apnea.
    d.   excessive daytime sleepiness.

46. Cataplectic attacks are most likely to occur during:

    a.   sleep.
    b.   periods of restfulness.
    c.   consumption of food.
    d.   an angry episode.

47. Cataplexy is associated with:

    a.   Stage 1 sleep.
    b.   Stage 3 sleep.
    c.   Stage 4 sleep.
    d.   REM sleep.

48. Hypnagogic hallucinations occur during:

    a.   dreams.
    b.   awakening from the night's sleep.
    c.   the transition from wakefulness to sleep.
    d.   nightmares.

49. Sleep paralysis occurs during:

    a.   periods of full wakefulness.
    b.   the transition from sleep to wakefulness.
    c.   Stage 3 sleep.
    d.   Stage 4 sleep.

50. Seizures during which the abnormal neural firing is confined to a specific area are called:

    a.   partial seizures.
    b.   generalized seizures.
    c.   absence seizures.
    d.   secondarily generalized seizures.

51. Seizures which involve the entire brain are called:

    a.   partial seizures.
    b.   generalized seizures.
    c.   temporal lobe epilepsy.
    d.   focal seizures.

52. What percentage of people report an aura prior to a seizure?

    a.   10%
    b.   30%
    c.   50%
    d.   70%

53. Which of the following is an example of an aura?

    a.   Stiffening of the body (tonic).
    b.   Jerking of the body (clonic).
    c.   Loss of consciousness.
    d.   Olfactory hallucination.

54. The period following a seizure is termed:

    a.   prodromal.
    b.   postictal.
    c.   postseizure.
    d.   the aura.

55. Stiffening of the body, jaw clenching, and a blue appearance to the face signify which type of seizure?

    a.   Complex partial.
    b.   Absence.
    c.   Focal.
    d.   Generalized.

56. Absence seizures are most likely to occur in which of the following age groups?

    a.   Infancy to 4 years.
    b.   4-14 years.
    c.   14-18 years.
    d.   Elderly.

57. Involuntary head turning, with no other symptoms, is likely to signify which type of seizure?

    a.   Simple.
    b.   Secondarily generalized.
    c.   Jacksonian.
    d.   Generalized.

58. A seizure which begins as simple jerking of an extremity but evolves into an episode represented by tonic and clonic symptomatology is likely a:

    a.   simple seizure.
    b.   generalized seizure.
    c.   secondarily generalized seizure.
    d.   absence seizure.

59. A seizure characterized by lip smacking and a feeling of fear, is likely a:

    a.   simple seizure.
    b.   generalized seizure.
    c.   complex partial seizure.
    d.   marching seizure.

60. What percentage of the population of the United States will experience at least one seizure in their lifetime?

    a.   1.2%
    b.   2.2%
    c.   5.2%
    d.   10.2%

61. During a complex partial seizure an individual may:

    a.   have a sense of déjà vu.
    b.   laugh.
    c.   wander around.
    d.   All of the above.

62. The eliptogenic focus is:

     a.   the neurological tissue which is affected by seizure activity.
     b.   the neuroanatomical site of seizure onset.
     c.   the abnormal concentration of neurotransmitters involved in any given seizure.
     d.   None of the above.

63. Seizures occur due to:

     a.   excessive inhibitory synchronous neuronal firing.
     b.   excessive inhibitory asynchronous neuronal firing.
     c.   excessive excitatory synchronous neuronal firing.
     d.   excessive excitatory asynchronous neuronal firing.

64. Which mechanism is implicated in absence seizures?

     a.   Suprachiasmic nucleus of the hypothalamus.
     b.   Reticular activating system.
     c.   Thalamocortical loop.
     d.   Brain stem.

65. Which neurotransmitter is implicated in absence seizures?

     a.   Serotonin.
     b.   Norepinephrine.
     c.   Gamma-aminobutyric acid.
     d.   None of the above.

66. Which neuropsychological ability is most likely to be preserved in individuals with complex partial seizures?

     a.   Memory.
     b.   Attention.
     c.   Language.
     d.   Motor skills.

67. The Wada test consists of:

     a.   EEG monitoring in order to localize seizure focus.
     b.   a clinical interview of the patient in order to establish a thorough history of the seizure disorder.
     c.   testing one cerebral hemisphere at a time to determine lateralization of memory and language.
     d.   surgical removal of epileptic tissue.

68. Seizures may be experienced secondary to:

    a.   alcohol withdrawal.
    b.   sleep deprivation.
    c.   high degrees of stress.
    d.   All of the above.

69. Treatment for epilepsy includes:

    a.   anticonvulsant medication.
    b.   neurosurgery.
    c.   stress management.
    d.   All of the above.

Essay Questions

1.   Discuss the purposes of both REM and Stage 4 sleep.

2.   Describe the characteristics of sleep apnea and narcolepsy as well as treatment options for both disorders.

3.   Discuss neuropsychological problems experienced by individuals with various types of seizures.

Answer Key

Chapter Exercises

1. Circadian (p.408)
2. REM (p.409)
3. Neglect (p.407)
4. epileptic syndrome (p.407)
5. agnosia (p.407)
6. Synthesthesia (p.407)
7. Ultradian (p.408)
8. True (p.409)
9. False (p.410)
10. True (p.410)
11. False (p.411)
12. False (p.412)
13. True (p.412)
14. True (p.411)
15. True (p.413)
16. False (p.414)
17. False (p.415)
18. True (p.415)
19. True (p.416)
20. True (p.416)
21. False (p.416)
22. True (p.416)
23. True (p.417)
24. False (p.417)
25. False (p.417)
26. True (p.418)
27. False (p.418)
28. False (p.420)
29. False (p.420)
30. False (p.420)
31. True (p.421)
32. False (p.422)
33. False (p.422)
34. True (p.423)
35. False (p.421)
36. True (p.421)
37. False (p.421)
38. True (p.423)
39. True (p.423)
40. False (p.423)
41. False (p.424)
42. True (p.424)
43. False (p.424)
44. True (p.424)
45. True (p.424)
46. False (p.424)
47. True (p.424)
48. False (p.425)
49. False (p.425)
50. False (p.425)
51. False (p.425)
52. False (p.425)
53. False (p.425)
54. True (p.426)
55. True (p.426)
56. True (p.426)
57. True (p.426)
58. True (p.426)
59. True (p.427)
60. True (p.427)
61. True (p.427)
62. True (p.427)
63. True (p.428)
64. True (p.428)
65. False (p.428)
66. True (p.428)
67. False (p.428)
68. True (p.430)
69. True (pp.430,431)
70. True (p.428)
71. True (p.428)
72. False (p.428)
73. True (p.429)
74. True (p.429)
75. True (p.432)
76. True (p.432)
77. False (p.433)
78. True (p.433)
79. False (p.433)

Post-Test

Multiple Choice

1.   A (p.407)
2.   C (p.407)
3.   B (p.407)
4.   A (p.407)
5.   A (p.408)
6.   D (p.408)
7.   C (p.409)
8.   D (p.409)
9.   B (p.410)
10. A (p.411)
11. A (p.410)
12. C (p.410)
13. C (p.411)
14. C (p.411)
15. A (p.412)
16. D (p.412)
17. D (p.412)
18. A (p.413)
19. C (p.413)
20. C (p.414)
21. D (pp.414,415)
22. D (p.415)
23. B (p.415)
24. D (p.415)
25. D (p.416)
26. A (pp.416,417)
27. B (p.417)
28. B (p.417)
29. A (p.417)
30. C (p.418)
31. D (p.419)
32. C (p.420)
33. D (pp.420,421)
34. B (p.422)
35. C (p.423)
36. B (p.421)
37. B (p.421)
38. D (p.424)
39. C (p.423)
40. A (p.423)
41. B (p.423)
42. D (p.424)
43. B (p.424)
44. B (p.424)

45. A (p.424)
46. D (p.425)
47. D (p.425)
48. C (p.425)
49. B (p.425)
50. A (p.425)
51. B (p.425)
52. D (p.426)
53. D (p.426)
54. B (p.426)
55. D (p.427)
56. B (p.427)
57. A (p.428)
58. C (p.428)
59. C (p.428)
60. B (p.430)
61. D (p.430)
62. B (p.428)
63. C (p.429)
64. C (p.429)
65. C (p.429)
66. B (p.432)
67. C (p.432)
68. D (p.432)
69. D (p.433)

Chapter 14

Neuropsychology in Practice
Neuropsychological Assessment

Chapter Overview

Overview

This chapter focuses on an overview of neuropsychological assessment, including the underlying assumptions, the evaluation process, and specific neuropsychological techniques. Simply put, the neuropsychological evaluation is a method of examining the brain by studying its behavioral product. Similar to other psychological assessments, neuropsychological evaluations involve the comprehensive study of behavior by means of standardized tests that are sensitive to brain-behavior relationships. In effect, the neuropsychological exam offers an understanding of the relationship between the structure and the function of the nervous system. Thus, the goal of the clinical neuropsychological exam is to be able to evaluate the full range of basic abilities represented in the brain. In practice, the neuropsychological assessment is multidimensional (i.e., concerned with evaluating many different aspects of neurofunctioning from basic to complex), reliable (i.e., stable across different situations and time), and valid (i.e., meaningful). Neuropsychological assessment has become one of the primary aspects of what neuropsychologists do. The many different facets of neuropsychological testing have made this area of neuropsychology one of the most interesting and dynamic ones.

Learning Objectives

- To understand the different psychometric concepts of reliability, validity, and base rates in neuropsychological assessment.
- To be able to review the different functional areas of neuropsychological assessment, including orientation, motor, and so on.
- To learn how traditional psychological testing, including intelligence and personality testing, is used in neuropsychological diagnosis and evaluation.

General Considerations in Neuropsychological Testing

True/False

1._____   Approximately 50% of neuropsychologists work in rehabilitation hospitals.

2._____   Neuropsychologists who are in private practice generally devote all of their time to neuropsychological evaluation and diagnosis.

3._____   Within a medical facility, the neuropsychologist typically engages mostly in neuropsychological evaluation, diagnosis, and intervention.

4._____   Within a medical facility, the neuropsychologist typically does not get involved in research.

5._____   Within a rehabilitation hospital, the neuropsychologist plays a prominent role in the remediation of cognitive difficulties related to brain impairment.

6._____   The largest patient population seen by neuropsychologists is that of learning disabilities.

7._____   More than half of all neuropsychological evaluations are for diagnostic purposes.

8._____   Neuropsychological evaluations are conducted for diagnostic and descriptive purposes.

9._____   A neuropsychological evaluation is a subjective assessment of cognition and behavior.

10. _____ The neuropsychological evaluation is often integrated with information collected from other medical specialties, such as neurology.

11. _____ One of the advantages of neuropsychological testing is that it is non-invasive and does not present a medical risk to the patient.

12. _____ Neuropsychological evaluations are relatively short and take approximately one hour on average to administer.

13. _____ A neuropsychological evaluation can differentiate between focal and diffuse brain impairment.

14. _____ Vocational potential can be assessed via a neuropsychological evaluation.

15. _____ A neuropsychological evaluation is the best way to assess for the presence of a brain tumor.

Psychometric Issues in Neuropsychological Assessment

Key Terms and Concepts

psychometrics   standardized test   reliability
validity   construct validity   content validity
criterion validity false positive   base rate

Matching

16. General meaningfulness of test interpretation.   a. base rate

17. The degree to which a test is related to a particular outcome.   b. psychometrics

18. Allows for systematic comparison between groups of individuals.   c. content validity

19. The detection of brain impairment in a non-impaired individual.   d. reliability

20. The science of measuring human traits and abilities.   e. false positive

21. The frequency of a given disorder in a specified population.   f. criterion validity

22. Ability of a test to measure a given psychological characteristic.   g. validity

23. Consistency of a psychological test upon repeated measurement of the same individual.   h. standardized test

24. The degree to which items of a test are representative of the behavior the test is supposed to measure.   i. construct validity

276

Neuropsychological Tests

<u>Key Terms and Concepts</u>

achievement tests	behavioral-adaptive scales	intelligence tests
neuropsychological tests	personality tests	vocational inventories
crystallized functions	fluid functions	orientation
sensation	perception	motor apraxia
ideomotor apraxia	dysgraphia	dyslexia
spelling dyspraxia	attention/concentration	language functions
visual-spatial abilities	memory	judgment/problem solving

<u>True/False</u>

25._____ An achievement test predicts what a patient will be able to accomplish in the future.

26._____ Behavioral-adaptive scales can measure activities of daily living in traumatically brain injured individuals.

27._____ An intelligence test measures both verbal and performance abilities.

28._____ A neuropsychological test measures changes in brain function.

29._____ A personality test measures intelligence in relation to emotional factors.

30._____ Vocational inventories measure an individual's interest in a certain occupation.

31._____ Fluid neuropsychological functions are strongly related to cultural factors and learning.

32._____ Crystallized neuropsychological functions are hypothesized to be independent of cultural factors and learning.

33._____ Spelling and factual information are considered crystallized functions.

34._____ Neuropsychologists typically use intelligence tests in conjunction with other tests within a test battery.

35._____ Orientation refers to level of awareness.

36._____ If an individual is oriented times three, it means they know who they are, who their family is, and where they are.

37._____ Following a traumatic brain injury, the GOAT is often administered.

38._____ The GOAT can only be administered one time a week to any given patient so that the patient cannot remember the answers and invalidate the test results.

39._____ A score of 10 on the GOAT is considered a "good" score.

40._____ Hearing your professor lecturing is considered a sensation.

41._____ Hearing your professor and knowing that he/she is "full of it" is considered a perception.

42._____ Sensory-perceptual tests may include visual, auditory, and tactile components.

43._____   There is one distinct form of attention.

44._____   Sustained attention is the ability to concentrate over a period of time.

45._____   Both auditory and visual attention can be measured by neuropsychologists.

46._____   Neuropsychologists are interested in simple and complex motor skills.

47._____   In order to measure graphomotor skills, neuropsychologists ask patients to draw complex figures.

48._____   Motor apraxia refers to the inability to speak.

49._____   The inability to perform motor sequences is referred to as ideomotor apraxia.

50._____   Neuropsychologists test both receptive and expressive language abilities.

51._____   A person with dysgraphia has problems reading.

52._____   A person with spelling dyspraxia is likely to have excellent spelling abilities.

53._____   Dyslexia is a disorder of reading skills.

54._____   The Token Test measures expressive language abilities.

55._____   The Controlled Oral Word Association Test measures receptive language abilities.

56._____   A neuropsychologist may measure spatial orientation, facial recognition, spatial organization, and visual sequencing in order to adequately measure visual-spatial abilities.

57._____   The Token Test and the Rey-Osterrieth Complex Figure Test are common tests used to assess visual-spatial abilities.

58._____   Attention is an important aspect of the ability to remember information.

59._____   Neuropsychologists measure both verbal and visual memory.

60._____   Memory can be thoroughly assessed after requesting that a person recall items in a list after 5 minutes.

61._____   A common battery of memory tests used by neuropsychologists is the Wechsler Memory Scale.

62._____   There are no neuropsychological tests available to measure abstract reasoning.

63._____   Neuropsychological tests exist only to measure an individual's ability to solve problems.

64._____   The Tower of London Test is used to measure problem solving abilities by tapping working memory, mental flexibility, attention, and response inhibition.

Traditional Psychological Testing and its Use in Neuropsychology

<u>Key Terms and Concepts</u>

objective personality tests   projective personality tests   intelligence
MMPI   Rorschach

<u>True/False</u>

65._____   Intelligence tests are believed to be good predictors of academic performance.

66._____   An intelligence test measures both verbal and performance abilities.

67._____   An average intelligence test score (i.e., IQ) is 100.

68._____   An IQ of 86 is considered to be in the mentally deficient range.

69._____   An IQ of 114 is considered to be in the superior range.

70._____   College graduates typically have an above average IQ.

71._____   Geniuses have been known to receive an IQ of 200 on the Wechsler Adult Intelligence Scale.

72._____   Ted Bundy and Jeffrey Dahmer scored in the mentally deficient range of intelligence.

73._____   The Wechsler Adult Intelligence Scale can provide information regarding an individual's intelligence and premorbid functioning.

74._____   A serious neurological event, such as a stroke, may have little effect on an individual's IQ score.

75._____   Personality may be defined as an individual's unique pattern of traits.

76._____   Personality is the result of brain functioning.

77._____   The MMPI-2 consists of 15 scales used to measure psychopathology.

78._____   The MMPI-2 is a good test for brain damage.

79._____   The MMPI-2 is often used as a part of neuropsychological evaluations.

80._____   Individuals with brain damage may score normally on personality testing.

81._____   Degree of brain damage is a predictor of level of emotional distress following a neurological event.

82._____   Projective personality techniques utilize true/false questions as the typical mode of testing.

83._____   The Rorschach Inkblot test is used more widely by neuropsychologists than the MMPI-2.

84._____   One use of personality tests in neuropsychological evaluations is to evaluate how an individual is adapting to a neurological trauma.

85._____   A neuropsychological test is one which is sensitive to changes in brain integrity.

86._____   Deficit measurement refers to the utilization of neurospychological testing to assess problem areas or dysfunction.

87._____   The utilization of personality tests in conjunction with neuropsychological tests assists in understanding any given individual more thoroughly than if neurospsychological tests were used alone.

Post-Test
Multiple Choice

1. What percentage of neuropsychologists work in private practice?

    e.   25%
    f.   33%
    g.   46%
    h.   85%

2. Within a medical setting, in which of the following will the neuropsychologist be involved?

    a.   Diagnosis.
    b.   Evaluation.
    c.   Intervention.
    d.   All of the above.

3. In which of the following settings will a neuropsychologist be most likely to be involved in research?

    a.   VA Medical Center.
    b.   Medical School.
    c.   Private Practice.
    d.   Rehabilitation Department.

4. Which is the largest represented patient population seen by neuropsychologists?

    a.   Psychiatric.
    b.   Various Dementias.
    c.   Rehabilitation.
    d.   Learning Disabilities.

5. Neuropsychological testing measures:

    a.   personality disorders.
    b.   brain functioning.
    c.   extent of seizure activity.
    d.   All of the above.

6. Which of the following is not a use for neuropsychological measures?

    a.   Differential diagnosis.
    b.   Identification of strengths and weaknesses.
    c.   Discharge planning.
    d.   None of the above.

7. What percentage of neuropsychological evaluations are given for the purpose of diagnosis?

   a. 96%
   b. 76%
   c. 56%
   d. 36%

8. Neuropsychological evaluation plays the major role in the diagnosis of what condition?

   a. Brain tumor.
   b. Learning Disability.
   c. Multiple Sclerosis.
   d. Epilepsy.

9. Which of the following is characteristic of the neuropsychological evaluation?

   a. Information gained from the neuropsychological evaluation is generally considered independent of data gained from neurology and brain scans.
   b. The neuropsychological evaluation is a subjective process.
   c. The neuropsychological evaluation is considered a comprehensive assessment of cognition and behavioral functioning.
   d. The neuropsychological evaluation is typically not integrated with intellectual assessment.

10. What is a reason that serial neuropsychological evaluations would be given?

    a. To provide better care when a patient changes healthcare providers.
    b. To determine if a given patient is improving.
    c. To make sure that the first results obtained for a given patient were accurate.
    d. To irritate insurance companies.

11. Which of the following cognitive abilities are assessed during a neuropsychological evaluation?

    a. Memory.
    b. Strength.
    c. Coordination.
    d. All of the above.

12. A neuropsychological evaluation takes approximately how long?

    a. 30 minutes to 8 hours.
    b. 1-2 hours.
    c. 3-4 hours.
    d. 6-8 hours.

13. Which of the following information is necessary when making a neuropsychological referral?

    a.   Inclusion of patient's IQ.
    b.   How the results will be used.
    c.   How the patient will pay for the neuropsychological evaluation.
    d.   All of the above.

14. Which of the following would be a valid reason to request a neuropsychological evaluation?

    a.   To differentiate between a focal versus a diffuse problem.
    b.   To evaluate an individual's vocation potential.
    c.   To assist in the development of a treatment program.
    d.   All of the above.

15. Psychometrics is the:

    a.   the science of measuring psychotic symptoms.
    b.   the science of measuring human traits or abilities.
    c.   the science of measuring psychopathology in individuals.
    d.   the science of measuring focal brain damage in mild brain traumas.

16. A standardized test is:

    a.   a task that has standard solutions which are answered in the same way by every patient.
    b.   a task which is used for a certain neurological disorder.
    c.   a task which is administered under consistent conditions.
    d.   a task which is either passed or failed by every individual with a specific neurological deficit.

17. For a neuropsychological test to be useful, it must be:

    a.   reliable.
    b.   valid.
    c.   subjective.
    d.   both a and b.

18. Reliability is:

    a.   the ability of a test to provide consistent results over multiple administrations to the same individual.
    b.   the ability of a test to measure what it is purported to measure.
    c.   the ability of a test to provide similar test findings in individuals with the same neurological injuries, such as mild brain trauma.
    d.   the ability of a test to prevent false alarms or false positives.

19. Validity is:

    a.   the ability of a test to provide consistent results over multiple administrations to the same individual.

    b.   the ability of a test to measure what it is purported to measure.

    c.   the ability of a test to provide similar test findings in individuals with the same neurological injuries, such as mild brain trauma.

    d.   the ability of a test to prevent false alarms or false positives.

20. Construct validity refers to:

    a.   the ability of a test's findings to relate to a specific outcome.

    b.   the degree to which a sample of test items represent a psychological domain.

    c.   the ability of a test to predict future behavior.

    d.   the ability of a test to measure an abstract psychological characteristic.

21. Content validity refers to:

    a.   the ability of a test's findings to relate to a specific outcome.

    b.   the degree to which a sample of test items represent a psychological domain.

    c.   the ability of a test to predict future behavior.

    d.   the ability of a test to measure an abstract psychological characteristic.

22. Criterion validity refers to:

    a.   the ability of a test's findings to relate to a specific outcome.

    b.   the degree to which a sample of test items represent a psychological domain.

    c.   the ability of a test to predict future behavior.

    d.   the ability of a test to measure an abstract psychological characteristic.

23. What is it called when a neuropsychological test incorrectly indicates the existence of a pathological condition?

    a.   A false positive.

    b.   A false alarm.

    c.   A Type I error.

    d.   All of the above.

24. A base rate is:

    a.   the abilities of any given individual prior to the development of a pathological condition.

    b.   the frequency of a pathological condition within a given population.

    c.   the measurement used to determine reliability and validity of any given neuropsychological instrument.

    d.   None of the above.

25. What is it called when a neuropsychological test fails to detect the presence of a pathological condition?

    a.   A miss.
    b.   A false negative.
    c.   A Type II error.
    d.   All of the above.

26. Which of the following is a test which measures how well an individual has profited by prior learning?

    a.   Intelligence test.
    b.   Behavioral-adaptive scale.
    c.   Achievement test.
    d.   Personality test.

27. Which of the following is a test, which measures what an individual usually does in everyday situations?

    a.   Achievement test.
    b.   Vocational inventory.
    c.   Neuropsychological test.
    d.   Behavioral-adaptive scale.

28. Which of the following measures achievement and aptitude?

    a.   Intelligence test.
    b.   Behavioral-adaptive scale.
    c.   Achievement test.
    d.   Vocational inventory.

29. Which of the following measures is sensitive to brain damage?

    a.   Intelligence test.
    b.   Neuropsychological test.
    c.   Vocational inventory.
    d.   Personality test.

30. Which of the following tests measures emotional states?

    a.   Neuropsychological test.
    b.   Intelligence test.
    c.   Behavioral-adaptive scale.
    d.   Personality test.

31. Which of the following measures assesses interest in various occupations?

    a.   Vocational inventory.
    b.   Personality test.
    c.   Achievement test.
    d.   Behavioral-adaptive scale?

32. Which of the following is believed to be crystallized?

    a.   Spelling.
    b.   Problem Solving.
    c.   Abstract Reasoning.
    d.   Attention.

33. Which of the following is believed to be fluid?

    a.   Spelling.
    b.   Abstract Reasoning.
    c.   Factual Knowledge.
    d.   Vocabulary.

34. Which of the following is assessed in a typical neuropsychological evaluation?

    a.   Motor Skills.
    b.   Memory.
    c.   Attention/Concentration.
    d.   All of the above.

35. Assessing orientation includes:

    a.   testing basic reflexes.
    b.   asking the patient where they are.
    c.   assessing basic sensation to pain and temperature.
    d.   asking the patient to count backwards from 100.

36. Which of the following tests is used to measure orientation?

    a.   d2.
    b.   COWA.
    c.   GOAT.
    d.   WMS.

37. Measuring sensation and perception includes assessing:

    a.   visual, auditory, and tactile function.
    b.   visual, auditory and memory function.
    c.   auditory, attention, and problem solving function.
    d.   visual functioning only.

38. Which of the following is a form of attention assessed by neuropsychologists?

    a.   Sustained attention.
    b.   Selective attention.
    c.   Attention span.
    d.   All of the above.

39. Which of the following is a standardized test of attention?

    a.   GOAT.
    b.   GCS.
    c.   SDMT.
    d.   COWA.

40. Which of the following is a test of selective and sustained visual attention?

    a.   d2.
    b.   COWA.
    c.   GOAT.
    d.   GCS.

41. The inability to perform common motor sequences is called:

    a.   aphasia.
    b.   ideomotor apraxia.
    c.   dyslexia.
    d.   dysgraphia.

42. Which of the following instruments measures grip strength?

    a.   Finger Oscillator.
    b.   WMS.
    c.   Dynamometer.
    d.   GCS.

43. Which of the following is the term for a deficit in the motor component of writing?

    a.   spelling dyspraxia.
    b.   aphasia.
    c.   dysgraphia.
    d.   dyslexia.

44. Which of the following is the term for a deficit in reading ability?

    a.   spelling dyspraxia.
    b.   aphasia.
    c.   dysgraphia.
    d.   dyslexia.

45. Which of the following is the term for a deficit in spelling skills?

    a.   spelling dyspraxia.
    b.   aphasia.
    c.   dysgraphia.
    d.   dyslexia.

46. Which of the following is a test of auditory comprehension?

    a.   d2.
    b.   COWA.
    c.   Token Test.
    d.   Tower of London.

47. Which of the following is a test of expressive language?

    a.   d2.
    b.   COWA.
    c.   GOAT.
    d.   GCS.

48. Tests of visual-spatial ability may measure:

    a.   visual sequencing.
    b.   facial recognition.
    c.   spatial orientation.
    d.   all of the above.

49. Which of the following tests are used to measure visual-spatial functioning?

    a.   Trail Making Test.
    b.   Token Test.
    c.   Tower of London.
    d.   Rey-Osterrieth Complex Figure Test.

50. Adequately testing memory includes testing:

    a.   attention, encoding, storage, and retrieval.
    b.   encoding, storage, and retrieval.
    c.   attention, storage, and retrieval.
    d.   encoding, problem solving, and storage.

51. A comprehensive neuropsychological memory test will include which components?

    a.   Immediate and delayed tasks with both free recall and recognition trials.
    b.   Immediate tasks with both free recall and recognition trials which allow for prompting from the examiner.
    c.   Several delayed tasks in case the individual remembers something later. In this way they are not penalized for false-forgetting.
    d.   Multiple learning trials so that delayed memory does not have to be tested, thus wasting testing time.

52. A standardized test of memory is the:

    a.   d2.
    b.   GCS.
    c.   COWA.
    d.   WMS.

53. Which of the following would be assessed in order to thoroughly evaluate judgment and problem solving?

    a.   Abstract reasoning.
    b.   Insight.
    c.   Ability to generalize.
    d.   All of the above.

54. The Wisconsin Card Sorting Test measures:

    a.   memory.
    b.   shifting sets.
    c.   sustained attention.
    d.   complex visual scanning.

55. The Tower of London measures:

    a.   insight.
    b.   auditory attention.
    c.   executive planning.
    d.   spatial orientation.

56. Intelligence tests are used to:

    a.   detect brain damage.
    b.   identify cognitive strengths and weaknesses.
    c.   localize brain dysfunction.
    d.   assess the severity of neurological impairment.

57. The Wechsler Intelligence Scales provide three different IQ scores. These are:

    a.   Verbal, Performance, and Aptitude.
    b.   Verbal, Performance, and Personality.
    c.   Verbal, Performance, and Achievement.
    d.   Verbal, Performance, and Full Scale.

58. The average IQ is:

    a.   80
    b.   100
    c.   120
    d.   140

59. What percentage of individuals score in the Very Superior range of intellectual functioning?

    a.   2%
    b.   5%
    c.   10%
    d.   20%

60. An IQ of 121 falls in the _____ range.

    a.   Average.
    b.   Below Average.
    c.   Above Average.
    d.   Superior.

61. An IQ of 59 falls in the _____ range.

    a.   Average.
    b.   Below Average.
    c.   Mentally Deficient.
    d.   Borderline.

62. College graduates have an average IQ of:

    a.   98
    b.   108
    c.   118
    d.   128

63. Intelligence tests measure:

    a.   mostly fluid abilities.
    b.   mostly crystallized abilities.
    c.   aptitude for future endeavors.
    d.   achievement in past endeavors.

64. Your personality is the result of:

    a.   brain damage.
    b.   brain functioning.
    c.   brain trauma.
    d.   your Kindergarten teacher.

65. What is the main objective personality test in use today?

    a.   Minnesota Multiphasic Personality Inventory.
    b.   Wechsler Adult Intelligence Scale.
    c.   Rorschach Inkblot Test.
    d.   Thematic Apperception Test.

66. Which of the following is measured by the MMPI-2?

    a.   Homosexual tendencies.
    b.   Aptitude for healthy emotional functioning.
    c.   Depression.
    d.   Intelligence.

67. Personality tests may be used in conjunction with a neuropsychological battery in order to:

    a.   assist in the diagnosis of brain damage.
    b.   assist in establishing the extent of brain damage.
    c.   measure psychosocial adjustment following brain damage.
    d.   predict future problems associated with brain damage.

68. What percentage of neuropsychologists includes the MMPI or MMPI-2 as a part of the comprehensive neuropsychological evaluation?

    a.   10%
    b.   20%
    c.   40%
    d.   60%

69. Which of the following is considered a projective personality test?

    a.   Minnesota Multiphasic Personality Inventory.
    b.   Rorschach Inkblot Test.
    c.   Wechsler Intelligence Scale.
    d.   Your next neuropsychology examination.

70. The Rorschach Inkblot Test has been shown to:

    a.   be a reliable indicator of brain damage.
    b.   aid significantly in the differential diagnosis of various types of brain impairment.
    c.   reveal the manner in which an individual is adapting to brain impairment.
    d.   predict the manner in which an individual will adapt to debilitating brain impairment.

71. What percentage of neuropsychologists utilizes the Rorschach Inkblot Test as a part of the comprehensive neuropsychological examination?

    a.   5%
    b.   7%
    c.   11%
    d.   60%

Essay Questions

1.   Briefly describe three reasons a neuropsychological evaluation might be requested?

2.   What are the main differences between intelligence tests, achievement tests, behavioral-adaptive scales, personality tests, and vocational inventories?

3.   Why would a neuropsychologist use personality tests as a part of a neuropsychological evaluation?

Answer Key

Chapter Exercises

1. False (p.440)
2. False (pp.440,441)
3. True (p.441)
4. False (p.441)
5. True (p.441)
6. False (p.441)
7. True (p.442)
8. True (p.442)
9. False (p.442)
10. True (p.442)
11. True (p.443)
12. False (p.443)
13. True (p.443)
14. True (p.443)
15. False (p.443)
16. g (p.444)
17. f (p.445)
18. h (p.444)
19. e (p.445)
20. b (p.444)
21. a (p.445)
22. i (p.445)
23. d (p.444)
24. c (p.445)
25. False (p.446)
26. True (p.446)
27. True (p.446)
28. True (p.446)
29. False (p.446)
30. True (p.446)
31. False (p.446)
32. False (p.446)
33. True (p.446)
34. True (p.446)
35. True (p.448)
36. False (p.448)
37. True (p.448)
38. False (p.448)
39. False (p.448)
40. True (p.448)
41. True (p.448)
42. True (p.449)
43. False (p.449)
44. True (p.449)
45. True (p.450)
46. True (p.450)
47. True (p.451)
48. False (p.451)
49. True (p.451)
50. True (pp.451,452)
51. False (p.452)
52. False (p.452)
53. True (p.452)
54. False (p.452)
55. False (p.452)
56. True (pp.452,453)
57. False (pp.452,454)
58. True (p.454)
59. True (pp.454,455)
60. False (p.454)
61. True (p.455)
62. False (p.456)
63. False (p.456)
64. True (p.457)
65. True (p.458)
66. True (p.459)
67. True (p.459)
68. False (p.459)
69. False (p.459)
70. True (p.459)
71. False (p.459)
72. False (p.460)
73. True (p.460)
74. True (p.460)
75. True (p.460)
76. True (p.460)
77. False (p.460)
78. False (pp.460,461)
79. True (p.463)
80. True (pp.461,463)
81. False (p.461)
82. False (p.461)
83. False (p.463)
84. True (pp.461,462)
85. True (p.464)
86. True (p.464)
87. True (pp.464,465)

Post-Test

Multiple Choice

1. C (p.441)
2. D (p.441)
3. B (p.441)
4. C (p.441)
5. B (p.441)
6. D (p.442)
7. C (p.442)
8. B (p.442)
9. C (p.442)
10. B (p.442)
11. D (p.443)
12. A (p.443)
13. B (p.443)
14. D (pp.443,444)
15. B (p.444)
16. C (p.444)
17. D (p.444)
18. A (p.444)
19. B (p.444)
20. D (p.445)
21. B (p.445)
22. A (p.445)
23. D (p.445)
24. B (p.445)
25. D (p.445)
26. C (p.446)
27. D (p.446)
28. A (p.446)
29. B (p.446)
30. D (p.446)
31. A (p.446)
32. A (p.446)
33. B (p.446)
34. D (p.447)
35. B (p.448)

36. C (p.448)
37. A (p.448)
38. D (pp.449,450)
39. C (p.450)
40. A (p.450)
41. B (p.451)
42. C (p.451)
43. C (p.452)
44. D (p.452)
45. A (p.452)
46. C (p.452)
47. B (p.452)
48. D (pp.452,453)
49. D (p.454)
50. A (pp.454,455)
51. A (p.455)
52. D (p.455)
53. D (p.455)
54. B (p.456)
55. C (p.457)
56. B (p.458)
57. D (p.459)
58. B (p.459)
59. A (p.459)
60. D (p.459)
61. C (p.459)
62. C (p.459)
63. B (p.460)
64. B (p.460)
65. A (p.460)
66. C (p.461)
67. C (p.462)
68. D (p.463)
69. B (p.461)
70. C (p.463)
71. C (p.463)

Chapter 15

Neuropsychology in Practice Interpretation and Diagnosis

Chapter Outline

Overview

Neuropsychological diagnosis remains an important component of the neuropsychologist's role. However, diagnosis is usually not the only question of interest when a patient is referred for neuropsychological testing. In fact, the neuropsychologist's role in evaluation has evolved from a diagnostic emphasis to one in which the current neuropsychological functioning is described and the individual's adaptation to the unique demands of his or her environment is evaluated. The focus is on performance in the testing setting as well as a task analysis of the cognitive requirements of home and work. In the role of diagnosis the neuropsychological testing profiles can aid in the identification of general categories of neurological disease and conditions. The purpose of evaluation is to examine the individual's strengths and weaknesses, their ability to deal with stress, their adaptation, and overall social and occupational functioning. It is in this latter more descriptive role that neuropsychologists have made their most recent advances. This chapter outlines the different roles of the clinical neuropsychologist and the different approaches to the interpretation of neuropsychological assessment data. The different approaches to interpretation and variables influencing such interpretation are important because they combine the different aspects of neuropsychological theory and what we know about brain behavior functions.

Learning Objectives

- To learn the different approaches to neuropsychological test interpretation.
- To understand the major subject variables that affect neuropsychological test performance.
- To learn the different roles of the clinical neuropsychologist.

The Roles of the Clinical Neuropsychologist

True/False

1._____ A neuropsychologist might be asked to differentiate between a psychosomatic reaction to an event and neurological damage.

2._____ An individual may experience cognitive problems even when CT and MRI are normal.

3._____ The main role of the neuropsychologist today is that of a diagnostician.

4._____ The neuropsychologist is often asked to provide information regarding the effect neurological damage has on behavior.

5._____ Neuropsychologists feature prominently in the diagnosis of ADHD and Alzheimer's disease.

6._____ Neuropsychologists are often asked to describe the current capabilities of an individual.

7._____ Neuropsychologists are often asked to predict future capabilities of an individual.

Interpretation of Neuropsychological Assessment Data

interpretive hypotheses	standard battery approach	process approach
normative data	cutoff score	specificity
sensitivity	normal distribution	deficit measurement
pattern analysis	lateralizing signs	pathognomonic signs

Matching

8. Comparison of a patient to the "norm" to determine existence and extent of deficits.

    a.   interpretive hypotheses

9. A score which is the set limit to determine impairment.

    b.   standard battery approach

10. The extent to which a test measures specific neuropsychological functions.

    c.   process approach

11. This method advocates adapting the neuropsychological evaluation to each individual patient.

    d.   normative data

12. A clinical observation which suggests brain dysfunction.

    e.   cutoff score

13. A brainstorming of potential explanations for a patient's difficulties.

    f.   specificity

14. This is reflected in the bell-shaped curve.

    g.   sensitivity

15. A test result which suggests right or left hemisphere dysfunction.

    h.   normal distribution

16. A comparison sample which considers age, gender, education, and intelligence.

    i.   deficit measurement

17. The degree to which a neuropsychological instrument measures impairment.

    j.   pattern analysis

18. Method of test interpretation which seeks to recognize patterns associated with specific neurological processes.

    k.   lateralizing signs

19. This method advocates giving exactly the same tests to every patient.

    l.   pathognomonic signs

Subject Variables Affecting Neuropsychological Test Performance

<u>Key Terms and Concepts</u>

age	premorbid functioning	dominance	sex
malingering	simulation	dissimulation	arousal
medication			

<u>True/False</u>

20._____ The older a person gets, the better they are expected to do on neuropsychological tasks requiring flexible problem solving.

21._____ Many neuropsychological tests exist with norms for elderly individuals over the age of 85.

22._____ Premorbid functioning refers to an individual's neuropsychological status prior to neurological disease or trauma.

23._____ In neuropsychological assessment, an individual's scores are compared to an estimate of their premorbid functioning.

24._____ Level of education is one indicator of premorbid functioning.

25._____ Dominance refers only to handedness.

26._____ The cerebral organization of speech is associated with handedness.

27._____ 70% of right-handed individuals are left-hemisphere dominant for speech.

28._____ Approximately 75% of the population is right-handed.

29._____ The majority of left-handed individuals have the same pattern of brain organization seen in right-handed individuals.

30._____ Individuals who are left-handed or ambidextrous are more likely to show a lateralization reversal for speech dominant hemisphere than right-handers.

31._____ Male and female brains are organized identically.

32._____ Women tend to perform better on visuospatial tasks than men.

33._____ Men tend to perform better than women on verbal tasks.

34._____ The exaggeration of neuropsychological deficits is referred to as malingering.

35._____ Simulation refers to a patient's test approach when he/she denies that there are any deficits in order to gain employment or avoid hospitalization.

36._____ Dissimulation refers to a patient's test approach when he/she fakes or exaggerates symptoms for secondary gain, such as awards in a lawsuit.

37._____ Malingering is easily detected using neuropsychological tests.

38._____ Level of arousal may impact neuropsychological test results.

39._____   Medications have not been found to influence neuropsychological test performance.

Other Roles in Neuropsychological Assessment

<u>Key Terms and Concepts</u>

forensic neuropsychology   criterion-related validity   construct validity

<u>True/False</u>

40._____   Forensic neuropsychology answers questions related to brain injury in the legal arena.
41._____   A forensic neuropsychologist might be asked to predict how neurological dysfunction will impact the individual's ability to be gainfully employed.
42._____   Potential for rehabilitation would not be an issue addressed by the forensic neuropsychologist.
43._____   The forensic neuropsychologist might be asked to determine a neurologically-impaired individual's competency to stand trial.
44._____   A neuropsychological test with criterion-related validity should be able to detect the presence or absence of brain damage.
45._____   A neuropsychological test with construct validity should be useful in describing behavior in relation to other areas of functioning.

Case Examples

<u>True/False</u>

46._____   Chlordane has commonly been used as a pesticide.

47._____   Chlordane impairs the normal functioning of the sodium-potassium adenosinetriphosphatase pump.
48._____   Chlordane poisoning may result in executive function and memory deficits.

49._____   Lyme's disease may result in neuropsychological deficits.

Post-Test
Multiple Choice

1. In the 1960s, what was the main role of the neuropsychologist?

    i.   Diagnostician.
    j.   Rehabilitation.
    k.   Forensic work.
    l.   Description of functioning, adaptation, and prognosis.

2. What development radically changed the early role of the neuropsychologist?

    a.   HMOs.
    b.   More effective medications with decreased side effects.
    c.   Advances in neuroimaging techniques.
    d.   The d2 test.

3. Which of the following is a role played by neuropsychologists today?

    a.   Rehabilitation.
    b.   Evaluation of quality of life.
    c.   Evaluation of functional abilities.
    d.   All of the above.

4. Why is a neuropsychological assessment required in addition to neuroimaging of various brain lesions?

    a.   Neuroimaging techniques are imprecise and require validation of neurological findings.
    b.   Neuroimaging cannot provide information regarding the level of functioning of a patient.
    c.   Radiologists need guidance as to which area of the brain to look at when evaluating neurological damage.
    d.   All of the above.

5. Which of the following do neuropsychologists play a major role in diagnosing?

    a.   Severe brain injury.
    b.   Brain tumor.
    c.   Alzheimer's disease.
    d.   · Hydrocephalus.

6. Which of the following statements regarding mild brain injuries is true?

    a.   Mild brain injuries are easily detected by MRI.
    b.   Mild brain injuries are easily detected by CT.
    c.   Mild brain injuries are diagnosed through the combined used of MRI and CT.
    d.   Mild brain injuries often are not detected on MRI and CT.

7. Which of the following questions will a neuropsychologist be interested in answering utilizing the neuropsychological evaluation?

    a.   Where is the lesion and exactly how large is it?
    b.   Are neuropsychological deficits impacting the patient's quality of life?
    c.   Will medication be effective in treating an individual's cognitive deficits?
    d.   All of the above.

8. Which approach advocates for administering the same neuropsychological tasks to all patients, regardless of the referral question?

    a.   Process approach.
    b.   Standard battery approach.
    c.   Pattern analysis.
    d.   Differential score approach.

9. Which of the following is an advantage of the standard battery approach?

    a.   Patients are evaluated for all basic neuropsychological abilities.
    b.   Minimal time is required when employing this approach.
    c.   The neuropsychologist has ample time in which to qualitatively evaluate the patient.
    d.   The evaluation focuses on the most important neuropsychological deficits.

10. Which of the following is the most frequently used assessment battery?

    a.   Dementia Rating Scale.
    b.   Luria Nebraska Neuropsychological Test Battery.
    c.   Halstead-Reitan Neuropsychological Test Battery.
    d.   Wechsler Adult Intelligence Scale-Revised.

11. Which approach advocates for adopting each neuropsychological evaluation to the individual patient?

    a.   Process approach.
    b.   Standard battery approach.
    c.   Pattern analysis.
    d.   Differential score approach.

12. Which of the following is an advantage of the process approach?

    a.   Patients are evaluated for all basic neuropsychological abilities.
    b.   This approach may yield more precise measurements of specific skills of individual patients.
    c.   There is little chance that a deficit may be missed.
    d.   This approach does not utilize tests which are unstandardized.

13. What percentage of neuropsychologists report using a strict standard battery approach?

   a.   10%
   b.   17%
   c.   25%
   d.   50%

14. Diagnostic and treatment decisions must be made via the integration of which of the following?

   a.   Neuropsychological test findings.
   b.   Neurological and medical findings/history.
   c.   The patient's developmental history.
   d.   All of the above.

15. Normative data takes which of the following into consideration?

   a.   Marital history, gender, and education.
   b.   Number of siblings, education, and intelligence.
   c.   Gender, education, and age.
   d.   Age, marital history, and education.

16. Scoring lower than the _____ indicates impairment.

   a.   rest of the class
   b.   cutoff score
   c.   average score
   d.   normative score

17. Which score is one reported in original test units?

   a.   Standard score.
   b.   Raw score.
   c.   Z-score.
   d.   T-score.

18. In the normal distribution, what percentage of cases fall within one standard deviation above or below the mean?

   a.   31.8%
   b.   68.2%
   c.   95.4%
   d.   99.7%

19. Which approach establishes the presence of statistically probable deficits by comparing test performance to normative data?

    a.   Pattern analysis.
    b.   Differential score approach.
    c.   Deficit measurement.
    d.   Pathognomonic evaluation.

20. Which approach compares a fluid and crystallized task in order to determine the presence of significant differences between the tasks, and subsequently the presence of neuropsychological impairment?

    a.   Pattern analysis.
    b.   Differential score approach.
    c.   Deficit measurement.
    d.   Pathognomonic evaluation.

21. Which approach examines the relationships among performance within a test battery?

    a.   Pattern analysis.
    b.   Differential score approach.
    c.   Deficit measurement.
    d.   Pathognomonic evaluation.

22. What is the term for test results which indicate right or left cerebral hemisphere dysfunction?

    a.   Pattern analysis.
    b.   Pathognomonic signs.
    c.   Lateralizing signs.
    d.   None of the above.

23. What is the term for qualitative observations which suggest brain impairment?

    a.   Pattern analysis.
    b.   Pathognomonic signs.
    c.   Lateralizing signs.
    d.   None of the above.

24. Older individuals should be expected to exhibit decreased performance in which area?

    a.   Factual information.
    b.   Flexible problem solving.
    c.   Motor speed.
    d.   Vocabulary.

25. Premorbid functioning refers to:

    a.   the initial decline in functioning seen following neurological trauma.
    b.   the neuropsychological status of an individual prior to neurological trauma.
    c.   the neuropsychological status of an individuals following neurological trauma.
    d.   None of the above.

26. Which of the following can assist in the determination of premorbid functioning?

    a.   Neuropsychological tasks measuring fluid abilities.
    b.   Tasks requiring new learning.
    c.   Level of education.
    d.   Marital status.

27. Dominance refers to:

    a.   the cerebral organization of the brain.
    b.   handedness.
    c.   eye preference.
    d.   All of the above.

28. What percentage of right-handed individuals are left-hemisphere dominant for speech?

    a.   43%
    b.   72%
    c.   96%
    d.   100%

29. What percentage of left-handed individuals are left-hemisphere dominant for speech?

    a.   50%
    b.   70%
    c.   80%
    d.   95%

30. On which neuropsychological tests do women generally outperform men?

    a.   Verbal abilities.
    b.   Visuospatial abilities.
    c.   Motor speed.
    d.   All of the above.

31. On which neuropsychological tests do men generally outperform women?

    a.   Verbal abilities.
    b.   Visuospatial abilities.
    c.   Memory.
    d.   Bilateral motor speed and coordination.

32. Which of the following refers to the intentional presentation of neuropsychological deficits?

    a.   Pathognomonic signs.
    b.   Malingering.
    c.   Depressive responding.
    d.   Litigious syndrome.

33. In the case of dissimulation, which of the following is a possible scenario?

    a.   An individual fakes a memory deficit in order to collect money in a lawsuit.
    b.   An individual exaggerates post-concussive headaches and concentration deficits to increase his workman's compensation claim.
    c.   An individual downplays attentional deficits so that he may continue to be actively employed as a pilot.
    d.   An individual displays no neuropsychological deficits on neuropsychological testing.

34. Which of the following may adversely impact neuropsychological test findings?

    a.   Patient fatigue.
    b.   Medication effects.
    c.   Level of motivation.
    d.   All of the above.

35. Which of the following might be a possible scenario in a civil court case?

    a.   A neurologically impaired individual kills another man and a forensic neuropsychologist is asked to determine his competency.
    b.   A brain-injured individual has sued the individual responsible for causing the brain injury and a forensic neuropsychologist is asked to determine the functional impact of the injury.
    c.   A forensic neuropsychologist is asked to evaluate a neurologically-impaired individual convicted of rape and make a recommendation regarding sentencing.
    d.   Everyone would be really, really nice to each other.

36. Which of the following should be taken into consideration when constructing a neuropsychological test?

    a.   Criterion-related validity.
    b.   Construct validity.
    c.   Sensitivity.
    d.   All of the above.

37. Which of the following statements is true regarding chlordane?

    a.   Chlordane attacks dendrites and leaves axons unharmed.
    b.   The use of chlordane as a household pesticide has been extremely limited.
    c.   Chlordane exposure can result in significant neuropsychological disabilities.
    d.   Chlordane exposure causes vomiting, headaches and nausea, but does not detrimentally impact cognitive functioning.

Essay Questions

1.   Describe three current roles of the neuropsychologist.

2.   What are the main advantages and disadvantages to the standard battery and process approaches to neuropsychological evaluation?

3.   Describe the various roles of the forensic neuropsychologist.

Answer Key

Chapter Exercises

1. True (p.468)
2. True (p.468)
3. False (p.469)
4. True (p.469)
5. True (p.469)
6. True (p.470)
7. True (p.479)
8. i (p.478)
9. e (p.476)
10. f (p.476)
11. c (p.473)
12. l (p.479)
13. a (p.470)
14. h (p.477)
15. k (p.479)
16. d (p.476)
17. g (p.476)
18. j (p.478)
19. b (p.471)
20. False (p.479)
21. False (p.480)
22. True (p.480)
23. True (p.480)
24. True (p.480)

25. False (p.480)
26. True (p.480)
27. False (pp.480,481)
28. False (p.481)
29. True (p.481)
30. True (p.481)
31. False (p.481)
32. False (p.481)
33. False (p.481)
34. True (p.482)
35. False (p.482)
36. False (p.482)
37. False (p.482)
38. True (p.482)
39. False (pp.482,483)
40. True (p.483)
41. True (p.484)
42. False (p.484)
43. True (p.485)
44. True (pp.483,484)
45. True (p.484)
46. True (p.486)
47. True (p.486)
48. True (p.488)
49. True (p.490)

Post-Test

Multiple Choice

1. A (pp.468,469)
2. C (p.469)
3. D (p.469)
4. B (p.469)
5. C (p.469)
6. D (p.470)
7. B (p.470)
8. B (p.471)
9. A (p.471)
10. D (p.473)
11. A (p.473)
12. B (p.473)
13. C (p.475)
14. D (p.476)
15. C (p.476)
16. B (p.476)
17. B (p.476)
18. B (p.477)
19. C (p.478)
20. B (p.478)
21. A (p.478)
22. C (p.479)
23. B (p.479)
24. B (p.479)
25. B (p.480)
26. C (p.480)
27. D (p.480)
28. C (pp.480,481)
29. B (p.481)
30. A (p.481)
31. B (p.481)
32. B (p.482)
33. C (p.482)
34. D (pp.482,483)
35. B (pp.484,485)
36. D (pp.483,484)
37. C (pp.486,487,488)

Chapter 16

Neuropsychology in Practice
Recovery, Rehabilitation, and Intervention

Chapter Outline

Overview
Learning Objectives
The Case of Jonathan
Adaptation and Recovery
Diaschisis
Brain Reorganization
        Axonal and Collateral Sprouting
        Denervation Supersensitivity
        Redundancy of Functioning
Overview of the Rehabilitation Process
Admission to Rehabilitation Programs
The Rehabilitation Team: Goal Setting, Treatment, and Evaluation
        Neuropsychology
        Physical Therapy
        Occupational Therapy
        Speech Therapy
        Therapeutic Recreation
Evaluation of Goals and Discharge Planning
Neuropsychological Assessment for Rehabilitation
Treatment Planning
Assessment of Everyday Activities
Treatment Methods for Neuropsychological Rehabilitation
Specific Functional System Training
        Attentional Retraining
Supported Employment
Computers as Compensatory Aids
Psychotherapy in Rehabilitation

Post-Test

Answer Key

Overview

What is the potential for the human brain to recover after brain injury? Are there areas or functions that may be able to repair themselves? Are other areas of the brain able to take over or compensate for destroyed brain functions? These are questions addressed in this chapter on rehabilitation and recovery from brain damage. This chapter is important to the neuropsychology student because it addresses the rationale for the rehabilitation process, including how team members work individually and together to foster the attainment of treatment goals. The neuropsychologist's role in the rehabilitation environment is examined as are theories and methods of neuropsychological rehabilitation, including selected strategies like cognitive remediation, "job coaching," and the importance of psychotherapy. The area of neuropsychological rehabilitation is clearly becoming one of the major areas of practice for neuropsychologists. The rehabilitation process is complex and dependent upon many factors including biological, personal, and environmental. It is the neuropsychologist's job to assess the degree to which spontaneous recovery will occur, evaluate cognitive functioning that can be restored, or assess other means of adaptation that can take place. Rehabilitation is best thought of as following a continuum from inpatient care, to outpatient treatment, to community re-entry, and follow-up. Rehabilitation of the brain-injured patient is the best example of a neuropsychologist working with a multidisciplinary team to gain a comprehensive picture of an individual within his or her environment.

Learning Objectives

- To appreciate the overall rehabilitation process and the role of the rehabilitation team.
- To understand the role of the neuropsychologist in the rehabilitation process.
- To be able to list the different treatment methods that are used in contemporary neuropsychological practice.

Adaptation and Recovery

Key Terms and Concepts

cerebral achromatopsia	diaschisis	redundancy of function
brain reorganization	axonal sprouting	denervation sensitivity

True/False

1._____ Cerebral achromatopsia refers to colorblindness.

2._____ Neuroscientists are able to successfully transplant healthy central nervous system tissue into damaged brains.

3._____ Brain damage results in emotional changes which are secondary to the cognitive effects.

4._____ Following brain damage, some spontaneous recovery of function is likely to occur.

5._____ The reorganization of neural connections is called restitution.

6._____ Premorbid intellectual level can impact recovery from a neurological trauma.

7._____   Diaschisis refers to the notion that the brain actively works to repair itself following neuronal damage.

8._____   Diaschisis refers to the notion that neurological regions away from the site of damage are rendered temporarily dysfunctional.

9._____   Brain reorganization is dependent on level of brain plasticity.

10._____   Collateral sprouting has both positive and negative effects.

11._____   Denervation sensitivity occurs when remaining neurons in a damaged area become less sensitive to neurotransmitters.

12._____   Redundancy of function is more likely to result in returned functioning if the damage to the brain is widespread.

13._____   Redundancy of function is represented by the potential of one hemisphere of the brain to "take over" for a corresponding, but damaged area in the other hemisphere.

Overview of the Rehabilitation Process

Key Terms and Concepts

| Physiatry | Speech Therapy | Occupational Therapy |
| Physical Therapy | Therapeutic Recreation | dysarthria |

True/False

14._____   The goal of rehabilitation is to medically stabilize the patient.

15._____   Rehabilitation requires active participation on the part of the patient.

16._____   The goal of rehabilitation is to return people to society at the highest possible level of functioning.

17._____   An average length of stay in a rehabilitation hospital for an individual surviving a traumatic brain injury, is currently 60 days.

18._____   There are approximately 160 traumatic brain injury treatment programs in the United States.

19._____   Data collection for the Traumatic Brain Injury Model Systems Project includes information obtained in the Emergency Room.

20._____   The Traumatic Brain Injury Model Systems Project attempts to document all aspects of a brain injury from the injury itself to the individual's return to the community.

21._____   There are currently 100 centers involved in the Traumatic Brain Injury Model Systems Project.

22._____   Most neuropsychologists working in rehabilitation work in acute-care hospitals.

23._____   Rehabilitation hospitals in many cases negate the need to transfer brain damaged patients to nursing homes.

24._____   The rehabilitation team typically consists of the Neurosurgeon, Microbiologist, and Physical Therapist.

25._____ A physician who specializes in physical medicine and rehabilitation is a physiatrist.

26._____ Once admitted to a rehabilitation hospital, a comprehensive neuropsychological evaluation is typically conducted.

27._____ In addition to traditional neuropsychological assessment, areas such as meal preparation and driving may also be evaluated.

28._____ Physical Therapists are concerned with self-care skills such as bathing, dressing, and grooming.

29._____ Occupational Therapists are concerned with increasing functional activities related to strength, balance, physical endurance, and range of motion.

30._____ Occupational Therapy focuses on return to work.

31._____ A Speech Therapist attempts to increase speech production and understanding.

32._____ Individuals with speech dysarthrias often experience word substitutions and problems with receptive speech.

33._____ Therapeutic recreation can include community outings which allow patients to practice skills such as mobility and money management.

34._____ Discharge planning can include determining whether or not a patient is safe to return home to live independently.

35._____ Within the rehabilitation setting, the neuropsychologist provides evaluation only for cognitive problems exhibited following neurological impairment.

Neuropsychological Assessment for Rehabilitation

Key Terms and Concepts

treatment planning   Cognitive Screening for Medication Self-Management

True/False

36._____ The purpose of neuropsychological evaluations in rehabilitation is diagnosis.

37._____ Neuropsychologists attempt to predict functional outcome following various types of neurological impairment.

38._____ In rehabilitation, it is important not only to neuropsychologically evaluate patients initially, but also to monitor their progress over time.

39._____ An ecologically valid measure evaluates such skills as working memory or expressive speech.

40._____ An ecologically valid driving test might include use of a driving simulator.

41._____ Medication taking is often a barrier in allowing an elderly individual to return home to live independently.

42._____ A means of assessing the ability to manage one's own medications is the Cognitive Screening for Medication Self-Management.

Treatment Methods for Neuropsychological Rehabilitation

Key Terms and Concepts

restitution
attentional retraining
selective attention
divided attention
generalization to neuropsychological testing
supported employment
job coach
orthotic
Amyotrophic Lateral Sclerosis

substitution
sustained attention
alternating attention
task improvement effects
generalization to daily life functioning
task analysis
compensatory aid
prosthetic
psychotherapy

Sentence Completion

43. _____ is a method of brain injury rehabilitation which emphasizes adaptations to the environment.

44. It is unclear if attention-specific cognitive retraining programs result in a _____.

45. In order to train _____ the Attention Process Training system adds distractions to tasks which require constant attention.

46. _____ results in loss of control of the muscles for speech.

47. A _____ outlines detailed steps required to complete a task.

48. _____ involves working with a job coach and an employer in order to maximize vocational outcome.

49. In order to train _____ the Attention Process Training system presents two tasks which must be performed simultaneously.

50. _____ (for example: cognitive retraining) is a method of brain injury rehabilitation which emphasizes the retraining of an impaired skill.

51. The use of a computer for assistance with money management and memory is an example of an _____.

52. _____ are generally good for the Attention Process Training system tasks and performance can reach that of a non-brain impaired individual.

53. Orthotics and prosthetics may be considered a _____.

54. In order to train _____ the Attention Process Training system presents a series of tasks which require constant attention.

55.   A computer aid used to assist an individual to speak is an example of a _____.

56.   _____ may be useful in assisting an individual in adjusting to their lifestyle and changes in functioning following a neurological insult.

57.   The Attention Process Training system did show a _____, showing improvement on standard tests of attention.

58.   A _____ assists an individual in learning a specific job by taking into account his/her abilities and the requirements of the work, as well as working with the employer.

59.   In order to train _____ the Attention Process Training system presents tasks which require switching between two attention demanding problems.

60.   _____ is attempted by the Attention Process Training system.

Post-Test
Multiple Choice

1. Cerebral achromatopsia is a condition characterized by:

   m.   the change of the color of healthy brain tissue.
   n.   complete color blindness.
   o.   inaccurate perception of the colors red and green.
   p.   inability to visually recognize objects.

2. Spontaneous recovery following brain damage is:

   a.   uncommon.
   b.   common but not enough to impact an individual's level of functioning.
   c.   expected.
   d.   almost always restores all neurological functioning to premorbid levels.

3. Knowledge of recovery from brain damage comes from:

   a.   prospective research that uses human volunteers.
   b.   animal studies.
   c.   human case studies.
   d.   both b and c.

4. For which of the following disorders has fetal tissue transplantation been attempted?

   a.   Hydrocephalus.
   b.   Fetal alcohol syndrome.
   c.   Anencephaly.
   d.   Parkinson's disease.

5. Why do neuroscientists believe that fetal tissue transplants have a good chance of treating various disorders?

   a.   Fetal tissue is not yet differentiated and is hypothesized to be adaptable to various areas of the brain.
   b.   There is a significant amount of fetal tissue available for research as opposed to limited adult neurological donor resources.
   c.   Fetal tissue has a greater concentration of neurons than adult tissue and thus even with expected neuronal death following transplant, there remain enough neurons to begin adapting to the new neurological environment.
   d.   None of the above.

6. When neurons are damaged, as opposed to destroyed, rehabilitation will probably focus on:

   a.   restitution.
   b.   substitution.
   c.   compensatory strategies.
   d.   prosthetics.

7. Which of the following will have an impact on recovery of function following neurological trauma?

    a.   Brain plasticity.
    b.   Premorbid intelligence.
    c.   Medical issues.
    d.   All of the above.

8. Recovery of neurological function due to a process which temporarily disabled working systems is called:

    a.   diaschisis.
    b.   substitution.
    c.   redundancy of function.
    d.   brain reorganization.

9. The ability of neurological tissue to reorganize after brain injury is called:

    a.   diaschisis.
    b.   substitution.
    c.   plasticity.
    d.   redundancy of function.

10. Brain reorganization is exhibited by:

    a.   diaschisis.
    b.   axonal sprouting.
    c.   redundancy of function.
    d.   neuronal death.

11. Hypersensitivity to neurotransmitters following brain injury is called:

    a.   denervation supersensitivity.
    b.   diaschisis.
    c.   collateral sprouting.
    d.   redundancy of function.

12. The potential for redundancy within neural systems is active:

    a.   from birth to age 5 years.
    b.   from birth to age 10 years.
    c.   from birth to young adulthood.
    d.   from birth to death.

13. Redundancy of function is mostly likely to be observed in:

    a.   neurological tissue which is geographically near the injured site.
    b.   neurological tissue which is represented similarly in the opposite hemisphere.
    c.   an individual without extensive neurological damage.
    d.   All of the above.

14. Neurons damaged through shearing, are most likely to be restored to functioning through:

    a.   plasticity.
    b.   redundancy of function.
    c.   neuronal transplant.
    d.   collateral sprouting.

15. The main goal of rehabilitation is to:

    a.   restore the individual back to premorbid levels of functioning.
    b.   improve the individual's level of functioning.
    c.   medically stabilize the patient.
    d.   All of the above.

16. Managed care has resulted in:

    a.   shorter inpatient and rehabilitation hospital stays following neurological insult.
    b.   shorter inpatient and longer rehabilitation hospital stays following neurological insult.
    c.   longer inpatient and rehabilitation hospital stays following neurological insult.
    d.   longer inpatient and short rehabilitation hospital stays following neurological insult.

17. Within a rehabilitation hospital, a neuropsychologist working with individuals with brain disorders is likely to:

    a.   address issues of adjustment with the patient.
    b.   evaluate cognitive strengths and weaknesses of the patient.
    c.   apply psychological principles to assist in recovery of the patient.
    d.   All of the above.

18. Approximately how many treatment programs exist for individuals with traumatic brain injury in the United States?

    a.   100
    b.   400
    c.   800
    d.   1600

19. Areas studied under the Traumatic Brain Injury Model Systems Project include:

    a.   computer technology.
    b.   costs of rehabiliation.
    c.   racial bias of outcome measures.
    d.   All of the above.

20. An acute care rehabilitation neuropsychologist is likely to:

    a.   administer an entire neuropsychological battery to an individual emerging from a coma.
    b.   administer neuropsychological evaluations in order to assess premorbid functioning prior to neurosurgery.
    c.   perform long-term follow-up evaluations in order to monitor a patient's progress.
    d.   All of the above.

21. Which of the following is not likely to be a member of the rehabilitation team?

    a.   The patient.
    b.   Neuropsychologist.
    c.   Neurosurgeon.
    d.   Physiatrist.

22. An example of a skill measured via an ecologically valid test would be:

    a.   attention.
    b.   meal planning.
    c.   executive functioning.
    d.   memory.

23. Which of the following professionals would evaluate an individual's ability to maintain their own personal hygiene?

    a.   Physical Therapist.
    b.   Occupational Therapist.
    c.   Recreational Therapist.
    d.   Speech Therapist.

24. Which of the following professionals would evaluate an individual's ability to utilize a wheelchair?

    a.   Physical Therapist.
    b.   Occupational Therapist.
    c.   Recreational Therapist.
    d.   Speech Therapist.

25. Which of the following professionals would evaluate an individual's ability to understand spoken language?

    a.   Physical Therapist.
    b.   Occupational Therapist.
    c.   Recreational Therapist.
    d.   Speech Therapist.

26. Which of the following professionals would facilitate a community outing so that a patient could practice his/her ability to manipulate a wheelchair?

    a.   Physical Therapist.
    b.   Occupational Therapist.
    c.   Recreational Therapist.
    d.   Speech Therapist.

27. A dysarthria is:

    a.   a lack of purposive action often observed in stroke victims.
    b.   a form of dysnomia.
    c.   articulation difficulties caused by injury to the motor strip.
    d.   the inability to write.

28. A neuropsychologist's main role in rehabilitation focuses on:

    a.   diagnosis.
    b.   treatment.
    c.   psychotherapy.
    d.   suicide prevention.

29. Which of the following is a question a neuropsychologist would be asked to assess?

    a.   What is the likelihood that an individual will be able to manipulate a wheelchair in his/her home following discharge from the rehabilitation hospital?
    b.   What is the likelihood that an individual will be able to utilize a communication prosthetic effectively?
    c.   What is the likelihood that an individual will be able to return to his/her job following discharge from the rehabilitation hospital?
    d.   What is the likelihood that an individual's family will continue to support him/her as needed?

30. Which of the following is a detailed list of all of the steps required to perform a given task?

    a.   Task requirements.
    b.   Task analysis.
    c.   Task measurement.
    d.   Task organization.

31. What is the biggest hurdle for independent living in the elderly?

    a.   Being unable to drive.
    b.   Taking medications incorrectly.
    c.   Having to live alone.
    d.   Financial problems.

32. Treatment planning is likely to incorporate:

    a.   standardized psychometric instruments and ecologically valid measures.
    b.   standardized psychometric instruments and physical therapy.
    c.   ecologically valid measures and personality tests.
    d.   None of the above.

33. Computer software which provides practice exercises for the purpose of the rehabilitation of attention is an example of:

    a.   substitution.
    b.   cognitive remediation.
    c.   an orthotic.
    d.   a prosthetic.

34. An example of lower order to higher order cognitive processes is:

    a.   focused attention, sequencing, and managing a household.
    b.   divided attention, executive tasks, and expressive speech.
    c.   sustained attention, sequencing, driving, and receptive language.
    d.   sequencing, divided attention, and managing a household.

35. An example of a contextually driven rehabilitation approach is:

    a.   job coaching.
    b.   driver training.
    c.   supported employment.
    d.   All of the above.

36. Contextually driven approaches are used mostly to:

    a.   completely restore function.
    b.   teach compensatory strategies.
    c.   assist the patient in adjusting to things that he/she will not be able to do at all anymore.
    d.   None of the above.

37. The main argument against cognitive retraining and the attempted restoration of brain systems is:

    a.   cognitive retraining has not shown to improve skills on the task being addressed.
    b.   cognitive retraining shows significant improvement in specific skill areas upon neuropsychological assessment but not on actual "real life" skills.
    c.   cognitive retraining fails to generalize to "real life" skills such as driving and return to work.
    d.   All of the above.

38. The retraining of _____ by the Attention Process Training system is accomplished through tasks, which require constant attention.

    a.   sustained attention
    b.   selective attention
    c.   alternating attention
    d.   divided attention

39. The retraining of _____ by the Attention Process Training system is accomplished through tasks, which require cognitive switching between two tasks.

    a.   sustained attention
    b.   selective attention
    c.   alternating attention
    d.   divided attention

40. The retraining of _____ by the Attention Process Training system is accomplished through tasks, which require simultaneous attention to two tasks.

    a.   sustained attention
    b.   selective attention
    c.   alternating attention
    d.   divided attention

41. The retraining of _____ by the Attention Process Training system is accomplished through tasks, which require sustained attention even when faced with distractions.

    a.   sustained attention
    b.   selective attention
    c.   alternating attention
    d.   divided attention

42. Effectiveness of attentional, memory and visual-spatial processing training on practice tasks is:

    a.   generally poor.
    b.   generally good.
    c.   good with attentional performance rising above premorbid functioning levels.
    d.   None of the above.

43. Generalization of cognitive retraining to daily life is:

    a.   proven through multiple prospective research studies.
    b.   good for skills such as attention but poor for visual-spatial abilities.
    c.   better than generalization to standardized neuropsychological assessment measures.
    d.   unclear due to other variables.

44. Supported Employment refers to:

    a.   the provision of easier jobs for brain-injured individuals, which provide for similar wages as pre-injury employment.
    b.   jobs provided for brain-injured individuals, which utilize temporary job coaches.
    c.   jobs provided for brain-injured individuals, which utilize permanent job coaches.
    d.   employment within a sheltered workshop.

45. A job coach is likely to:

    a.   construct task analyses for various job demands.
    b.   fade out over time.
    c.   determine the social demands of the workplace.
    d.   All of the above.

46. An example of an orthotic is:

    a.   a computerized schedule.
    b.   a device which allows an individual, who cannot speak, to communicate.
    c.   a computer monitor.
    d.   All of the above.

47. An example of a prosthetic is:

    a.   a computerized schedule.
    b.   a device which allows an individual, who cannot speak, to communicate.
    c.   a computer monitor.
    d.   All of the above.

48. Following brain injury, psychotherapy may be used to:

    a.   evaluate neuropsychological functioning.
    b.   provide motivational strategies for rehabilitation.
    c.   provide antidepressant medications to individuals who are experiencing depression secondary to their brain injury.
    d.   read the patient's mind.

Essay Questions

1. Discuss the ways an individual might regain neurological functioning following an insult to the brain.

2. Describe who is on the rehabilitation team, and briefly discuss each of their roles.

3. Construct a task analysis for washing dishes.

Answer Key

Chapter Exercises

1. True (p.494)
2. False (p.495)
3. True (p.495)
4. True (p.495)
5. False (p.496)
6. True (p.496)
7. False (p.496)
8. True (p.496)
9. True (p.497)
10. True (p.497)
11. False (p.497)
12. False (pp.497,498)
13. True (p.498)
14. False (pp.499,500)
15. True (p.500)
16. True (p.500)
17. False (p.500)
18. False (p.500)
19. True (p.502)
20. True (p.502)
21. False (p.502)
22. False (p.500)
23. True (p.501)
24. False (p.501)
25. True (p.501)
26. True (p.504)
27. True (p.504)
28. False (pp.504,505)
29. False (pp.504,505)
30. False (pp.504,505)
31. True (pp.505,506)
32. False (p.506)
33. True (p.506)
34. True (pp.506,507)
35. False (p.507)
36. False (p.507)
37. True (pp.507,508)
38. True (p.508)
39. False (p.510)
40. True (p.510)
41. True (p.510)
42. True (p.511)
43. Substitution (p.512)
44. generalization to daily life functioning (p.514)
45. selective attention (p.513)
46. Amyotrophic Lateral Sclerosis (p.520)
47. task analysis (p.515)
48. Supported employment (p.515)
49. divided attention (p.513)
50. Restitution (p.512)
51. orthotic (p.520)
52. Task improvement effects (p.514)
53. compensatory aid (pp.520,521)
54. sustained attention (p.513)
55. prosthetic (pp.520,521)
56. Psychotherapy (p.519)
57. generalization to neuropsychological testing (p.514)
58. job coach (pp.516,517)
59. alternating attention (p.513)
60. Attentional retraining (p.513)

Post-Test

Multiple Choice

1. B (p.494)
2. C (p.493)
3. D (p.494)
4. D (p.495)
5. A (p.495)
6. A (p.496)
7. D (p.496)
8. A (p.496)
9. C (p.497)
10. B (p.497)
11. A (p.497)
12. D (pp.498,499)
13. D (pp.497-499)
14. D (p.499)
15. B (p.499)
16. A (p.500)
17. D (p.500)
18. D (p.500)
19. D (pp.502,503)
20. B (p.501)
21. C (p.501)
22. B (p.504)
23. B (p.505)
24. A (p.504)

25. D (pp.505,506)
26. C (p.506)
27. C (p.506)
28. B (p.507)
29. C (p.507)
30. B (p.515)
31. B (p.510)
32. A (pp.509,510)
33. B (p.512)
34. A (p.512)
35. D (p.512)
36. B (p.512)
37. C (p.512)
38. A (p.513)
39. C (p.513)
40. D (p.513)
41. B (p.513)
42. B (p.514)
43. D (p.514)
44. B (p.517)
45. D (pp.516,517)
46. A (p.520)
47. B (p.520)
48. B (p.519)